SECOND EDITION

Put It in Writing

COMPOSITION
AND GRAMMAR

DAVID GATES

JOANNE BUCKLEY

Prentice Hall Canada Inc., Scarborough, Ontario

Canadian Cataloguing in Publication Data

Buckley, Joanne Lorna, 1953 - .

Put it in writing: composition and grammar, 2nd ed.

ISBN: 0-13-123100-6

1. English language - Rhetoric. 2. English language - Grammar. 3. English language - Rhetoric - Problems, exercises, etc. 4. English language - Grammar - Problems, exercises, etc.

I. Gates, David Philip, 1952 - . II. Title.

PE1408.B82 1995 808'.042 C94-931246-0

Prentice-Hall, Inc., Englewood Cliffs, New Jersey
Prentice-Hall International (UK) Limited, London
Prentice-Hall of Australia, Pty. Limited, Sydney
Prentice-Hall Hispanoamericana, S.A., Mexico City
Prentice-Hall of India Private Limited, New Delhi
Prentice-Hall of Japan, Inc., Tokyo
Simon & Schuster Asia Private Limited, Singapore
Editora Prentice-Hall do Brasil, Ltda., Rio de Janeiro

ISBN 0-13-123100-6

Acquisitions Editor: Michael Bickerstaff
Developmental Editor: Edward O'Connor
Production Editor: Kelly Dickson
Copy Editor: Shirley Corriveau
Cover and Interior Design: Monica Kompter
Cover Image: The Image Bank/Pierre-Yves Goavec
Text Illustration: Deborah-Anne Barley
Page Layout: Zofia Moczulak

5 RRD 99

Printed and bound in the U.S.A.

Every reasonable effort has been made to obtain permissions for all articles and data used in this edition. If errors or omissions have occurred, they will be corrected in future editions provided written notification has been received by the publisher.

TABLE OF CONTENTS

INTRODUCTION

Starting out as we mean to go on

In *Put It in Writing,* we work from the premise that writing, rather than grammar rules, comes first. It is, after all, only by writing that your work will improve. As we have discovered from our teaching experience, students are more interested in the practice of writing, producing clear correct prose that expresses their own ideas, than they are in theories of composition. This book will afford you plenty of opportunities for classroom writing practice. Writing in the classroom can seem like an empty exercise, but once you master the essentials, you'll be free to use the forms as you wish.

The first part of this book will concentrate on composition as a whole, giving you a chance to get acquainted with forms of writing used in the classroom, as well as in your professions. You will find a number of hypothetical writing situations which will allow you the opportunity for role playing and for creative writing within a professional framework. These are meant to start you thinking about your writing in relation to purpose and audience. These situations can be the basis for either a one paragraph or a longer composition, as class time and the needs of the students dictate.

The second part of the book focusses on grammar, in particular on the correction of common errors. The correction of errors is, of course, not the only criterion of good writing, but it is a necessary step in your development as a writer. The weight and distribution of exercises reflects our experience of the most common problems in writing.

You can use the book either on your own, as a self-help guide, or in the classroom. You may choose to work through the book systematically or to refer to specific chapters relevant to your writing needs. Answers to the exercises in chapters 3 to 7 can be found in the back of this book.

We hope that you will find this book both useful and enjoyable. Covering a wide variety of subjects, both serious and otherwise, this book should have something for everyone. It uses student work as the basis for discussion and exercises, and emphasizes Canadian themes. We hope that it will defuse some of the anxiety connected with the writing process and help you clarify your thought and put it in writing.

ACKNOWLEDGMENTS

We would like to thank our students, who allowed us to use samples of their work throughout this text, and our reviewers, Susan Braley, Fanshawe College; Cheryl Dahl, Fraser Valley College; William Main, Douglas College; and Margaret van Dijk, Centennial College, all of whom gave helpful suggestions and encouragement. The authors would also like to thank each other, and Kim Harrison and John Stracuzza for those moments when inspiration was flagging.

Finally thanks go to the reviewers of the book: Rudi Aksim, Algonquin College; Martin Hallett, Vanier College; Vernon McCarthy, Campion College, University of Regina; Diana Patterson, Mount Royal College; Donald W. Pimm, Concordia College; Carole Reed, Dawson College, and to the copy editor, Shirley Corriveau.

PART ONE

THE WRITING SITUATION

Where to Start
—and How

GETTING STARTED

An experienced author once said that nobody but a blockhead ever wrote except for money. That may have been all right for Samuel Johnson, but a lot of people face their fears of writing with no expectation of financial gain. In spite of the dread that many of us feel at the prospect of writing anything more complicated than a shopping list, writing can have rewards, if not financial, then at least emotional or intellectual. Writing can be troublesome if you think of it only as a task imposed upon you instead of a genuine expression of your opinion. Writing can also be intimidating if you think you have to produce a polished draft the very first time you sit down to face a blank page or empty computer screen. There are several ways to deal with the typical fears of writing:

1. Reconcile yourself to producing more than one draft. Think of the first version as being "for your eyes only," a reflection of your thoughts on a subject that does not have to withstand the scrutiny of others.

2. Keep a notebook to capture thoughts and questions as they occur. Consider this collection as a source of "raw material" to be mined (written up, revised, edited) later.

3. Don't approach the assignment by asking "What does the instructor want me to say?" or "What am I supposed to say?" Use it as a springboard to explore what you think; you might not realize that you have an opinion about a particular issue until you begin to turn it over in your mind.

4. Talk to other people. Although you may feel you have nothing to say about unemployment, for example, it might be worthwhile to think about conversations you and your friends have had recently. You might have talked about the lack of job prospects or thought about ways of writing your résumé in order to attract an employer's attention. If you think about it, you will find that your own experiences or those of your friends will supply ideas and material for writing.

All good expository writing meets certain requirements. This kind of writing does not tell a story; it explains or makes a point. It can show the reader something or present an argument. A good essay takes a clear position or viewpoint toward a subject; it selects only those details that are relevant to the treatment of that subject or that create a unified impression. An essay always has an introduction, a body, and a conclusion, a beginning, a middle, and an end. The introduction sets the stage for what is to come and usually culminates in a statement of the essay's main point. The body develops supporting details. The conclusion summarizes and considers the implications of what has been said.

What follows will help you master the demands of the essay form.

When you sit down to write a paragraph or an essay, you need to ask yourself four questions.

1. Why are you writing? What is your **motive**?

2. Who are you writing to? Who is your **audience**?

3. What do you want to say? What is your **main point**?

4. How will you defend your main point? What **support** can you offer for it?

MOTIVE

Why do we write? All writing has an object in mind. In the classroom, you are asked to write to develop your thinking and communication skills. Outside the classroom, you may be prompted to write by a need to express clearly all the details of your idea or to make sure that your thoughts are on record. In business, short pieces of writing are the main forms of communication and documentation. You may, for instance, write to request information, or to register a complaint, or to make a proposal.

AUDIENCE

Read the following sentence:

> You'd probably think that all used car salespersons are crooks, but you'd be wrong.

This sentence alienates its readers because it assumes something negative about them. It is often better to avoid the use of the second person pronoun "you," except when you are teaching someone how to do something, as is the case in this book.

> People who are pro-choice ought to have their heads examined.

Although this sentence expresses its point of view clearly, it is overstated, emotional and antagonistic.

> It is the opinion of this author that the financial institutions of this dominion must realign the parameters of mortgage interest to coincide more closely with the bank rate.

This sentence is overwritten and pretentious. The writer's meaning would be better expressed in a much simpler form, such as the following:

> The bank rate should be in line with interest rates.

5

You and Your Audience

As the above examples show, the use of pronouns can make a significant difference in the effect of your writing. Be especially careful of references to yourself or to your reader. Using the pronoun "you" often involves making assumptions about the reader's experience or beliefs. Similarly, it may be more straightforward to refer to yourself as "I" than as "this writer."

MAIN POINT

All of your writing will be organized around, or developed from, a main point. The main point of an essay is usually called a thesis statement, and of a paragraph, a topic sentence. Although in expository writing the topic sentence can be a statement of fact, in most of the writing you will be asked to do, it will be a statement of opinion that can be supported by facts. For a main point or thesis statement to function effectively, it has to be arguable. If all readers would accept your thesis without question, then the statement will not serve as the foundation for your argument, for your interpretation of the facts. In essence, your main point must make some kind of claim that is not self-evident; avoid saying things like "Corruption is bad."

Whatever the intention, remember that most writing is fundamentally persuasive in nature. Whether you are writing to convince someone that you are the right person for the job or to get someone to take action on your behalf, you need to establish your point firmly. Even in most expository or explanatory writing, you will be imposing your opinion upon the facts that you present. If, for example, you are writing to teach someone how to scramble eggs, your explanation will be based on what you consider to be the best method. Your selection and ordering of the steps in the process and the suggestions you include will reflect your interpretation. Hence, even simple instruction depends on your opinion, your sense of the main point.

A main point has to be narrow enough to be handled in the length you plan to use. For instance, a main point like "The Industrial Revolution led to many social and political problems" is too broad to be dealt with in any detail, except perhaps in book-length form.

Examples

> Hiking is a sport that tests your mental perceptions as well as your physical abilities.

This sentence has a good main point because it makes a claim about hiking, that it can challenge you. It is also effective because it suggests the direction that the rest of the paragraph, or longer piece of writing, will take: it will go on to discuss both mental and physical capacities. This main point acts as the introduction to an expository paragraph or essay since its function is to explain something about its subject.

> This paragraph will discuss recent developments in the automotive industry.

This sentence does not really make a main point; it describes the subject of the writing, but it neither narrows the topic sufficiently nor does it tell you what the writer thinks about the recent developments. A better version of this sentence would be something like this:

> One of the recent developments in the car industry is the shotgun alliance of Japanese management techniques and North American initiative.

This version expresses a point of view, and makes the subject much more specific.

> The train is the most relaxing way to travel.

Here the main point is to persuade the reader that train travel has an advantage over other means of transportation. From this main point, there are several directions the writer could take: he or she could describe the stress-free nature of train travel or compare various modes of transport to demonstrate the train's superiority.

> What are the pros and cons of placing an ad in the personal column?

Although it may appear to set up the topic, this question leaves the reader guessing about the writer's attitude. Even if your purpose is to consider both sides of the question, you need to establish where you stand at the beginning of the paper. You write to convince the reader of your point of view, not to convince yourself. You might say instead something like this: Although a popular practice, placing an ad in a personal column can be an embarrassing experience. This sentence acknowledges that advertising in the personal column has some attraction, but it prepares us for a piece of writing that will defend the claim, perhaps by giving examples.

> The squid is a ten-armed cephalopod found in both coastal and oceanic waters.

Here there is no main point because the sentence is simply a statement of fact. While it demonstrates some knowledge of the squid, a paper using this as a thesis statement or topic sentence would be just reporting facts without declaring any position on them.

> Sooner or later everyone has to run away from home.

This main point is effective even though it leaves the reader in some suspense.

This kind of claim gets attention because of its unconventionality. Provided the piece of writing goes on to demonstrate that the statement is, in fact, true, it should work well. Perhaps the most contentious part of the claim is indicated in the verb "run," and a good writer would make that the focal point of the writing.

A good main point fulfills these functions:

1. It makes a claim that you are prepared to defend.

2. It works to explain something to the reader or to persuade the reader of something.

3. It is sufficiently narrow to be discussed in the piece of writing it introduces.

4. It catches the reader's attention.

A good main point should also lead to the development of smaller topic sentences that will serve as the basis for each of the paragraphs to follow. For example, a main point like the following can be broken down into three smaller units.

Main Point: Health care benefits should be provided by government programs.

Topic Sentence 1: Good health care is one of the rights of a citizen.

Topic Sentence 2: Good health care should not be given only to those able to afford it.

Topic Sentence 3: Having a good health care system is ultimately beneficial to the welfare of the country.

Each of these reasons can be developed by a supporting paragraph. Each topic sentence has a controlling idea that governs what the rest of the paragraph is about. For a topic sentence to work effectively, it should be narrow enough to be dealt with in the space of a paragraph, it should be focussed on something relevant to the larger main point, and it should make a definite claim that the rest of the paragraph goes on to defend.

To check to see if the entire essay is unified, you need to ask if the topic sentences relate to and support the main point.

EXERCISE 1-1

Decide whether each of the following expresses a suitable main point or thesis statement for an essay. Try rewriting any that are unacceptable, making sure that your statements are narrow and arguable.

1. Low barometric pressure causes migraines.

2. Aunt Eva enjoys poor health.

3. This paper will discuss the advantages and disadvantages of liposuction.

4. Windsurfing is a sport everyone can enjoy.

5. I preferred Timothy Findley's earlier novels to his most recent one, *Headhunter*.

6. The old age pension system is in serious trouble.

7. With his lottery windfall from *Reader's Digest*, Randy Feldspar bought a mobile home.

8. Although Kevin Major's books are controversial, they present a realistic view of adolescence.

9. Aesop's *Fables* was first printed in English in 1481.

10. Doing volunteer work can be rewarding.

EXERCISE 1-2

Decide whether each of the following expresses a suitable main point or thesis statement for an essay. Try rewriting any that are unacceptable, making sure that your statements are narrow and arguable.

1. To survive economically, you need to have two careers.

2. According to the dictionary, an epidemic is a disease that attacks many people in the same country.

3. Each year I watch the hawks migrate.

4. To relieve stress, you should change your life.

5. Ermentrude goes to Florida each winter with all the other Canadian snowbirds.

6. Eighty-five percent of all avalanches are caused by yodelling.

7. Origami is the Japanese art of paper folding.

8. Cross-country, downhill, and slalom are three kinds of skiing competition.

9. The post office should not be allowed to raise postal rates without improving services.

10. This paper will tell you everything you need to know about snowmobiles.

EXERCISE 1-3

Make the following main points more specific, by sharpening the controlling idea.

1. Medicine has changed a lot in the last fifty years.

2. I enjoy quilting.

3. You can learn a great deal by having your own garden.

4. Hairstyles can make a difference.

5. Home renovation, although costly, is worthwhile.

EXERCISE 1-4

Make up three unified topic sentences for each of the main points you wrote in the exercise above.

EXERCISE 1-5

Check to see if the following topic sentences provide unified development for the main point.

1. **Main Point:** New homes have some disadvantages compared to older homes.

   Topic Sentences: They are expensive.
   They have higher property taxes.
   They are often unlandscaped.
   They are served by super mail boxes and not home delivery.
   All my friends have purchased new homes.
   New homes are built at a faster rate in urban centres than in rural ones.

2. **Main Point:** Donating to a food bank is a good way to make a contribution to your community.

   Topic Sentences: Food banks provide food for people who are out of work.
   Food banks often run drives during major holidays.
   Donations of food are easy to make.
   Food banks provide nourishing meals for children who might not otherwise be provided for.

3. **Main Point:** TV can be a good educational device for a child.

   Topic Sentences: Many programs are written expressly for children.

Television programs allow children to gain a wider perspective of the world.

Taped programs can enable children to have a story repeated beyond the patience of a human storyteller.

Children can develop an aesthetic sense through television.

Children can have the same consumer impulses instilled in them as in everyone else.

4. **Main point:** Everyone would benefit from an auto mechanics course.

Topic sentences: Having your car fixed is very expensive.
Understanding how your car works can make you a better driver.
Auto mechanics is easier than people think.
Doing a job well yourself is very satisfying.
Knowing about your car will be helpful in emergency situations.

SUPPORT

Your main point needs to be supported if it is to be persuasive. A reader will not necessarily agree that vegetarians are healthier than meat eaters. You need to back up this idea with some evidence to enable the reader to see its value. There are four different kinds of support: examples, authorities, statistics, and reasons.

Examples

The most common way to back up a main point is through the use of examples. These can be drawn from your own experience or knowledge and do not necessarily require research. Examples should be detailed enough to allow the reader to visualize them and understand the point being illustrated.

Example

Although amateur theatre productions often lack funding or polish, they compensate by being energetic and resourceful. My friends and I recently attended a performance of *Macbeth,* put on by students at a local college. The costumes revealed a shortage of money: Lady Macbeth's wardrobe consisted of one unflattering dress with yellow ruffles, that looked like a reject from *Gone with the Wind.* On the other hand, the outdoor setting, which created echoes when the actors shouted, was appropriately atmospheric. A flock of crows arrived as if on cue, and branches felled by a recent storm made a convincing Birnam Wood. The many battle scenes, in which both women and men played soldiers, were fought vigorously.

This paragraph uses personal experience and specifics to develop the topic sentence in a vivid way.

Authorities

When you cite the opinion of an expert in a particular area, you make your argument more believable than it would be if dependent on your perspective alone. You should be careful not to rely solely on the ideas of others without expressing any of your own.

Example

> Some people argue that fairy tales are too violent or escapist and should be removed from libraries. What they should realize is that fairy tales can aid in the process of psychological growth. Bruno Bettelheim, in *The Uses of Enchantment,* argues that fairy tales are therapeutic because they allow children to find solutions to their own problems, based on the implications of the stories. In his study, Bettelheim shows how the individual tales reflect patterns of inner conflict that the child might face, for example, the problem of sibling rivalry that is an important theme of "Cinderella."

When using authorities as support, you should set up the point in your own words and then follow it by quoting or paraphrasing your source. This way the authority is employed as support for *your* ideas. Usually it is not enough to refer to a source and then leave the reader to draw his or her conclusions about it. You need to elaborate on the words of the authority so that the reader understands how you are using them to substantiate your case.

Statistics

In some cases, numerical data or statistics will be the most effective way of proving your point.

Example

> Asthma is becoming more prevalent than in recent years.
>
> According to Statistics Canada, in 1985 it was the seventh leading cause of hospitalization among men and the thirteenth leading cause among women. It is estimated that $120 million dollars worth of hospital bills were related to asthma in 1987–88.

Try to make the statistics meaningful to the reader; here they are effective because they are higher than might be expected and would surprise readers.

Reasons

Unlike examples, authorities, and statistics which are accumulated kinds of evidence, reasoning refers to your sense of what constitutes a fair and rational argument. When you support your main point with reasons, you are interpreting other kinds of evidence to build your case.

Example

> Abortion should not be an option beyond four months into a pregnancy. Since it has been shown that a fetus is viable after twenty weeks, and a fetus able to sustain itself independently is a living human being, any intervention after that point should be considered murder.

This example uses some statistical evidence to argue against abortion. While this approach to the evidence is not conclusive, it offers a reasonable interpretation that hinges upon a definition of "life."

SOURCES

It is important to remember that when you cite an example, an authority, or a statistic not taken from your own experience, you should acknowledge your source. Failure to indicate clearly where your information comes from can be considered theft or plagiarism. You need to cite your sources whether you quote the original words exactly or whether you paraphrase the idea. If the reader is inclined to ask "How do you know this?" then you should provide the answer to the question. To achieve credibility and avoid charges of theft, acknowledge your sources by using a method of documentation suggested by your instructor or the system described in one of the following books. They should be available in the reference section of the library; your instructor will tell you which one is appropriate.

American Psychological Association. *Publication Manual of American Psychological Association.* 3rd ed. Washington: American Psychological Association, 1983.

Gibaldi, Joseph, and Walter S. Achert. *MLA Handbook for Writers of Research Papers.* 2nd ed. New York: Modern Language Association, 1984.

Turabian, Kate L. A *Manual for Term Papers, Theses, and Dissertations.* 5th ed. Chicago: University of Chicago Press, 1987.

FORM—THE PARAGRAPH

In your writing class, you will be asked most often for paragraphs and short essays, usually three to five paragraphs in length. Generally, the paragraph will consist of four elements: a clear and concise topic sentence, some support for the main point, some elaboration or explanation of that support, and a concluding statement, which echoes or highlights the main point that has been made. As part of a larger piece of writing, this summary statement may be replaced by a connective, by means of which the reader is given a link to what will follow. Because of these requirements, it is common for a paragraph to be composed of at least three sentences, though this characteristic is arbitrary.

Consider the following example:

> (1) Although polio has been virtually wiped out in North America since 1954 with the introduction with the Salk vaccine, the effects of the poliomyelitis virus are being felt once more. (2) It has been estimated that up to a quarter of 700,000 North Americans who survived polio in childhood will experience post-polio syndrome, as late as fifty years after the initial contact with the virus. (3) A victim of this syndrome will experience a return of the symptoms of polio: respiratory difficulties, fatigue, and muscle weakness or pain. (4) Dr. Laura Halstead, who has studied the syndrome, says, "There are people who run a marathon each week, and they look gaunt and old because they are pushing their bodies to the limit all the time. For people with post-polio, it's just walking around the house that may push the body to the limit." (5) Although there is no cure, symptoms can be relieved by following a program of strengthening exercises and avoiding muscle stress. (6) These coping strategies, however, offer little comfort to those who thought they had put the disease behind them. (7) A doctor who has seen more than 200 post-polio patients since 1987 comments, "They thought they were finished with this and see it coming up again. Patients are very scared."

Sentence 1 introduces the main point while the others develop this central idea by providing information about it. Sentence 2 uses statistics to explain the numbers of people affected and the length of time that may elapse between the disease and the syndrome. Sentence 3 defines the subject by giving examples of the symptoms that may recur. Sentence 4 uses a quotation from an authority to give the reader a sense of the syndrome's impact. Sentence 5 highlights ways of coping with post-polio syndrome. Sentences 6 and 7 conclude by echoing the opening statement.

The author of this paragraph would also have to acknowledge the source for the information according to the format of one of the manuals listed above under "Sources." (Douglas Powell, "Polio: A Childhood Enemy Makes a Comeback." *The Globe and Mail,* 18 September 1993, D8.)

Besides these requirements, a paragraph should also have unity, coherence, and emphasis.

14

Unity

Unity refers to the relevance of all details to the point being made. One way of ensuring unity is to place your topic sentence at the beginning of the paragraph and use it as the core of your thinking. For example, in the paragraph above, everything that is included relates to post-polio syndrome, who is likely to be affected, when the disease is likely to recur, how it is manifested, and how its effects may be alleviated.

Topic sentences often appear at the beginning of a paragraph and they are clearer there, but you will sometimes find them as summary statements at the end. When you begin a paragraph with a topic sentence, as above, you are organizing your material according to a deductive pattern of logic. If, on the other hand, you proceed from examples and evidence to a concluding statement, which is in effect your topic sentence, you are employing an inductive pattern.

Look at the following example of an inductive paragraph:

> I consider myself a reasonably capable individual, but recently all sorts of things seem to be beyond my control. The automatic coffee maker I purchased last month has already ceased to work, and I can't remember whether I sent in the warranty. I can't figure out how to program the VCR. And trying to choose between two competing telephone networks which both offer savings but under different conditions and with different fee structures is something I cannot get my mind around. A friend who fancies himself a computer whiz installed a new "more convenient" desktop system on my computer which is slower and more cumbersome to use than the old one. Technology holds out the promise of easier work and more leisure time, but in fact, it only makes us more dependent and confused.

Here the concluding sentence states the main point by making a general claim based on the specific examples.

Coherence

A paragraph is coherent if all details are connected. Repetition of key words, the use of pronouns, parallel structures, and transitions all can be used to create coherence. In the paragraph on post-polio syndrome, repetition of words like "virus," "syndrome," and "symptoms" helps to establish coherence. Similarly, the muscle weakness that is listed as a symptom in Sentence 3 is firmly connected to the quotation in Sentence 4 and to the mention of muscle stress in Sentence 5.

Transitions

Transitions are signal or key words that connect ideas or mark changes in the direction of your thought. They are a useful tool for the writer. Do not leave them out or assume that the reader will automatically know when you are moving from one step in your argument to another. In the sample paragraph on polio, words like "however" and "although" serve as transitions.

Here is another example of how transitions work:

Main point: There are three ways to prevent the spread of mosquitoes: insecticides, repellents, and proper drainage.

First supporting point—insecticides

Use approved equipment to apply chemicals to control the growth of larvae.

Second supporting point—repellents

Look for sprays containing the chemical DEET.

Third supporting point—drainage

Drain potential sources of standing or stagnant water such as pool covers or plant containers.

Change water in bird baths frequently.

The three points outlined (insecticides, repellents, and drainage) need to be introduced by transitional phrases that mark the steps of the argument. You might use as a first point "Insecticides are one important method of controlling the mosquito population." In this sentence the word "one" is transitional, signalling to the reader that the first supporting point is being introduced. Notice too that this is linked to the original topic sentence so that the reader understands how this part of the paragraph serves as its support. The next sentence might begin "Repellents are also useful as a means of warding off mosquitoes." Here the word "also" flags the reader.

Sometimes in the haste of creating a rough draft, writers omit these necessary links. When you edit the rough draft, check first to see that the arguments are all clearly related through transitions to the thesis statement.

Emphasis

In a paragraph, an idea can be given emphasis by its position. Just as we tend to remember the last thing someone says to us, so a point can be made emphatic by appearing towards the end of the paragraph. In the sample paragraph above, the recurrence of the syndrome is emphasized by the two final sentences.

While it is a good idea to summarize your thinking in a concluding sentence, conclusions need not be elaborate: don't feel that you must include a resounding or obvious conclusion that adds nothing to what you have already said. For example, don't say "Thus we have seen that Albert Einstein was a great thinker."

It can be said, though, that paragraphs are small units of thought that, like the essay, usually have a discernible beginning, middle, and end. If your essay succeeds as a whole, your paragraphs need to be unified, coherent and emphatic.

Read the following essay and study the relationship of the paragraphs to the entire structure.

A CONFUCIAN'S NEW WONDERLAND

When I emigrated from China to Canada, I felt I was like a young frog coming out from a very deep old well. The sky was so much bigger. This world was such a different one. I was excited. I was nervous.

I started looking at the people of this country. Whites, blacks, yellows—what a colourful society! The people were so friendly and relaxed. Their way of talking and acting was very interesting.

I put away the chopsticks and started using a fork and a knife to eat "Grandma's Tofu." I wanted to learn Canadian customs. I wanted to be a real Canadian.

"Don't throw away the Ten Thousand Mile Spiritual Wall I built for you," a deep voice resounded from the eastern sky waking me up from a dream. I looked at the picture of Confucius on a book which I brought with me when I left "the old well." "I am living in Canada now," I replied to the sky, "I don't know if this western land has a place to put your Spiritual Wall or not. I've got to do things in the Canadian way, even though I am still searching for that way."

I started looking for a job. The Human Resource Manager, a smart-looking gentleman, at my first job interview asked me, "What is your five-year career goal if we hire you?"

After I failed to get the job, I highlighted the answer "To be a boss," which I found in a career guide brochure. I put a question mark beside the answer and went to the teacher of my class in English as a Second Language. "So what was your answer?" the teacher asked me. "To be a good employee," I told her. She smiled and said, "I guess people with an eastern background don't like to give too haughty an impression to others, but many North Americans are the opposite." Incomprehensible, I thought.

After dinner I thought about the teacher's words. Obviously there are many differences between eastern and western cultures. I walked over to my

Chinese cabinet and looked at some eastern curios. "Some parts of the Spiritual Wall seem in my way," I said.

"What are you mumbling about?" My wife closed the cabinet and continued, "You know there were more than forty candidates who wanted to get that job. It's competition. There is nothing wrong with your Wall."

"My eastern teaching made me too restrained. It seems it's not good for me to carry the eastern standards in this competitive world," I said.

"Confucius said that education is of crucial importance in the universe of man. You should go back to school," she suggested.

"Confucius? Confusing." I said.

Two months later, I received a letter from Centennial College informing me that my application for the Business Program had been accepted. The program was going to start in the fall.

I began bombarding my wife with all kinds of questions about Canada because I really wanted to find out "the Canadian way." My wife belongs to the second generation of a Chinese-Canadian family. I had wondered why the traditional Chinese customs did not bother her; she simply accepted them alongside North American customs. However, she sure was bothered by my questions, such as "What are the main moral standards of Canadians?" and "How does the educational system teach these standards to the children?" One day she came home with two Canrail passes and said, "Let's get on the train and go across Canada to look around. That may be the best way to learn about Canadians."

"Super idea," I said. The Canrail passes were good for one month. There was enough time to travel to many parts of Canada.

What an amazing country Canada is. We travelled east to Halifax and west to Vancouver Island. The land is vast and beautiful, the people gracious and nice, the history old but also young. This is an international country, an international food mart, an international cultural centre. So many things we saw were new to me, but many were also familiar, things from "the old well." I seemed to see a divining rod which showed me "the Canadian way," but what the rod showed was not very clear.

"Ya-hoo!" My wife gave a big yell when we got off the train in the Land of the Cowboy. Later, while I was watching the cowboys chasing cows in the Calgary Stampede, my brain started flipping from the Blue Jays' fans in SkyDome to P.E.I.'s little red-haired girl of Green Gables, from the sample of Confucius' work on the wall of the O'Keefe Centre to Montreal's Notre Dame Basilica, from the Indian village at Sioux-Lookout to the big whales off Vancouver Island.

"Giddyap! Giddyap!" I suddenly jumped up and joined the cheering cow-boys, cowgirls, cowladies and cowgentlemen. I was so excited. I saw my divining rod clearly. It was showing me "the Canadian way." Canadians are never afraid of challenge; they have something like the wonderful cowboy spirit. They look after the land and wildlife carefully. They are generous and peaceful; they respect human rights. They welcome all kinds of cultures; they believe it's beneficial to preserve and study them.

I came back from my tour happily. I am no longer nervous in this coun-try. Now the Ten Thousand Mile Spiritual Wall is only one part of my spiri-tual shelter. I believe I will be very rich, not only because I am studying Canadian business skills, but also because I am rebuilding my Spiritual Wall. The more I learn about Canada, the more I love her. Canada is my new home, a beautiful wonderland. I will do my best to keep her beauty and to add to it.

1. What images does the writer use to establish unity in the essay?

2. How do the introduction and conclusion connect?

3. How does the writer's thinking develop from questions about Canada to an-swers about Canada?

4. How does he use dialogue to illustrate the development of his thoughts?

5. What details are used to amplify this writer's definition of Canadian identity?

6. How does the writer manage to bridge intervals of time which would damage the coherence of the argument?

FORM—THE ESSAY

Longer compositions or essays are in some ways extended versions of the para-graph form. An essay offers some discussion or analysis of factual informa-tion. It does not just report the facts; it also offers a point of view about them. Conventionally, essays have a three-part structure. They have a thesis statement, similar to a topic sentence, placed in the introduction; a body constructed of points in support of the thesis statement; and a conclusion that recaps the steps of the argument. The argument defends a particular point of view. For example, a good essay might include the following thesis statement: "Free trade is bad for Canada because it causes slowdowns or layoffs in industry, curtails government-subsidized programs, and interferes with the book trade." Notice that this thesis statement contains a preview of the points to be developed in the body of the essay. A thesis statement should always express a point of view and provide a direction. It would not be enough to say "This essay will discuss whether or not free trade is good for Canada," since that would leave the reader wondering what the point of the essay is.

When you devise a thesis statement, you could use this formula as a starting point: "——is good/bad because——." However, thesis statements are not always so contentious. You could say "Raquetball is fun because——." This statement would lead to an expository, rather than a persuasive, essay, but both kinds depend on a similar basic structure for the argument.

Essay writing can be formal or informal based on the topic you select and the audience you address.

Consider the following example:

Cars are such an essential part of modern life that it is difficult to imagine being without them. We depend on them to take us where we want to go and, even more, to get us back again. Despite decades of research and development, despite all the resources, the money, and the brainpower that have gone into the evolution of ever more improved automobiles, every one that has ever been built has some troublesome quirk designed to disrupt the life of its owner. Car problems can vary from the merely bothersome to those that threaten life and limb, but the majority of them fall into the category of highly annoying.

My vehicle is no exception. It has its own unique and extremely vexatious habit. Drive it a short distance, say eight kilometres. Stop for a short time, say five minutes. Try to restart the car, and the problem reveals itself. Nothing will persuade the engine to restart for at least two hours. This has caused me to be stranded in the parking lots of variety stores and farm markets all around the area. It has caused me to meet people that I would not ordinarily get to meet, most notably the irate owners of parking lots and those ever helpful people who believe that they know all there is to know about the automobile.

The former are generally excitable people who are not impressed with my faithful patronage of their establishments. They prefer the quick turnover of customers' vehicles to having their best parking spot inhabited by one immobile car. They seem to believe that I was sent by their archrivals to inhibit their business or perhaps that I take some perverse pleasure in spending long hours in their parking lots.

The latter, invariably large men smelling vaguely of diesel fuel and tobacco, driving vehicles which are massive, rusty, and sounding as though an efficiently working muffler were just a distant memory, are always ready to help a lady in distress whether or not she needs help. They ignore my protests, which are based on months of experience and a simple faith in the continuation of a pattern, that the car will start eventually, and insist on delving into the inner workings of the balky engine. Poking at this wire, pulling at that connection, they become steadily more chagrined as my motor resists all their attempts at revival. Each in turn walks away, wiping his hands and muttering that only a towtruck will move "the ***** thing" from its resting place. Invariably, given enough time, my car starts up as though there had never been a problem.

This annoying little habit can turn a quick trip to pick up milk and bread into a half-day adventure. It has enabled me to develop skills of diplomacy for dealing with store owners and would-be rescuers. It has given me the opportunity to sort out the contents of my glove compartment, and it has provided me with many uninterrupted hours for contemplation. Like most of the perplexing problems of automobiles, this one never happens in the presence of a mechanic. Cars, with their quirks, seem designed to cause aggravation and frustration to their owners, but where would we be without them?

The structure of this essay is fairly typical of the short essay form:

Paragraph 1 consists of the introduction, the general idea that cars are essential in modern life, and the thesis statement, the main point, that cars can be annoying to their owners.

Paragraph 2 develops the thesis statement by describing the writer's own car troubles and the people she meets as a consequence.

Paragraph 3 describes one group of people she meets, the parking lot owners.

Paragraph 4 describes another group of people she meets, those who try to fix her car.

The conclusion summarizes the "advantages" of car problems and reinforces the point that cars are necessary.

Or consider this example:

Professional baseball is a billion-dollar industry in the United States and Canada played by an elite group of highly skilled athletes. Slo-pitch, a derivative of the game of baseball, is the common person's version of the game. Although slo-pitch has developed from the game of baseball, there exist many contrasting elements between the two sports. The differences between professional baseball and slo-pitch may be contrasted in terms of the participants, fields of play and the rules for each respective game.

Professional baseball involves an elite group of male athletes performing in front of an audience of millions. Each professional baseball team consists of nine players on the field at once. Alternates bring the team size up to a total of twenty-five players. To make it to the "big leagues," a player must prove his talents as a teenager and throughout the minor league system as a young adult. Only the best players in this feeder system make their way to the highest level. As a result, there is a great deal of competition for the 700 roster spots in the major leagues.

The rewards for making it to the top in professional baseball are quite substantial. Most of the major league ball players reap the benefits of a large salary combined with public notoriety. The average annual salary per player is over one million dollars in the major leagues. When endorsements are considered, a professional baseball player could easily increase his total income several times over that of his salary. For example, Roberto Alomar of the Toronto Blue Jays more than doubles his three million dollar salary through endorsements. Players like Roberto Alomar become as well known for what they endorse as for their abilities on the field.

Slo-pitch, on the other hand, allows amateurs to participate. There are male, female and co-ed teams. The skill level of these players is minute when compared to the professionals. To be a member of a slo-pitch team requires no previous experience. Each slo-pitch team consists of ten players on the field with alternates taking the total team size to between fifteen and twenty players. Although an individual slo-pitch team may contain fewer players than a major league team, the total number of slo-pitch teams greatly outnumbers the twenty-eight teams in the major leagues. In fact, the total number of slo-pitch players exceeds ten million in the United States and Canada.

There is no financial reward awaiting the slo-pitch enthusiast. What the game offers is the opportunity to enjoy a simplified version of baseball where fun replaces the emphasis on winning or losing. A slo-pitch player must "pay to play" as there is a participation fee a player must pay at the beginning of each season. This fee is used to offset the operating costs of a slo-pitch team. Unlike professional baseball, there is no celebrity status associated with slo-pitch. It is inconceivable that a slo-pitch player would ever achieve public notoriety to the same extent as Nolan Ryan or Dave Winfield.

The second contrasting element between baseball and slo-pitch is the fields of play. In professional baseball each of the 28 teams plays in an elaborate baseball park. These ballparks vary from open-air stadiums with natural grass to covered domes with artificial turf. Skydome in Toronto, through modern technology, may be a covered or uncovered stadium depending upon the weather. Another characteristic of these ballparks is their ability to seat many spectators. To enhance viewing pleasure, these stadiums provide visual and audio aids. Again, Skydome offers a state of the art Jumbotron to relay information and replays to the spectators.

In comparison, a slo-pitch ballpark offers none of the elaborate fixtures found in the big league parks. Slo-pitch fields exist only in an open-air environment. Unlike the manicured grounds where the professionals perform, most slo-pitch fields consist of dirt infields and sparsely grassed outfields. Slo-pitch parks provide wooden bleachers with close proximity to the field; however, these seats offer little comfort to the spectator. For the few spectators that attend slo-pitch games there are no audio or visual aids to enhance viewing pleasure. Consequently, spectators attending a slo-pitch game must be alert to all on-field action.

The final contrasting element between professional baseball and slo-pitch is the rules governing each respective game. A professional pitcher throws a small, tightly wound, leather-bound ball from a mound of dirt sixty feet six inches from home plate. When thrown, this ball could near a speed of 100 miles per hour. In support of the pitcher there are eight position players in the field (three outfielders, four infielders and a catcher). The objective of the pitcher is to prevent the batter from reaching base. Sometimes, the pitcher may attain this goal directly by striking out the batter. In the event that the batter hits the ball, the pitcher then relies on his teammates to keep the hitter off base. A wooden bat is the professional ball player's weapon against the pitcher and his formidable defense. The odds of a batter getting a hit are less than 50 percent. Actually, obtaining three hits in ten opportunities is looked upon as highly successful.

In the game of slo-pitch the rules, although derived from the game of baseball, are significantly different from those of professional baseball. In slo-pitch a larger, less tightly wound ball is used. The pitcher, situated forty-six feet from the batter, lobs the ball with an arc of between six and twenty feet toward a home plate that is two feet wide by three feet long. A slo-pitch pitcher does not stand on a mound but throws from field level. (The speed of the pitch is not important; in slo-pitch accuracy becomes most important.) Because of the high arc and slow speed, it is much easier to hit the ball in slo-pitch than in baseball. Batters should hit successfully at least 50 percent of the time; seven hits out of ten is above average.

The defensive players in slo-pitch take on a much larger role than in baseball. Because the ball is so much easier to hit and the pitcher seldom strikes out a batter, defense becomes very important in slo-pitch. (This is not to imply that defense is unimportant in baseball. A professional baseball game can be dominated by an overpowering pitcher whereas this situation is highly unlikely in slo-pitch.) Slo-pitch batters have access to the latest in bat technology; some may use wooden bats, but most use lightweight, aluminum bats that further benefit them.

Upon examining the three main contrasting elements, one finds significant differences between professional baseball and slo-pitch. After comparing the two games, a sports enthusiast can decide either to watch a professional game of baseball or to participate in a leisurely game of slo-pitch.

1. What is the thesis statement?

2. Where is the route map?

3. How does the introduction function to prepare you for the thesis statement?

4. What are the main points of comparison?

5. Find the topic sentences in each paragraph.

6. What kinds of support does the writer offer for each point?

7. What changes might you make to turn this paper into a persuasive essay rather than an expository one?

8. Show what an outline for this essay would look like.

9. This paper compares two things in a point by point way. One could also write this paper using block comparison, by describing first one thing and then the other. How would your outline look if you were doing such a comparison? Which kind is more effective in this case?

EXERCISE 1-6

When developing support for a topic sentence, it is important to focus on the burden of proof. Find some examples of sensational tabloid "news" stories ("Boy

Gives Birth to Second Child"); look at the authorities, statistics, examples, and reasons offered in support of the claims and consider their degree of credibility.

EXERCISE 1-7

Consider each of these proverbs as a main point to be developed into a topic sentence. Provide support to develop each into a paragraph.

1. A stitch in time saves nine.
2. Many are called but few are chosen.
3. A watched pot never boils.
4. It never rains but it pours.
5. You can catch more flies with honey than you can with vinegar.
6. Better late than never.
7. Beauty is only skin deep.
8. An ounce of prevention is worth a pound of cure.
9. Time waits for no man.
10. You can lead a horse to water, but you can't make him drink.

EXERCISE 1-8

For each of the following topics construct a topic sentence and write a paragraph to develop it.

1. the benefits of regular participation in sports
2. why I spend most of my time _____
3. politics
4. what I hate most
5. the advantages/disadvantages of education
6. what it means to be an adult
7. marriage
8. being in style
9. my least favourite person
10. what I consider funny

25

EXERCISE 1-9

For each of the following topics construct a topic sentence and write a paragraph to develop it.

1. the generation gap

2. disappointments

3. weightlifting

4. feuds

5. lumberjacks

6. board games

7. waiting

8. the beach

9. making do

10. people with too much money

OUTLINE

As you have seen, a paragraph consists of a main point which is presented in a topic sentence, some support for it, and some elaboration of that support. These elements constitute the outline of a paragraph. When you write longer compositions, with perhaps three to five paragraphs, you need a more complex outline. In fact, you should have an outline before you start to write. The outline for an essay or research paper or report will include the main point or thesis statement and a plan of the direction your writing will take. Your plan is a preview of the points the paragraph or essay will explore.

Main point or thesis statement: Using sex in advertising is inappropriate.

Plan: Exploiting sexuality to promote consumerism misrepresents the product, degrades women, and exposes children to unsuitable material.

In your introduction, you would state your thesis statement which establishes both the main point of your essay and the plan for your argument. Next you would develop topic sentences outlining the steps in your argument, each of which will be considered in detail in one or more paragraphs.

Topic sentence 1: Advertisers falsely promise that their products will make you more sexually attractive, even if the products themselves have nothing to do with physical appearance.

Topic sentence 2: Advertisers use women in skimpy or revealing clothes to sell products unrelated to sexuality—everything from beer to chewing gum.

Topic sentence 3: Seductive advertising is so widespread on television and in magazines that children cannot be protected from it.

You will also need to include in your outline your concluding statement which will briefly echo the main point of the writing, pose a question about it, or call for some action in response to it.

Conclusion: Because of its insidious nature, the use of sex in advertising should be monitored by both consumers and legislators.

EXERCISE 1-10

For each of these thesis statements, write an outline based on the model above.

1. Having a part-time job is an effective way to put yourself through school.
   Plan:
   Topic Sentence 1:
   Topic Sentence 2:
   Topic Sentence 3:
   Conclusion:

2. Dogs make better pets than cats.
   Plan:
   Topic Sentence 1:
   Topic Sentence 2:
   Topic Sentence 3:
   Conclusion:

3. Walking through a shopping mall can provide insight into human nature.
   Plan:
   Topic Sentence 1:
   Topic Sentence 2:
   Topic Sentence 3:
   Conclusion:

4. Bicycle riders should be required to pass a driving test.
   Plan:
   Topic Sentence 1:

Topic Sentence 2:
Topic Sentence 3:
Conclusion:

5. Public speaking can be an instructive and entertaining experience.
Plan:
Topic Sentence 1:
Topic Sentence 2:
Topic Sentence 3:
Conclusion:

EXERCISE 1-11

Find an editorial in a newspaper or magazine and locate its thesis statement and the points of its argument. Can you find a topic sentence for each of the paragraphs?

EXERCISE 1-12

Look at a piece of your own writing (one that has previously been handed in and marked by an instructor). Does it have a clear thesis statement and topic sentences? If not, can you revise the writing to make the outline of your argument clearer?

Methods of
Organization

Now that you know that a paragraph is composed of a topic sentence (its main point or thesis statement), support, elaboration, and a conclusion, you must next consider some of the different methods by which a paragraph or series of paragraphs can be organized.

Seven methods of organization will be described here: description, narration, definition, classification, process, comparison, and cause and effect. You can use each of these methods to develop either individual paragraphs or longer compositions.

Any of these methods of organization can be used either alone or in combination depending on your purpose. For instance, if your subject was censorship, you could develop your argument according to whichever aspect of the question you wanted to address.

If your main point was that some forms of censorship are necessary, you could, for example, *describe* in concrete detail a film scene that you consider gratuitously violent and therefore unsuitable for certain audiences.

Using narration, you might outline the history of recent protests against the inappropriate depiction of women in advertising.

You could try to *define* the term "censorship," explaining what you mean by it. You might say that censorship is the restriction of access to printed or recorded materials.

In order to *classify* the term, you might differentiate between censorship guidelines, like provincial ratings of films, and censorship laws, forbidding the distribution of certain books and media.

If you were outlining a *process* related to your main point about censorship, you might explain how you would decide what forms of censorship should be implemented.

To show that some kinds of censorship are necessary to protect society, you might *compare* the crime rates in places that have censorship laws to those that do not.

Using *cause and effect,* you might examine the social consequences, as you see them, of having no censorship laws.

No one paper would necessarily incorporate all of these methods of organizing an argument, but experimenting with these approaches might help you discover the best way to present your opinion. Further, an argument can be developed by using several of these methods in combination. Suppose you were arguing that censorship was actually good in some contexts. You might narrow the focus by saying that extreme violence in film and on television should be censored. You would have to *define* what you mean by extreme violence. You could present the *example* of the influence of the television movie *The Burning Bed;* this movie is said to have provoked a woman in the United

States to murder her husband. Using this example, you could argue that extreme violence on television is dangerous for impressionable or unstable minds, because it offers them a model of behaviour *(cause and effect)*. In conclusion, you might explain how potentially dangerous materials (those that make extreme violence attractive) should be dealt with *(process)*.

DESCRIPTION

What is Description?

Description provides a picture in words of a particular person, place, or thing in order to create a sense impression for the reader. Description focusses on the physical details in an attempt to recreate what the writer has seen.

Look at this passage describing a piece of sculpture:

Cyril Reade's installation consists of a found dining room suite surrounded by an eight-foot-high chain link fence. The *Weathering Table*, installed for one year in the Wolf Sculpture Garden at the London Regional Art and Historical Museums, is exposed to the natural processes of weathering and decay. It is clearly visible from various vantage points both inside and outside the gallery. Placed at the periphery of the site are signs reading "wait to be excused" and "provided you sit quietly," reminders of the kinds of rules taught to children and learned at the dining room table. Reade's signs resemble the neighbouring traffic signs in material, format and colour. *Weathering Table*, with its empty chairs casually arranged around a bare table, draws attention to an anonymous missing family. The absence adds to the ominous impenetrability of the barbed wire and chain link fence.

Reade has interwoven the complex issues of racism, genocide and suburban alienation into the innocuous domain of the dining room. The materials he has used are familiar and, in themselves, unremarkable. It is the combination of contrasting images of comfort and enclosure, refinement and brutality, that make the installation disconcerting.

The passage begins by describing the elements of the sculpture in objective terms, what actually can be seen. The last two sentences of the first paragraph begin to move the description from the visual to the interpretive. While also descriptive, the second paragraph is more subjective, explaining the meaning of what is seen.

In your writing, description can be a useful technique for presentation and interpretation of experience.

Using Description

1. Use language that is concrete, rather than abstract. Even though you may be trying to evoke a particular emotional response in the reader, it is usually best to concentrate on physical features of who or what is being described to create that impression. For instance, rather than writing "a scary-looking mask," you might write "a white-faced, eyeless mask with a protruding forehead."

2. Make use of figurative language to conjure up the effects that you want. Figurative language refers to such devices as similes, metaphors, and allusion. Similes and metaphors use comparison to make the unfamiliar familiar; similes use the words *like* or *as* to set up the comparison, while metaphors imply the relationship by means of an imaginative leap.

> Just before Lynette was due to arrive, Gareth vacuumed his apartment, like one possessed. (simile)

> Just before Lynette was due to arrive, Gareth became a maniac with a vacuum cleaner. (metaphor)

An allusion is a reference to something well known, meant to elucidate something less immediately recognizable. Allusions can be drawn from many sources, famous people, books, films, and places. To be effective, however, allusions should be common knowledge.

> Sabrina was considered the Madonna of the third grade.

> Its critics called it the Disneyland of Canadian universities.

3. Use spatial elements as a means of organization. You might, for instance, tour the reader through your home by moving from the front door to the back, taking in only those aspects of the house that distinguish it as characteristic (or uncharacteristic) of a student's living quarters.

4. To select the details you will describe, establish a dominant impression that you wish to convey to the reader. Test the effectiveness of your paragraph to create such an impression when you reread it. This tactic should help you avoid a common trap of descriptive writing—the tendency to describe too much or to no purpose.

Transitions

Some of these signals will be useful in developing description:

above	against
below	across
beside	next
beneath	to the right, to the left

The following essay uses description to develop its main point.

Whenever I think of Saskatchewan, I think of my home—not my parents' house so much as the city of Saskatoon and the surrounding area. Wherever I went inside this territory, I belonged. It was home to me. It was home to other people too, but I had no problem with that. There was plenty of room, physically and mentally. Perhaps it was because that was all I knew. Part of the self-centredness of being young meant feeling that nothing else and nowhere else mattered.

The most vivid memories that come back to me at the mention of the name Saskatchewan are of hunting, fishing, driving to hockey tournaments, exhibition baseball games, things that meant driving in the country. Strange that the first wave of memories for me were of the country—I grew up in the city. While I was taking classes in Canadian literature, in city classrooms, I kept hearing about how the land shaped the psyches and the art of the writers and especially the prairie writers. And when I drove across that land, I thought I understood. On the surface it all sounds exaggerated, but it is not. To this day, I still have an instinctive bias in support of prairie artists.

Saskatchewan's style is pure prairie. It does not even have a non-prairie province or state on its borders. Duck hunting was my favourite pastime of all. Although it is now politically incorrect, it was such a cherished part of my past that I still have my shotgun. I do not tell many people about it, but I remember hour after hour of standing out in the bald prairies in a small bunch of weeds, staring at the powerful sunrises and sunsets that I have not seen duplicated anywhere since. I never really caused a lot of damage to the duck populations, but I had a lot of Zen-like moments of inner peace and solitude that I cannot say I have had anywhere else.

Along with these times of bliss, I had times of great discomfort. I froze my ass over and over again. I clearly remember getting back to the car as fast as possible after dark, turning on the car immediately, and as soon as the car began to blow hot air, jamming my frozen, wet hands and feet in front of the air outlets. When my fingers or toes began to thaw enough for the feel-

35

ing to come back into them, the excruciating pain would leave me speechless. I sucked air through clenched teeth, eyes shut, waiting for the pain to go away.

Growing up on the prairies meant being cold, very cold much of the time. The cold could be inhibiting to anyone, but less so to us Saskatchewanians. We were born into it, understood it. Cars, trucks, and animals suffered terribly in prairie winters. I could only admire and wonder at my animal brothers and sisters who had no choice except to try to survive Old Man Winter's death grip. I thanked God that it was not me who had to live out in the raw country. I can remember being around large farm animals in the winter and recall clearly the condensing steam coming off their broad backs and the breath shooting out of their large nostrils, turning instantly to ice fog. They amazed me. The sounds were very localized. The snow absorbed sounds so well that I could hear only the sounds immediately around me—the crunching snow, breathing cows, an idling truck that seemed to idle louder. The sense of other animals living in the country was missing. The whole world would shrink down to whatever I could see or hear close to me. All else was frozen. This was far from the truth, of course, because life and death were continuing for many species, but to me, it just did not seem possible. Spending a night outside seemed like dying. How very humbling. Of course, writers from the prairies write about the power of the elements. How could they not?

Until I moved from Saskatchewan to the Northwest Territories and then to Vancouver, I did not realize how little contact I had had with peoples of other races. All of the people in my childhood were of European origin. In my high school of over one thousand students, there were small handfuls of Oriental students or Indo-Asian students. Strangely enough, there were even very few Native Canadians. I consider this to be unfortunate for us European Canadians, as well as the small visible minorities. Coming out of my childhood, I was left with a perspective that was sadly narrow and inexperienced. I think I still resent that fact.

Economically, Saskatchewan is ill. The illness shows in the eyes of the people too young to retire. The youth of my generation have little to look forward to. Just getting by seems to be the goal of far too many young people. The dreams and delusions of grandeur of youth have been replaced with a waiting out the storm mentality. I fear the storm may never end. In the early seventies, jobs were plentiful, farmers were prosperous and life seemed easy. Not anymore, I am sorry to say. The streets are badly in need of some maintenance, and commercial buildings for rent are cropping up faster than the wheat. The wheat once kept all these buildings in business. The success or failure of the grain farmer is the success or failure of Saskatchewan—its government, its commerce, and its people. Today wheat is selling for about ten dollars and fifty cents a bushel or about one fifth of the value of the same product grown and sold in the seventies. I will not defend those numbers with my life, but they are close enough to make anybody realize that everybody in Saskatchewan who is not a civil servant is worried. European and American grain price subsidies have driven the open market price of grain down to a level where no grain farmer in the western world can survive without government subsidies. Unfortunately, for Saskatchewan farmers, their provincial and even their federal governments are small players on the world market. They are powerless to control the situation. There is more grain on the market than people who want to buy it. People are dying by the thousands in Somalia and Ethiopia and other similarly stricken countries around the world, but the sad truth is they do not have any money to buy the grain. The countries that have the money have plenty of grain because it is cheap.

Saskatchewan farmers are repeatedly planting and harvesting a crop that nobody wants anymore. As might be predictable, whenever I offer this prognosis to anybody involved in farming, the response is icy silence. It is akin to talking about the black sheep in one's family; everyone knows it is a fact, but it is in poor taste to mention it. People do not want to hear it. They do not want to believe that everything the preceding three or four generations strove for may be coming to an end. If it comes to an end, then what?

Saskatchewanians do not want drastic change in their communities. They seem to be holding on, waiting for some form of miracle to bring the price and demand for grain back up to past lelvels. They do not want to change who they are, and, deep down inside, I do not want them to change who they are either.

Saskatchewan is my ancester. Watching my ancestors pass their peak, age, and fade is hard to accept. Seeing a large part of my past grow old and weak, psychologically breaks me a little more from my youth and my past. As each preceding generation fades and dies, we are a little more alone in the world.

1. What is the main point or thesis statement of this essay?

2. What is the dominant impression of this essay?

3. What details contribute to the creation of this impression?

4. Can you find any examples of figurative language?

5. Which elements of this essay are subjective and which objective?

6. What transitions are used in the course of this paper? Could any transitions be added or improved?

EXERCISE 2-1

Write a descriptive paragraph using one of these topics:

1. your dreamhouse

2. the car you own or would like to own

3. the experience of participating in a favourite sport

4. a walk in the woods

5. a walk in a shopping mall

6. fashion follies

7. the view out a window

8. a cherished object

9. an exotic pet

10. the face of someone you know

11. a meal you enjoyed

EXERCISE 2-2

Find some examples of descriptive passages in magazines like *Equinox*, *National Geographic*, or in the travel section of the newspaper. What tactics do you find there to make description clear and engaging?

NARRATION

What is Narration?

Although expository writing does not tell a story, one of the tactics you can use to explain your point is narration. Narration can dramatize your central idea by means of brief or extended, factual or hypothetical anecdotes that serve as examples. Narrative can create suspense in your writing. While you should not keep your reader in suspense about the point of your argument, you can make your work more interesting by using dramatic examples.

Using Narration

1. Narration should be employed, not for its own sake, but for the purpose of illustrating the main point of the writing.

2. All details should be selected with an eye to relevance and the development of the argument. Watch for unnecessary frills, "artistic touches" and verbal clutter: keep a tight rein on adjectives and adverbs.

3. Because narration outlines events over time, it is essential for the reader to have a clear sense of chronological sequence. Monitor your verb tenses; if you begin in the past tense, stay with it. Casting the narrative in the present tense, however, makes it more dramatic and creates immediacy. Either tense will work as long as you are consistent in its use. Also, make sure your transitions are sufficient indicators of the passage of time.

4. Your point of view should be consistent through the narrative example, whether you are describing events through your eyes or from the perspective of someone else. If, for example, you begin by using the pronouns "I" and "me," you should not shift to "you."

5. Narrative examples can be enlivened with dialogue, but the speakers must be clearly identified and the language should ring true. Again, relevance should be the guiding principle.

Transitions
Some of these signals may help in organizing narration:

next	now
later	then
before	after
while	since
during	again
at the same time	suddenly

The following essay uses narration to develop its main point.

VANCOUVER MARATHON

A year ago I would never have imagined running a marathon. But here I was, with number 1726 on my chest and adrenalin pulsing through my body. Bang! The sound of the starting gun vibrated through the crowd at the Plaza of Nations. The mass of runners surged towards the starting line. Exhilaration filled my body as I realized how significant this race was to the rest of my life.

I have always been goal oriented, but running a marathon was the ultimate test. I wanted to see what I was made of, to find out just how far I could go. The marathon tested my physical and mental limits and challenged my discipline. Several of my friends had run marathons, so I was well aware of the commitment. It was during a casual gathering with these friends that I dared to mention my desire to run a marathon. I was enthusiastically handed a book on "Running Your First Marathon."

I began my training the next day. Starting very slowly, listening to my body, I gradually began to increase my miles. I endured 6 a.m. runs through wind, slush, snow, and anything else nature had to offer. Eating properly was important as well as knowing when to rest and when to apply ice to my various minor injuries. On bad days, when my body was aching and my morale was down, I used visualization to get me out of bed, imagining the glory of running through the finish line. Anticipating the feeling of satisfaction I would gain from completing the marathon helped through my training. I was determined to succeed.

The day of the race soon arrived. Was I ready? Accompanied by my friends, Allan, Marie, and Lorne, I joined with the others at the starting point. These three special people, whom to this day I call my "Pit Crew," played an important role in getting me through this event. Allan, without fail, met me at every three to five mile point to encourage me and supply me with fluids. Marie, who shares my running ambitions, was always at the right place at the right time to cheer me on. Lorne managed to pull me through the last six miles by running alongside me.

Bang! We were off. I knew that the only way to complete the 26.2 miles was to pace myself. It is very tempting to kick into high gear and pass everyone. This approach, I learned from previous runs, only results in early burnout. Even though the crowds of runners passed me, I still had full rein on my ego.

What I love the most about a run is the great mood and friendliness of the crowd. From my perspective (at the back of the pack), meeting people from all over the world was much of the fun. We all have our own special reason for running, but we, in the back, have one thing in common: the hope of finishing.

We ran down Beach Avenue toward Stanley Park. The wind felt like ice. Once in the park, we were protected by trees which allowed the sun to work on our frozen muscles. At three miles we reached our first water station, and there was Allan's smiling face, making sure I was O.K. The course took us through Lost Lagoon, past Deadman's Island, Brockton Point, the Girl in the Wet Suit statue, back around to the zoo and onto the next water station. The six-mile point came, and I was feeling great. Heading along Stanley Park Drive, I felt a twinge in my knee. Moving away from the crowd, I stopped to stretch. Stretching helped a little, but I knew I was headed for trouble. I had never had knee pains in any of my other runs. The prospect of defeat weighed heavily on me.

What perfect timing—I looked away and saw Marie cheering me on. She wiped away any negative feelings I had, and new energy swept over me.

Running over the Lion's Gate Bridge was a thrill that made me forget the pain. I was halfway there. I knew Allan would be at Park Royal with the Gatorade, and we would celebrate. Fortunately, the road was flat along Welsch Street, Esplanade and the lower levels; however, my knees started to seize, and the pain was excruciating. As I approached the Second Narrows Bridge, I felt devastated. The possibility of not finishing the marathon became too real. My bottom lip started to quiver, and tears fell on my already salty face. I was nose to nose with "The Wall," something I had read about but never experienced. Looking up at the bridge, I realized I was at the twenty-mile mark.

If I could make it across, surely I could manage the last six miles. Besides, I knew Allan was waiting on the other side.

Planting my focus at the end of the bridge, I did some fast walking to give my knees a rest. Allan cringed when he saw me limping but did not say a word. I had FINISH written all over my face. At different times along the route, Allan had been taking pictures, and I thought how interesting it would be to see the play by play of my deterioration. Crazy thoughts were making their way through my head. Just as I thought I was losing my mind, Lorne appeared from out of nowhere to coach me through the last six miles. The pain was almost unbearable. I knew the sensible thing to do was to stop, but I needed to finish. Lorne talked me in. "Let's just make it to that stop sign. Come on ... Now how about passing the guy in the yellow shorts?" He would count to ten, and we would walk for ten counts. Little things started to annoy me; in fact, at one point I had this sudden urge to punch Lorne. But, really, I was glad he was there.

I was about to admit defeat when I saw B.C. Place. Lorne left me about one hundred yards from the finish line. People were cheering, and I could see Allan throwing up his arms, a bouquet of flowers in one hand.

Mentally, I felt fabulous, but my body, on the other hand, was hurting. My tag was removed as I walked through the gates and headed for the muffins and juice. Then I headed out to the common area where my "pit crew" waited for me. I felt extremely close to them for what we had just been through together.

Now that it is all over, I know it was foolish not to stop running when the pain in my knee first started. Completing the marathon meant more to me than the physical ordeal. In fact, the challenge of the marathon itself was not my prime motive. I needed to know whether it was possible to reach beyond a lifetime of personal boundaries that kept me safe and comfortable. Now I feel that each goal I set is possible to accomplish. One other valuable insight I had as a result of this event is how fortunate I am to have friends who believed in me more than I believed in myself. I found a new confidence and greater understanding of friendship.

1. What expository purpose does this narrative serve?

2. How do the details of the narration add to its effectiveness?

3. How does the author handle the passage of time?

4. What transitions are used throughout the essay?

EXERCISE 2-3

Write a short essay using narration to develop one of the following topics:

1. the worst date of your life

2. the best party you gave or attended

3. your appearance on your favourite game show or soap opera

4. an embarrassing moment

5. an accident or a dangerous experience

6. an interview

7. the first day of school (any year)

8. a family get-together

9. a significant moment in your life

10. how your parents met

11. the experience of having a roommate

12. my day off

13. finding an apartment

14. a day at the beach

15. an argument

DEFINITION

What is Definition?

We often need to explain certain words in order to be understood. Definition relies on specific details and examples to clarify meaning. Usually when you define a term, you describe not only what the term is but also what it is not. If you were asked to define the crime of stealing, for instance, you would, in order to be precise, have to distinguish between several legal terms: theft, burglary, and armed robbery. Although all of these terms describe the same form of crime, there are differences a careful definition would indicate.

Theft is the general term for the act of stealing:

The *theft* at the video arcade meant the loss of $300.

Burglary involves illegal entry into a building for the purpose of theft:

> There was a *burglary* at the Mac's Milk store: a door was forced open, and the contents of the cash register and twenty bags of potato chips were taken.

Armed robbery is the use of violence to obtain goods illegally:

> The victim of the *armed robbery* spent three weeks in hospital recovering from his injuries.

We make use of **definition** every time we look up the meaning of a word in a dictionary.

ill-use (v. il′yüz′; n. il′yüs′)v.-used,-**us•ing;** n.—v. treat badly, cruelly, or unfairly.—n. bad, cruel, or unfair treatment.

Optical Illusions

il•lu•sion (i lü′zhən) n. **1** an appearance or feeling that misleads because it is not real; something that deceives by giving a false idea: *an illusion of re-ality.* **2** a false impression or perception: *an optical illusion.* **3** a false idea, no-tion, or belief: *Many people have the illusion that wealth is the chief cause of happiness.* **4** a fine, delicate, net fabric used especially for veils and trimmings. [< L *illusio,-onis* < *illudere* mock < *in-* at + *ludere* play]

Syn. **1. Illusion, delusion** = something mistakenly or falsely believed to be true or real. **Illusion** applies to something appearing to be real or true, but actually not existing or being quite different from what it seems: *Good motion pictures create an illusion of reality.* **Delusion** applies to a false and often harm-ful belief about something that does exist: *The old woman had the delusion that the butcher was always trying to cheat her.*

Usage. Do not confuse **illusion** and **allusion**. An **illusion** is a misleading appearance: *an illusion of wealth.* An **allusion** is an indirect reference or slight mention: *He made several allusions to recent novels.*

il•lu•sion•ist (i lüzhən ist) n. **1** a person who produces illusions; con-jurer. **2** a person who has illusions; dreamer.

Source: *Gage Canadian Dictionary* (Toronto: Gage Publishing Ltd., 1983).

Using Definition

1. Decide what the term means, drawing on the dictionary and your own experience. The dictionary will tell you the precise denotation of the word or what it means in common use. In addition to its essential meaning, a word may have associated or implied meanings, the connotations that the word has picked up through use.

   The denotative meaning of the word "fox" is a red-furred, sharp-snouted, bushy-tailed, carnivorous quadruped preserved in England and other places as a beast of chase.

   The connotative meanings of the word "fox" include a crafty person or an attractive woman.

   For the most part, a dictionary definition is not enough. While you may need to know what the word means, the focus of your writing will be on what *you* mean by the word:

What does the word mean?	*dictionary definition*
What do I mean by the word?	*your working definition*

2. Decide what category the word belongs in. What kind of thing is it? When you formulate a definition, you will find it helpful to see the term in the context of similar things.

   A chihuahua is a small, smooth-haired *dog* of Mexican origin. A Doberman pinscher is a large, smooth-haired *dog* of German origin.

   Knowing the category will prevent you from writing imprecisely worded definitions like this one:

   Education is when your talents and abilities are brought out.

   "Education" is not a time so you should revise the sentence:

   Education is a process by which your talents and abilities are brought out.

3. Make distinctions. How is the term different from related things? Notice how this example distinguishes between two apparently related professions.

   Many people confuse psychiatrists and psychologists. Unlike the psychiatrist, the psychologist has no medical training and is not able to prescribe drugs. A psychologist may have a degree in counselling and may often work under the supervision of a psychiatrist.

   This kind of definition frequently has a "not this ... but that" structure.

4. Determine function. What does it do? How does it work? Give examples to illustrate its characteristics.

   A compact disc player is a computerized audio system that reads coded

45

messages from a specially prepared disc by means of a laser in order to produce high-quality sound.

Transitions

Some of these signals may help in organizing definitions:

in other words	in general
to put it another way	generally speaking
in particular	usually
to be specific	often
especially	for the most part
to some extent	frequently
to a degree	

The following essay uses definition to develop its main point.

NODDERS

What are nodders you ask? This is a small group of people, composed of students of only the highest intellectual calibre. Nodders are preprogrammed. They respond with a head-bobbing movement several times throughout each class. They always assume front-row positions in a classroom so that their nods are highly visible to the instructor and to all those stiff necks who sit behind them.

Opportune moments for a good nod occur when a remote but, of course, very interesting point is raised in the class or when an item of trivia known only to experts on a particular subject is pointed out. When teachers ask questions that nobody in the class can answer, they are often forced to answer themselves. This is an excellent opportunity for an "oh yeah, now I remember" nod.

The funny thing about nodders is that when it comes right down to enlightening everybody on their vast knowledge of the topic, for some reason they only know a little, or, well, it was a long time since they read that book, or watched that movie, or saw that play. Some nodders get right out of saying anything. They just repeat the club motto: "Oh, I thought you were talking about something else."

I wasn't allowed in the nodders' club because they couldn't get me to stop shaking my head.

1. What is the thesis statement of this essay? Where is it located? Is another more effective location possible?

2. How are nodders characterized?

3. What transitions are used to signal the movement from one step in the argument to the next?

4. What supporting details are used to develop the steps of this definition?

5. Can you strip the essay down to its outline?

EXERCISE 2-4

Write a paragraph defining one of these terms:

hero	villain	underdog	loser
rebel	show-off	trouble-maker	fanatic

EXERCISE 2-5

The words that appear below are called "the seven deadly sins." Choose the one that most applies (or appeals) to you and develop a definition of it in either a single paragraph or a three-paragraph essay, making sure that you follow the four steps outlined above:

avarice	envy	gluttony	lust
pride	sloth	wrath	

EXERCISE 2-6

Invent a term for a group of people you have observed and create an extended definition for it, using the short essay "Nodders" as a model.

EXERCISE 2-7

Write a definition of yourself. What are the special qualities, the strengths and weaknesses, likes and dislikes, that constitute you?

EXERCISE 2-8

Write a definition based on one of the following:

What makes a good parent?	What makes a good pet?
What makes a good employer?	What makes a good party?
What makes a good friend?	

CLASSIFICATION

What is Classification?

Classification is a method of sorting information about a subject into logically defined categories. Classification is used as a system of organization in such things as want ads, libraries, supermarkets, and horoscopes. Classification is a logical extension of definition: once you have the general term *trees* in mind, then you can begin to classify kinds of *trees* according to certain categories, for instance, coniferous and deciduous.

Using Classification

1. Generally you should have a main point or thesis in mind when you classify items. This may simply be a statement explaining why you chose a particular method of classification. You might want to explain that you have sorted food processors by their features, rather than by their price, in order to evaluate their capabilities.

2. Use only one principle of classification at a time. For instance, if you write about motorcycles, you need to decide whether you will categorize them according to size, horsepower, or manufacturer.

3. Divide a subject up in as many ways as possible. Try to consider all the potential categories. Keep in mind that opinion polls not only include the categories of *Agree* and *Disagree*, but also offer the option of *Undecided*.

4. Make sure that your topic is narrow enough to be classified into a reasonable number of categories. Instead of trying to write about religions of Canada, a topic which would generate perhaps a hundred separate categories, limit your topic to Canada's four major religions, and base your selection on numerical criteria.

5. Remember that classification, like any labelling, is a partial way of understanding a subject. Subjects can often be placed in different categories, depending on your motive. You can classify people according to the labels passive or aggressive, but you need to be aware that people are seldom entirely passive or aggressive in every area of their lives.

CLASSIFICATION KEYS

You want to classify five animals that you have found, to differentiate them from each other by certain of their features. Biologists have made up classification keys to help you sort the information about these animals into logically defined categories.

   In this simple key you will classify the animals by their appendages and, in the last instance, also by their body shape. Start with the first animal and work down the key until you have identified that animal. Then do the same for the other four animals.

1. Butterfly

2. Spider

3. Crayfish

4. Centipede

5. Millipede

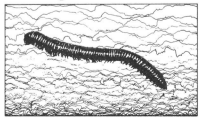

1a	Has wings	Butterfly
1b	Has no wings	Go to classification 2
2a	Has 8 or fewer legs	Spider
2b	Has more than 8 legs	Go to classification 3
3a	Has 10 or fewer legs	Crayfish
3b	Has more than 10 legs	Go to classification 4
4a	Body flattened; 1 pair of legs per body segment	Centipede
4b	Body rounded; 2 pairs of legs per body segment	Millipede

Remember that you could also classify these animals in many other ways: by their body weight, by their eating or mating habits, by their life spans, and so on.

Transitions
Some of these signals will be useful in developing classification:

first, second, third ...	as well
another	in contrast
then	although
similarly	though
equally	even though
likewise	whereas
again	on the one hand ... on the other hand
in the same way	

Consider how the following passage uses classification:

'TIS THE SEASON TO BE KISSING

By Sidney Katz*

Kissing, a delightful human activity which peaks at Valentine's Day, is a simple enough act: two people saluting or caressing each other with their lips. But depending on how it's done, the kiss can convey a wide variety of messages—duty, gratitude, curiosity, respect, friendship, sexual passion or undying love. In unsentimental medical jargon, a kiss is described as "the anatomical juxtaposition of the two orbicularis oris muscles in a state of contraction."

50

*Copyright, Sidney Katz Enterprises Limited, 1990.

But to the romantic Greeks, a kiss is "the key to paradise," while Cyrano de Bergerac defined it as "a rosy dot placed on the eye of loving: 'tis a secret told to the mouth instead of the ear."

A widely respected standard for "the perfect kiss" was set more than 50 years ago by Hugh Morris, author of *The Art of Kissing*. The secret, said Morris, lies in concentration. "Kiss as though at that moment nothing else exists in the world. Kiss as though your entire life is wrapped up in the period of the kiss. Kiss as though there is nothing else you would rather be doing."

The main types of commonly used kisses can be listed as follows:

The blow kiss. This comes highly recommended for people who want to avoid physical contact. With a quick gesture of hand and mouth, you can dispatch a kiss to someone at the other end of the room—or to anyone in sight.

The cheek peck. Widely used, it's a kiss without substance consisting of a quick touch to the cheek. This kiss is for casual acquaintances only.

The cheek nuzzle. This is more personal than the perfunctory cheek peck and takes longer. You warmly touch the cheek of the recipient with your lips and cheek. This kiss is limited to people you genuinely like.

The ear kiss. Thoughtful people will resort to this kiss if the recipient is a heavily made-up lady who's in fear of seeing her handiwork smeared.

The low-voltage lip kiss. This kiss is meant for friends you like or for people to whom you wish to express sincere gratitude.

The high-voltage lip kiss. This kiss is intended to express intense passion and/or love. You should be warned that this kiss triggers a physiological earthquake in the body. The pulse rate shoots up from 72 to 100, the blood pressure and blood sugar level rise and there's a flutter around the heart—the result of spleen contraction and the addition to the blood of millions of red blood corpuscles.

Although kissing is a pretty safe form of recreation, there are still some hazards to be reckoned with. During a kiss, anywhere between 23 and 280 colonies of bacteria are exchanged, most of them harmless unless you happen to have a cold or some other ailment. In the so-called "Hollywood Kiss" (duration 10 to 12 seconds), twice as many bacteria travel mouth-to-mouth as are transmitted during a perfunctory kiss on the lips. Men with a mustache deliver more bacteria during a kiss than do smooth-shaven ones.

Wearers of contact lenses are urged to exercise caution during high-voltage kissing: the vigorous movement of the cheek and jaw muscles during kissing can work the lenses loose and you stand a good chance of losing them. The amount of high-voltage kissing which prevails at any given time must have some bearing on the prosperity (or lack of it) in the optical supplies business.

1. What is the thesis statement of this essay?

2. What factors determine the categories of kissing?

3. Why do you think the author uses classification to approach this subject?

4. What supporting details are used to develop the steps of the argument?

5. What part does humour play in a classification of this kind?

EXERCISE 2-9

Write a composition on one of the following topics, using classification.

sports fans	outdoor activities
television commercials	shoes
students	stores
attitudes towards death	jocks
beer	opinions about money
video games	friends
waiters and waitresses	areas of the city
siblings	attitudes towards marriage
teachers	bosses
fast food	lies
jobs	attitudes towards warfare
attitudes towards children	irritations
hairstyles	parties
cars	movies
leaders	dates

PROCESS

What is Process?

When you write a paper employing process, you are outlining actions that take place in a sequence. Process writing usually takes the form of a set of instructions. The main point or thesis statement of writing based on process is your recommendation that this is the best or most efficient way to do something. The most common example of process is a recipe. In a recipe you find a list of ingredients followed by a description of how to proceed in order to achieve the desired result. Process writing, although it often does not use a numbered list of steps as a recipe might, develops in the same ordered fashion.

RECIPE FOR CHOCOLATE CHIP COOKIES

1. Combine, in one bowl, 1 1/2 cups all-purpose flour, 1 tsp. baking powder, and 1/2 tsp. salt.

2. Blend together, in a separate bowl, 2/3 cup butter (softened to room temperature), 1/2 cup white sugar, and 1/2 cup brown sugar. Then beat in 1 egg and 1 tsp. vanilla. Finally, blend the dry ingredients and the creamed mixture together.

3. Stir in 1 cup chocolate chips and drop by teaspoonful onto well-greased baking sheets. Bake for 8 to 10 minutes in a 375 degree (F) oven.

4. Loosen from pan as soon as they come out of the oven.

5. Let cool and remove from pan.

Using Process

1. Make sure all terms are defined.

2. Make sure the process follows a logical and effective order.

3. Make sure all the necessary steps are included.

4. Develop one step fully before going on to the next.

5. Anticipate the reader's questions about the process or potential problems that may arise.

Transitions
Some of these signals may help in organizing process writing:

to begin	all the while
to end	while
first ... second ... third	until
now	before
then	during
later	after
meanwhile	in conclusion
in the mean time	finally

The following essay uses the process pattern.

HOW TO BE A DICTATOR

First choose a small country with a suitable climate, preferably mediterranean or tropical. This country should have an unstable government ripe for a *coup d'état*. To ensure support for your ambitions, mobilize the army by making friends with several highly placed generals. The best ways to cultivate such friends are by making outrageous promises about what you will do once in power and exchanging a little currency. Have them overthrow the current regime, bloodlessly if possible.

The proper way to celebrate your victory is to make an appearance on the balcony of the presidential palace, making sure that your wardrobe reflects your humble origins and your status as "one of the people." You should now make a speech promising free and democratic elections, increased access to education, freedom of the press, and lower taxes. Next you must organize a press conference in order to shore up your position with a media blitz; release photographs of you and the rebel forces marching amid the friendly crowds. Ensure that these photographs are prominently featured in all the major western newspapers and magazines.

Once in power, design new uniforms for your elite corps of army supporters, heavy on the gold braid and epaulets. An important dictator needs a wife, so you marry a glamorous socialite who will become known for her shopping skills, conspicuous consumption, and her appearances in *Vanity Fair* magazine. To guarantee the support of western nations and to demonstrate your dedication to culture, you should build a fabulously expensive opera house, hold a major film festival, and host many parties with the jet-set televised on the national network so that all your people, including the poor, can enjoy them in the comfort of their own hovels.

To establish a firmer socioeconomic base, you must now declare yourself President-for-life. This announcement should be accompanied by a change in your wardrobe to indicate the prestige of the new office: Polo and Gucci are two of the names of choice. This shift in political ideology necessitates raising taxes. Sensing some opposition to the new policy, you now regretfully shut down the newspapers and close the schools. It might be wise at this point to schedule an interview with Morley Safer on "60 Minutes" to defend yourself against the press who have failed to understand your political reality and the need for detainment without arrest. In case you are unable to control public support, you should open a Swiss bank account in your own name as a safe place for government funds. Keeping a packed suitcase at your bedside might also be advisable now. Begin secret negotiations with a large democratic nation, preferably the United States, to secure political refugee status.

When the situation gets too hot, flee the country, making sure that you take your "insurance": the photo album showing you and many friends, media celebrities, and world leaders in familiar poses. In your safe haven, set about writing your memoirs and confirming your place in the history of your former nation.

1. What is the thesis statement of this essay?

2. What are the steps in the argument?

3. What supporting details are used to develop the steps of the argument?

4. Are other steps possible in this particular process?

5. Can you strip the essay down to its outline?

EXERCISE 2-10

There's a bomb in the building; give someone directions on how to get out of the building safely from where you are.

EXERCISE 2-11

Write a process paper on one of these subjects:

how to make a million	how to make the right impression
how to be famous	how to be very popular
how to write a best-seller	how to be the life of the party
how to find true love	how to be healthy
how to run the country more effectively	how to get a job

EXERCISE 2-12

Write a process paper explaining how you do something.

EXERCISE 2-13

Write a process paper explaining how you got to know X (a person, a place, a thing, a subject of interest).

EXERCISE 2-14

Write a process paper explaining what you as the next Prime Minister of Canada would do to fix the country.

COMPARISON

What is Comparison?

The most important thing to know about comparison is why you are using it. Comparison assumes a relationship between two or more things and asks what you can know about them by putting them next to each other. By pointing out similarities, however, comparison also highlights differences.

When you write a comparative essay, you should not assume that the points of similarity and difference are obvious; you must bring those points into sharp focus.

COMPARISON

When you compare two things, you want to keep the reader's focus on the main point of the comparison. In this advertisement, the point is clearly how much a toupee can improve your looks—and your life.

Using Comparison

There are two ways to structure a comparative essay.

1. The first method, best suited for short papers, is to describe one side of the comparison completely and then the other, making sure that you present the details of the second subject in exactly the same order as the first.

Main point or thesis statement: Working full time is more rewarding than working part time.

a) Full time employment
   —responsibilities
   —hours
   —wages
   —benefits

b) Part time employment
   —responsibilities
   —hours
   —wages
   —benefits

c) Conclusion

2. The second method of organization is to alternate between the subjects being compared, discussing them under common headings.

Main point or thesis statement: Working full time is more rewarding than working part time.

a) Responsibilities: full time—part time

b) Hours: full time—part time

c) Wages: full time—part time

d) Benefits: full time—part time

e) Conclusion

Transitions
Some of these signals may help in organizing comparison writing:

also	however
on the other hand	in comparison
likewise	and yet
similarly	instead
the same as	nevertheless
more	on the contrary
less	by the same token
by contrast	at the same time
but	

The following two essays develop the two different methods of comparison, block comparison and point by point comparison. Read them carefully to discover which method is used in each. Consider how you would organize the same material using the other method.

THREE DIFFERENT STUDY METHODS

When preparing for examinations, I have found that methods of study are often as diverse as the kinds of students who use them. The degree of ease, or lack of it, with which students prepare themselves for exams quite often reflects the quality as well as the quantity of work carried out in the course of the term. As a result, the student's activities on the night preceding an exam can vary from watching television, to rigorously cramming a full term's study into one night, to calmly and confidently reviewing the work of the term in a rational and systematic manner.

Three students, Mitch, Mei-Ling, and Kirsten, illustrate these methods in the "case histories" that follow.

Mitch begins his evening's study by first attempting to assemble what lecture notes he does have. As he leafs through the assortment of dog-eared, coffee-stained lecture notes of the past term, he notices that they account for only half the lectures set out in the course outline. "I can't have missed that many lectures," he tells himself. "Oh well, I never could make sense of what that instructor was talking about half the time anyway!" Then Mitch shifts his efforts toward the course textbook which he finds buried beneath a pile of dust under his bed. He bends back the stiff cover and turns to the Table of Contents, realizing to his horror that he has ten chapters to read that night.

It is at this point that Mitch concedes defeat; his lack of preparation and poor attitude have again proved to be his undoing. This student's nervousness and concern subside as he faces the fact that his chances of passing the exam are virtually nil. Mitch's tendency toward rationalization helps reduce his worry even more: "That course wasn't important anyway. There's always summer school." At this point, Mitch concludes his study, turning his attention to the nearby television set: "I can still catch part of 'Wheel of Fortune.' "

By contrast, Mei-Ling is hard at work organizing her collection of meticulously kept notes. A full term of writer's cramp has resulted in a complete set of notes which she believes will guarantee her a good mark. "I got down every word that professor ever said," she thinks as she riffles through the thick pile of notes. However, her hopes for easy study soon fade as she faces the same problem as her lazy fellow classmate Mitch: she has too much material to cover in too little time. Although she has taken great pains to compile her notes, they amount to little more than scribbles on a page. She was so anxious to get down every word the instructor said that she missed several of the major ideas.

Desperately Mei-Ling seeks help from the text she has thoroughly highlighted. Upon opening the book, she is nearly blinded by the glare of blazing yellow ink radiating from almost every line on every page. Highlighting the textbook seemed like a good idea at the time: why bother trying to understand the material in the book when the key points can be emphasized with the simple sweep of a marking pen? It is unfortunate that so much of her hard work was for nothing. Mei-Ling faces the prospect of having to put in an all-night study session with only average results to show for her efforts.

With further development of her study skills, Mei-Ling might be able to share the success of Kirsten. Unlike either of her previously mentioned classmates, Kirsten started studying for the exam during the first class. Instead of trying to copy down the instructor's every word, this student focussed her energy upon copying down key words and ideas discussed in the classes. The result of this method of note-taking is a set of clear, concise notes which cover the major topics. If Kirsten is unsure of any of these points, she can check them against the textbook which often contains a list of suggestions for further reading.

Kirsten has simply to go over these notes, while remembering the relative importance of certain chapters in the text to conclude, "The emphasis seemed to fall on Chapters 2, 3, 5, and 9." She can read these chapters over in depth and skim over the key points in other chapters.

This method of study results in maximum efficiency, permitting the student to use the valuable time before the exam to its full potential. The time saved by having the term's work condensed allows Kirsten to focus on the central themes of the course and get a good night's sleep before the exam.

Comparing these three examples of study methods, you can see that the method of study is as important as the amount of study. By focussing your attention upon significant elements of class discussion and being able to distinguish this material from the less important, you will achieve maximum benefit.

WINNING BY LOSING

Fatty, fatty, two by four,
Can't get through the bathroom door.

We live in a society obsessed with size and shape. Magazines are continually offering fool-proof ways of achieving the perfect silhouette. In spite of supposedly painless "secrets," "tips," and "miracles," there are only two ways to lose weight: one is to decrease input (translate that to mean "eat less"); the other is to increase output ("do more"). The first will probably make you cranky; the second will undoubtedly make you sweat. Whichever of these methods you choose as the answer to your weight problem, you will need to do the same three things: cultivate discipline, change your habits, and develop realistic goals.

In either case, the discipline is essential. You see, a pound is made up of 3500 calories, or units of energy. You can find 3500 calories in about one whole cheesecake. Roughly speaking, you need 12–15 calories per pound each day to maintain your body weight. Burning 500 calories more each day or reducing your intake by 500 calories each day should thus result in a weight loss of about a pound a week.

If you decide to increase your rate of activity, you're going to need that discipline. It may mean getting up at five o'clock in the morning in order to run off these offensive bulges. And the exercise should be regular. A half hour of running, though it is sound aerobic exercise (which means it increases your heart rate), won't help unless you persist on a daily basis, or at least three times a week.

If you choose to diet, rather than to work so hard, you're going to have to watch your calories. It is usually a good idea to choose a level between 1200 and 1500 calories a day for safe weight reduction. Less than that, and your body won't get the nourishment it needs to carry you through the day. If you don't know much about the calorie content of foods, you can buy a simple guide in your grocery store. Take note that many foods have labels to inform you of their caloric value as well. A less complicated method, but one which requires firm discipline, is to train yourself to eat smaller portions of everything, with the possible exception of edibles laden with "empty calories" like potato chips and chocolate bars.

Changing your habits is an important part of any weight reduction program. If, for example, you intend to increase your activity substantially, you might consider sleeping fewer hours per night. Sleeping 6–7 hours, and no more, should help to reduce your weight and increase your metabolic rate. In addition, you should try to learn new activities, not only regular (and perhaps boring) exercises, but also sports, like tennis or skiing, which offer pleasurable ways of burning off that extra piece of cake or bottle of beer.

Habit plays a major role in eating less as well. Do you eat something as soon as you get home from school whether you are hungry or not? Do you find yourself eating without thinking—nibbling at the supper vegetables before they are cooked, for example? Studying your typical eating patterns, you may discover that you eat when you are depressed or angry or bored. Taking note of these bad habits and setting about to change them will help you maintain more conscious control over the shape you're in.

Another important thing to remember about weight control—your goals must be realistic. You simply cannot expect to start running three miles a day if the most strenuous exercise you normally engage in is opening the refrigerator door. Overexertion will only result in fatigue or injury. If you concentrate on increasing your activity rate by joining a gym, taking up a sport or doing sit-ups in front of the television set, you must remember that changes do not occur overnight. Only regular, slow, and sustained effort will be rewarded.

Dieting isn't magic either. Do not set goals that are impossible for you to achieve. If you have a big frame or bulky proportions, dieting cannot transform you into calendar art. Weighing yourself every day will do little for you if you have exaggerated expectations. Besides, starvation diets are self-defeating: too much deprivation will only result in uncontrollable craving, cheating in the middle of the night, and binge eating. The changes in your shape can come about only through realistic goals and practices.

The best approach to weight loss is a combination of these two methods. You may wind up being sweaty AND cranky, but it will ultimately pay off.

1. What is the main point, or *thesis* statement, of each piece of writing and where is it placed?

2. Which method of organization is used for each of these essays?

3. What are the points of comparison in each essay? What support is used to develop them?

4. What signals are used to emphasize the comparison?

5. Are there places where clearer signals could be added?

EXERCISE 2-15

Write a comparison of one of the following pairs:

dogs and cats
cars and motorcycles
watching TV at home and
going to the movies

glasses and contact lenses
rock music and country and western
love and lust
walking and driving

EXERCISE 2-16

Think of a subject on which you and a family member or a friend disagree. Write a comparison of your attitudes to persuade the reader that you are right.

EXERCISE 2-17

Write a comparison of yourself at the age of six or the age of twelve and yourself now. Limit your discussion in order to focus the writing.

EXERCISE 2-18

Write a comparative study of how your life will be different from that of your parents.

EXERCISE 2-19

Choose two different brands of the same product and write a comparison of them, deciding which is superior.

CAUSE AND EFFECT

What is Cause and Effect?

We use cause and effect to explain why things happen and what the results are. There are two possible cause and effect relationships that you can develop in short pieces of writing: you can examine the causes in detail, or you can examine the consequences in detail. In a longer piece of writing, you might try to explicate both the causes and effects of a particular thing.

Generally speaking, cause and effect development would follow a pattern like this: Because of A, B occurs. You could develop causes (the A side of the cause-effect relationship). For example, an accident occurs, and traffic stops for forty-five minutes. A van is in the ditch, and three people are taken to the hospital. Suppose that you have to explain the causes of the accident. Your topic sentence might look something like this:

Because of weather conditions and driver error, the accident occurred.

In the paragraph which follows this topic sentence, you would explore the causes in detail: weather conditions and driver error. For example, you might say that the pavement was wet and therefore slippery and that the driver was distracted by a wasp which had flown in the window.

If you want to develop the effects which spring from a particular cause, you would focus on the B side of the cause-effect relationship. For instance, you might wonder what the consequences of using calculators are upon the mathematical ability of those who use them. Your topic sentence might look like this:

> Using calculators diminishes ability to perform simple mathematical functions, promotes dependency upon technology, and reduces quick-thinking skills.

In the paragraph which follows, you would elaborate these three effects by providing details that support your point and persuade the audience of its credibility. For example, to prove that today's students cannot perform simple mathematical functions well, you might cite a study that indicates that elementary students in the 1980s were less proficient in multiplication and division than students in the 1960s.

CAUSE AND EFFECT

A cause and effect essay should clearly make the connection between an event and its outcome. This diver's lack of foresight was the cause of his disaster.

Using Cause and Effect

1. Make sure that your claim about cause and effect is narrow enough so that you can provide adequate support for it: generalizations are dangerous. You can't claim that Upper Canada won the War of 1812 because of Laura Secord's espionage activities.

2. Make sure that there really is a cause and effect relationship. You can't argue that there is a cause and effect relationship just because every time you get into the bathtub, the phone rings. The two events occur in sequence, but there is no direct causal relationship between them.

3. Avoid oversimplification. Remember that most effects have multiple causes, and most causes have many effects. You can't argue that Napoleon lost the battle of Waterloo solely because he suffered from hemorrhoids, although they may have been a contributing cause.

Transitions
You may find these signals useful when developing cause and effect relationships.

so	because
hence	for
thus	then
therefore	accordingly
as a result	so far
consequently	thus far
since	

Consider how the following example uses cause and effect:

THE RISE OF STREET GANGS IN CANADIAN CITIES

If you see a group of kids in Toronto all wearing black Doc Marten boots, sunglasses, and sweats, you might be looking at the Untouchables. Or they might be the Impossibles, the Dreadnox, or the Jungle Posse. These are not rock groups; they are street gangs. In the last few years, gangs have become increasingly active in major Canadian cities. Typical activities for these bands of young people include beatings, rape, and "swarming," mass attacks on other teenagers or adults. Virtually no place in a downtown area is safe; a school playground in Montreal, a movie theatre in Vancouver, and the Eaton Centre in Toronto have all been scenes of gang violence.

What has led to these nation-wide outbreaks of modern barbarism? Experts disagree about the causes of such brutal behaviour but have made some suggestions: the disintegration of the family, the attempt to achieve status and power, and the influence of certain movies.

Some argue that parents in the last two decades seem to have adopted a policy of benign neglect, letting their kids "do their own thing." This attitude, coupled with a disintegration of the family through divorce and an increase in the number of single parents, has relaxed controls on young people and given them complete license to act as they please. The gang, as a result, becomes a surrogate family, offering structure and a code of behaviour.

Another suggested cause of this increase in street gangs is socioeconomic. Some young people drop out of school, feeling that further education is pointless. They then become frustrated at the prospect of unemployment and poverty. Street gangs provide a sense of power and tangible rewards: money, watches, leather jackets, and stereos. It is a reflection on mainstream consumerism that most of the goods lifted by gangs are luxury items.

Even some movies, according to police, have contributed to the development of gangs in urban areas. For example, *Colors*, a depiction of gang life in Los Angeles, has been criticized as presenting violence in a glamorous light. Police say that *Colors* has become a cult film and that many gang members know the film by heart.

All of these causes suggest that controlling gang violence requires some hard thinking about improvement of social conditions.

1. What is the main point or thesis statement of this essay?

2. What are the steps in the argument of this essay?

3. What causes are identified here? Can you think of any other causes that might have been included?

4. What transitions are used to signal the movement from one step in the argument to the next?

5. Can you strip the essay down to its outline?

EXERCISE 2-20

Write a paragraph speculating on the effects of the following:

television   day care
heavy metal music   acne
pesticides   having too much money

EXERCISE 2-21

Write a paragraph speculating on the causes of the following:

adult education   feminism
vandalism   cancer
anti-smoking laws   increased numbers of pets
the current obsession   the popularity of a music group (your choice)
with physical image/
physical fitness

EXERCISE 2-22

Develop the following statements into a paragraph:

     Why I believe in _____.
     Why I would never _____.
     Why I enjoy _____.

EXERCISE 2-23

Write a cause and effect composition explaining how you wound up where you are today.

EXERCISE 2-24

Write a cause and effect composition explaining how a particular sport originated.

EXERCISE 2-25

Selling the Whatchamacallit—write a composition based on the following:

a) Create a new product—something original or a new version of a product already in existence. Define it and classify its features.

67

b) Using process, explain how the new product works or how it could be used.

c) Compare it to other similar products on the market and explain why your product is superior.

d) Devise an advertising strategy, describing how this product will make the purchaser's life better.

EXERCISE 2-26

You are employed by the Ministry of Tourism. Choose a place—somewhere you have been or somewhere you would like to go—and create a brochure promoting this place, making sure you do some of the following:

a) Define what makes this place interesting.

b) Classify the kinds of attractions it offers.

c) Compare it to similar kinds of places.

d) Explain how you can get there.

e) Explain what a visit to this place would do for you or for someone else.

Writing Situations: Assignments

SECTION A

In business, the most commonly used brief forms of communication are the memo (short for memorandum) and the letter. Despite their varying lengths and purposes, both forms of writing are composed of a main point and support.

Sample Memo

TO: All volunteers

DATE: May 11, 199–

FROM: Tamara-Lee Pratt

SUBJECT: The Society for the Prevention of Cruelty to
              Plant-Life booth at the Fall Fun Fair

As you know, we will be selling candy bars as part of our fundraising for charity at the upcoming Fall Fun Fair. Volunteers in teams of two (one man and one woman) will be required at the booth over the course of two days. Shifts will last two hours.

I want to encourage all of you to volunteer. The proceeds ($1 a candy bar) will go to the Society for the Prevention of Cruelty to Plant-Life. This should be an easy way to raise money. All you need to bring is your sweet tooth.

In the following assignments you are asked to take on different roles and write memos based on the information provided. You may also have to invent details.

1. You are the vice-president in charge of marketing for the Around the World Yo-Yo Company. You have to call a meeting to discuss the marketing strategy for your new fluorescent product. Write a memo to convince your co-workers that their attendance is vital. Your memo should include the main selling features of the yo-yo and details of time and place.

2. As part of the Human Resources Management team for a major company, you have noticed how flabby the employees have become recently. Write a diplomatic memo urging the employees to take part in a weekly fitness class and offering three incentives.

3. Your salesperson, Olympia Delaney, has been having a difficult time in her personal life lately. You have been understanding, but recently she has been coming back from lunch with a noticeable scent of liquor on her breath. In a memo, explain the company's policy about drinking on the job and offer suggestions about where she might find help for her problems.

4. Elliot Wadke, your boss, is retiring, and frankly, most of the employees are glad to see him go because of his rigid adherence to company policy and his bad temper. Unfortunately, you have the thankless task of collecting money to buy him a present and of organizing the retirement party. Write a discreet memo persuading fellow employees to contribute to the present and come to the party.

5. You are running for the position of treasurer of your local union. As part of your campaign, explain why you should be elected instead of your opponent, providing three reasons.

6. Your secretary, Rudi, has requested an extra week of holidays so he can go on a Caribbean cruise. The dates he has given coincide with the busiest time of year for your company, which manufactures ball bearings. Write a response turning down his request and explaining how valuable he will be to you at this time.

7. Sales have been down, and there has been talk of layoffs at your plant, which presses records. Write a memo designed to dispel the rumours and boost employee morale, giving several reasons for optimism.

8. The computer department in your company is going to offer a series of workshops concerning the use of database files for recording and storing information. Announce these workshops and convince your employees that participating in them would be a good idea.

9. You're in charge of a sales force promoting a new electronic home security system. Write a memo to the staff outlining the promotional strategy for the sales campaign.

10. You want to offer Angelo McVittie, the shop foreman, a place on the management team, but he has to upgrade his education by taking several courses in management training. Write a memo convincing him that the investment of his time and effort will be worthwhile.

SECTION B

The following exercises ask you to write complaint letters which address a problem that needs to be resolved. When you write this kind of letter, keep in mind these suggestions:

- Explain what you perceive the problem to be. A complaint letter should contain a statement of the problem.
- Provide sufficient background information and detail.
- Request some specific action.
- Keep your cool; make the tone controlled and reasonable.

Sample Letter: Full-Block Style

July 14, 199-   *Date line*

Pizza in a Jiffy   *Inside*
107 Eagle's Nest Rd.   *Address*
Burnaby, B.C.
V5E 9N7

Dear Manager (of Pizza in a Jiffy):   *Salutation*

I am writing to complain about the service I received last night from your employees. At 7:30 p.m. I called to order a large pizza with everything on it, including anchovies and hot peppers. According to your takeout menu, the pizza was to be delivered within 30 minutes. After waiting an hour, I called to ask what had happened.

The person who answered the phone was surly and uncooperative, saying that the pizza was not delivered because the employee who took the order assumed that my request was a prank call. Apparently, he could not confirm my order because he had taken down the telephone number incorrectly and decided that my request for a pizza with everything was a prank. As a result, I had to reorder the pizza and wait another 30 minutes.

I would like to point out that most prank callers are not middle-aged women and hence would advise your employees not to jump to conclusions. I would further suggest that they be more careful when they take down information and that they repeat phone numbers to check them.

Yours sincerely,   *Closing*

I.M. Peeved

In the following assignments you are asked to take on different roles and write complaint letters based on the information provided.

1. You have just heard that there are plans to open a bar in your neighbourhood. This bar will feature strippers and table dancers. As a parent and homeowner, you are opposed to this development in your primarily residential area. Write a letter to city council giving reasons for your position.

2. In the student newspaper you read that tuition fees will be raised substantially in the coming semester. Since you think that they are already too high, draft a letter to the administration, explaining why you believe this fee hike should not take place.

3. Yesterday your friend bought an egg salad sandwich at the cafeteria and, after eating it, was stricken with food poisoning and rushed to the hospital. This is not the first incident that has occurred at the college in the past year. Write a letter to the head of Food Services criticizing the poor quality control and demanding improvement.

4. Last week you went to the cosmetic counter of a major department store and bought a large bottle of Perversity, the newest and most expensive cologne on the market. Unfortunately, when you put it on, your skin broke out in an ugly and painful rash. When you tried to return it, the salesperson insisted that promotional items cannot be returned and refused to refund your money. Write a letter to the store manager, explaining your problem.

5. Because of recent policy, there is no longer any place to smoke inside the college. People who want to smoke have to go out to the parking lot. Your student activity fee contributes to the maintenance of the student lounge which you, as a smoker, cannot use. Write a letter to the president of the college, explaining why you feel you are being discriminated against and requesting a smokers-only lounge.

6. Write your own letter of complaint.

SECTION C

You have just inherited a newspaper, *The Morning Blast*, from your late Uncle Albert. Unfortunately, you have no money to hire staff, so in addition to being the editor, you have to write all the other columns yourself under different names.

Newspaper writing tends to be less formal, livelier, and more direct than essay writing. Use these exercises as opportunities to have some fun with your writing.

1. As editor, you are in charge of the Births, Marriages, and Deaths column. Write an obituary profiling the life of one of the following:
   a) a celebrity from the entertainment world
   b) a politician or world leader
   c) someone you know
   d) a fictional character (from books, TV, movies, or cartoons)

2. As financial consultant, you have received the following letter:

   Dear Financial Consultant:

   I have just won a million dollars in a lottery. I want to buy a Corvette and take a trip around the world, but my parents want me to invest it sensibly for the future. What do you advise me to do?

   Sincerely,

   Confused but Rich

   Write a three-paragraph response to the writer's question.

3. As Mr. Fixit (handyman), explain one of the following:
   a) how to change a washer in a tap
   b) how to rotate tires
   c) how to paint a room
   d) how to frame a picture

4. As a psychologist, you are asked to give advice on the following matters. Write a response to one of these queries.
   a) how to deal with a problem child
   b) how to cure the blues
   c) how to handle meddling relatives
   d) how to cope with low self-esteem

5. As sports editor, write a column on one of the following topics:
   a) the profile of a sports personality
   b) how to play a sport
   c) sports injuries
   d) the future of the Olympics

6. As medical writer, write a short column on one of the following topics:
   a) treatment of the common cold
   b) "the heartbreak of bad skin"
   c) the value of cosmetic surgery
   d) allergies

7. As entertainment critic, review one of the following:
   a) a movie or play
   b) a record
   c) a book
   d) a concert or "event"

8. As political correspondent, write a commentary on one of the following:
   a) your favorite political party
   b) a recent political scandal
   c) the advantages or disadvantages of democracy
   d) a political figure who should be removed from office

9. As etiquette adviser, provide an answer to one of these questions:
   a) how do I tell a coworker he has bad breath?
   b) what should I do with my engagement presents now that the wedding is off?
   c) how should I conduct myself on a first date?
   d) how do I break off a relationship?

10. As food editor, write about one of these subjects:
    a) healthy snacks
    b) barbequing
    c) eating out
    d) cooking lessons

11. As science writer, write a column on one of the following topics. Some research will be necessary before you begin.
    a) constellations
    b) hurricanes
    c) curiosities of nature (plants or animals)
    d) the greenhouse effect

12. As editorial writer, compose an editorial for the paper, using one of the following topics. In each case, decide whether you are for or against the issue and draft the column accordingly.
    a) nuclear disarmament
    b) the funding of abortion clinics
    c) euthanasia
    d) gay rights
    e) sex education in public schools
    f) Sunday shopping
    g) mandatory French classes in local schools
    h) taxes to support day care
    i) the projected expansion of a nearby shopping mall

j) compulsory military service for women

k) the abolition of rent control

l) an issue of your choice

THE WRITER'S CHECKLIST

Argument

❑ 1. What is your *MAIN POINT?* Where is it positioned? Generally, the strongest place for the main point is at the beginning—if it is the topic sentence of a paragraph, then have it open the paragraph, and if it is the thesis statement of an essay, then place it within the first or second paragraph of the composition.

❑ 2. Is your *MAIN POINT* as clearly expressed as possible?

❑ 3. What *IDEAS* are you using to develop your main point?

❑ 4. Do all your ideas have *RELEVANCE* to the main point?

❑ 5. Do your ideas have adequate *SUPPORT* in the form of authorities, statistics, examples, or reasons?

❑ 6. Is the *ORDER* of ideas logical?

❑ 7. Are there *TRANSITIONS* to lead from one idea to the next?

❑ 8. Is there a clearly identifiable *STRUCTURE* to the writing? Does it have an *INTRODUCTION* which sets up the main point and indicates the direction of the ideas? Does the *BODY* of the writing elaborate the main point satisfactorily? Does the *CONCLUSION* sum up the main point of the writing effectively?

Language and Style

❑ 1. Have you defined any *UNFAMILIAR TERMS?*

❑ 2. Have you avoided unnecessary *REPETITION?*

❑ 3. Does your writing have the proper *TONE* for the purpose?

❑ 4. Have you checked your sentences for *VARIETY* and *CONCISENESS?* Does your writing flow easily when you read it aloud?

❑ 5. Is your *WORD CHOICE* reasonably original, expressive, and free of clichés and jargon?

Accuracy

❏ 1. Have you consulted a *DICTIONARY* to check words you have trouble spelling?

❏ 2. Does your *PUNCTUATION* make sense?

❏ 3. Have you checked for and corrected the *ERRORS* you most frequently make in writing?

A WORD ABOUT COMPUTERS

If you are lucky enough to have a computer, there are a number of advantages you should remember when faced with a writing assignment:

1. You don't have to write a draft from start to finish; you can begin wherever you want and fill in the gaps later on.

2. You can change order of information as your argument develops to make it more coherent.

3. You can compare two drafts of an assignment on the screen at the same time.

4. You can read back your ideas on the screen as well as on the hard copy.

5. You can take advantage of spelling and grammar checks, bearing in mind that these programs aren't foolproof and are no substitute for a solid grounding in grammar and style.

6. You can use the Search Function to help you find areas where you need to fill in details or answer questions you have left unanswered. You can mark such areas with an * as you work so you don't disrupt the rhythm of composing.

7. You can make significant changes in shorter periods of time. Even 15 minutes can make a difference when working on a computer.

8. As long as you know how to Save correctly, you have the security of being able to return to your work exactly as you left it.

9. Because you aren't "committed" until you print your work, the whole process of brainstorming, composing, and revising can be freer and more private.

PART TWO

GRAMMAR

Sentence Construction

THE PARTS OF SPEECH

In order to understand sentence construction and punctuation, you need to be able to identify the parts of speech. Every word in a sentence can be categorized according to the part it plays. You will need to know the following: noun, pronoun, verb, adjective, adverb, preposition, conjunction, and article.

Nouns

Nouns are the names of persons, places, and things.

> The *member of Parliament* from *Kingston* was noted for her quick thinking and her *determination*.

A word is a noun if you can place *a, an, the* or a word like *my, your, his, her, its, our, their* before it without turning the sentence into nonsense.

> Smoking is bad for your *health*.

You can tell that *smoking* is a noun because you can put *your* in front of it without losing the meaning of the sentence.

Pronouns

Pronouns take the place of nouns.

Personal Pronouns

	Person	Subjective	Objective	Possessive	Absolute Possessive	Reflexive
Singular	1st	I	me	my	mine	myself
	2nd	you	you	your	yours	yourself
	3rd—					
	feminine	she	her	her	hers	herself
	masculine	he	him	his	his	himself
	neuter	it	it	its	its	itself
	one	one			oneself	
Plural	1st	we	us	our	ours	ourselves
	2nd	you	you	your	yours	yourselves
	3rd (all genders)	they	them	their	theirs	themselves

Zoltan gave the cuckoo clock to Pete and Angela.

He gave *it* to *him* and *his* fiancée.

Demonstrative Pronouns—*this, that* (singular); *these, those* (plural)

This is a fine mess.

Those tigers in the garden will have to go.

Expletive Pronouns—*it, there*

To everything *there* is a season.

It is important to look both ways before crossing the street.

Indefinite Pronouns—include *another, each, either, neither, many, few, more, enough, some, such, less, any, much, nothing*

Nothing comes of nothing.

Many are called, but few are chosen.

Intensive Pronouns—same as reflexive form of personal pronoun

I did it all *myself.*

Interrogative Pronouns—same as relative pronouns, also *what*

Who has seen the wind?

Which of the iguanas did you choose for a pet?

Reciprocal Pronouns—*each other, one another*

They hated *one another* on sight.

Relative Pronouns—*that, which, who* (subjective, both singular and plural), *whom* (objective, both singular and plural), *whose,* and compounds formed by adding "*ever*" (for example, *whatever*).

I know *who* did it.

Never seek to know for *whom* the bell tolls.

Verbs

Verbs express action or condition (state of being). They often (but not always) appear after a noun or pronoun. Verbs change form and tense, depending on the meaning of the sentence, the subject of the action, and the time the action takes place (past, present, or future).

Margarita *performs* every night at the casino. (present)

Branwell *was* sickly. (past)

Gunther's Body Shop *will sponsor* this year's snowshoe race. (future)

81

Adjectives

Adjectives describe or qualify nouns.

> The *little* girl wore her red riding hood when she went to visit her bedridden granny.

> The coffee maker's instructions were *difficult.*

Adverbs

Adverbs describe or qualify verbs, adjectives, and other adverbs. Adverbs explain where, when, how, and how much.

> Clark attaches the harness *carefully.*

> Ruthann was *rather* upset by Larry's peculiar behaviour.

Prepositions

Prepositions precede nouns or pronouns to form prepositional phrases.

> He is reputed to be the richest man *in* the country.

> Mona and Spencer are *behind* the barn picking raspberries.

> *For* their thirtieth anniversary, my parents are going *around* the world.

Conjunctions

Conjunctions join words, phrases, or clauses. There are three kinds of conjunctions: coordinate, subordinate, and correlative.

In English there are seven **coordinate** conjunctions: *and, or, nor, for* (meaning because), *but, yet, and so.*

> Rock *and* roll is here to stay.

Subordinate conjunctions join a dependent or subordinate clause to a main clause. (We have listed subordinate conjunctions under the next section, "Parts of the Sentence.")

> *Until* your homework is done, you are not going out.

Correlative conjunctions are pairs of conjunctions that appear together: *either ... or, neither ... nor, both ... and, not only ... but also.*

> *Either* you *or* the maid must answer the door.

Articles

In English, there are three articles: *the*, the definite article, and *a/an*, the indefinite articles. These precede nouns and function as adjectives. Definite articles refer to specific things; indefinite articles are used to refer to general examples. *A* is used with a noun beginning with a consonant, and *an* is used with a noun beginning with a vowel *sound*.

> Reba saw a man watering *the* flowers.
>
> *The* man was using a hose.
>
> *An* honest politician is a rare bird.

EXERCISE 3-1

Identify the parts of speech in these sentences, using the following code:

① Nouns   ② Verbs   ③ Adverbs   ④ Conjunctions
⑤ Pronouns   ⑥ Adjectives   ⑦ Prepositions   ⑧ Articles

1. Sometimes people in trouble turn to a minister for counselling.

2. Counsellors are expected to minister to the needs of their clients confidentially.

3. Remember to consult the computer manual if you can't get the program to function.

4. Manual labour, though it's hard on the muscles, is good for the soul.

5. The arrows will guide you to the nearest washroom.

6. The tour guide at the Festival Theatre showed the audience the gong.

7. Don't ruffle your feathers; I'm coming.

8. The ruffle on his dress shirt needs to be starched.

9. Poindexter felt that life was short, transient, and basically dull.

10. The transients huddled in the bus station for warmth.

EXERCISE 3-2

Identify the parts of speech in these sentences, using the following code:

① Nouns   ② Verbs   ③ Adverbs   ④ Conjunctions
⑤ Pronouns   ⑥ Adjectives   ⑦ Prepositions   ⑧ Articles

1. Bertram would like to preface his remarks with a warning to the audience to keep silent during the remainder of his speech.

2. The preface of his first book was long winded, tiresome, and full of typographical errors.

3. Dara wore a tangerine dress to her prom.

4. The camel ate the tangerine greedily.

5. Huck noticed that the table was covered with a beautiful piece of linoleum.

6. A linoleum floor is not as stylish as hardwood.

7. The collector discovered to his chagrin that the painting he had been duped into buying was a counterfeit.

8. Counterfeit money is sometimes very difficult to spot if the serial numbers are done correctly.

9. The would-be actor wants to audition for a part on the new soap opera, *The Old and the Ruthless*.

10. His audition went well, but he didn't get the role of the veteran hockey player because he still has all his teeth.

EXERCISE 3-3

Identify the parts of speech in these sentences, using the following code:

① Nouns   ② Verbs   ③ Adverbs   ④ Conjunctions
⑤ Pronouns   ⑥ Adjectives   ⑦ Prepositions   ⑧ Articles

1. The Montgolfier brothers invented the balloon in France in 1783.

2. The first balloon flight covered a distance of a mile and a half before it landed safely.

3. Other early balloonists were not so lucky.

4. Superstitious peasants attacked one "monster" with scythes and pitchforks as it descended from the sky.

5. Balloons were used to carry mail and passengers and for military surveillance.

6. Both the North and the South used observation balloons during the American Civil War.

7. The world's first practical powered airplane was invented by Orville and Wilbur Wright.

8. Orville made the first manned mechanical flight in history at Kitty Hawk, North Carolina.

9. Charles Lindbergh, in his plane "The Spirit of St. Louis," made the first non-stop flight from New York to Paris in thirty-three hours and thirty-three minutes.

10. Whatever happened to Amelia Earhart?

PARTS OF THE SENTENCE

The essential components of a sentence are a subject (stated or implied) and a verb. A sentence must also be able to stand alone as a grammatically complete unit.

> Anna and Vronsky fight constantly.

As you already know, verbs express action or condition. The verb in this sentence is the action word *fight*. The subject of the verb often comes before the verb and is the performer in the action. You can find the subject by asking WHO or WHAT fights. In this case, *Anna and Vronsky* are the subject of the sentence; they are the ones who fight.

Usually, though, a sentence has three main parts: a subject, a verb, and either an object or a complement, often in that order. Let's begin by looking at a sentence following the subject-verb-object pattern.

> They often throw things at each other.

Start by finding the verb. Here it is the action word *throw*. Then ask WHO or WHAT throws. The subject is *they*. To find the object, or the receiver of the action, ask WHO or WHAT is thrown. The object is *things*.

If a sentence follows the subject-verb-complement pattern, it will look something like this:

> Theirs is a tempestuous relationship.

The verb here does not express an action, but rather a condition or state. The verb is *is*. In this kind of example, the subject is WHO or WHAT is being described. Here the subject is *theirs*. The complement follows the verb and completes the subject. Here it is the group of words, or phrase, *a tempestuous relationship*.

85

A sentence, because it stands alone, can be described as an independent, or main, clause. All clauses have a subject and a verb: some can stand alone; others cannot. Clauses which cannot stand by themselves are called subordinate or dependent. The first of these sentences has only a main or independent clause, and the second has an independent and a subordinate clause.

Tallulah, Helmut and Concepcion get together for a beer every Saturday night. (main or independent clause)

Although they are on rival bowling teams, they play poker regularly.

Although they are on rival bowling teams is a subordinate or dependent clause. It has a subject (they) and a verb (are), but it cannot stand by itself. *They play poker regularly* is a main or independent clause. It has a subject (they) and a verb (play), and it can stand by itself as a sentence.

Note the function of *although* in this sentence. If it were not there, *they are on rival bowling teams* could stand by itself as a sentence. With the addition of *although,* however, this clause must be joined to another. *Although* is called a subordinator. There are many words that can act as subordinators in English. Here is a list of some of them:

after	how	that
although	if	though
as	since	unless
because	than	until
before		

Subordinate clauses often begin with words that start with "wh-."

when, whenever	where, wherever	whether
who, whoever	what, whatever	while
which, whichever		

The addition of any of these words to a clause will make it dependent or subordinate.

It is raining. (main clause)

Because it is raining ... (subordinate clause—not a sentence)

Because it is raining, Delbert will take his umbrella. (a sentence composed of a subordinate clause and a main clause)

The beach volleyball star was on television. (main clause)

Whom they admired. (subordinate clause)

The beach volleyball star whom they admired was on television.

EXERCISE 3-4

Underline the subjects and verbs in the following sentences. Use one line for subjects and two lines for verbs.

1. The elderly couple acted as godparents to the new baby.

2. They bought new clothes to wear to the ceremony.

3. The godmother even purchased a hat with a feather and a veil.

4. The godfather wore a new silk tie and a camelhair jacket.

5. The baby was not impressed and screamed in protest.

6. The minister baptized her in spite of her apparent resistance to the procedure.

7. The godparents swore to protect their charge against evil.

8. Screaming, the baby was carried from the church.

9. Perhaps her godparents should have brought a magic wand with them.

10. Where were Flora, Fauna, and Merriweather?

EXERCISE 3-5

Underline the subjects and verbs in the following sentences. Use one line for subjects and two lines for verbs.

1. Boredom can be a problem in the classroom.

2. Falling asleep is occasionally the result.

3. What can be done to counteract this problem?

4. Try listening to the sounds outside the window, rather than to the teacher's droning voice.

5. Just for safety's sake, prop your head up with your hand.

6. For variety, scribble down a few notes.

7. Passing notes to the person next to you can be an interesting way of livening up a dull class.

8. Failing that, students sometimes make paper airplanes.

9. You should be careful, however, not to attract unwanted attention.

10. Skipping class altogether might be a better idea.

87

EXERCISE 3-6

Underline the subjects and verbs in the following sentences. Use one line for subjects and two lines for verbs.

1. As a child, Emmeline loved Home Economics classes.

2. She made a flannel nightgown two sizes too big.

3. She also designed a stuffed poodle made out of corduroy.

4. She especially enjoyed the cooking classes.

5. Spaghetti noodles, however, must be added to boiling water, not cold water.

6. Norbert's experience in Industrial Arts class was equally rewarding.

7. He did, admittedly, dislike the skill saw.

8. Stories about past tragedies in shop class worried him.

9. He managed to produce a wooden lamp shaped like an elephant.

10. He became a chef after graduation.

EXERCISE 3-7

Underline the subjects and verbs in the following sentences. Use one line for subjects and two lines for verbs.

1. Asleep in the corner was the Sealyham terrier.

2. Coddled and pampered, she was a beloved pet.

3. In fact, she ate better than her master.

4. He was perpetually on a diet.

5. She, on the other hand, ate T-bone steaks on a daily basis.

6. Her master took her health very seriously.

7. She had eyedrops, eardrops, pills, and regular visits to the veterinarian.

8. The health of the master, by contrast, was neglected shamefully.

9. The terrier was, of course, a spoiled brat, always in need of medical attention.

10. Do you think she was a hypochondriac?

EXERCISE 3-8

Underline the subjects and verbs in the following sentences. Use one line for subjects and two lines for verbs.

1. Max always has trouble sleeping at night.

2. He drinks warm milk, eats hot cereal, and does exercises to calm his nerves.

3. Despite all his efforts, sleep does not come to him.

4. Counting sheep has no discernible effect.

5. Frankly, Max is afraid of sheep.

6. Should he hang upside down like a bat?

7. Perhaps a bedtime story would soothe him.

8. Reading fairy tales might prove alarming, though.

9. Think of all the trolls and witches.

10. Staying up to watch test patterns on television might be the best solution.

EXERCISE 3-9

Underline the subjects and verbs in the following sentences. Use one line for subjects and two lines for verbs.

1. Having worked all day, Griselda needed a hot bath.

2. She took off her clothes and stretched out in the tub.

3. Then the telephone rang.

4. Dripping, she ran to answer it.

5. The caller was doing a survey on varieties of pet food.

6. Griselda had not owned a pet in fifteen years.

7. Her mother had flushed her neglected guppies down the toilet.

8. Hanging up, she vowed silently to buy an answering machine.

9. Disgusted with the interruption, Griselda returned to the bathtub.

10. There ought to be a law against telephone surveys.

EXERCISE 3-10

Underline the subjects and verbs in the following sentences. Use one line for subjects and two lines for verbs.

1. Making dinner after a hard day at work can be exhausting.

2. What should you cook: a meal in a box or a meal in a can?

3. There is one very useful solution to this dilemma.

4. Go out to eat.

5. In the back of the cupboard behind the half-used jar of peanut butter are stacked some packages of stale macaroons.

6. Eating sandwiches every night can be very dull.

7. Why don't we buy candy bars, soda pop, and potato chips?

8. At least that way we won't need dinner plates.

9. Nothing is more annoying after a hard day than washing a lot of dishes.

10. Wouldn't you rather have the services of a full-time cook and house-keeper?

SENTENCE FRAGMENTS

When a group of words is punctuated like a sentence but does not contain at least one main (or independent) clause, it is a sentence fragment. Although we often use them in conversations, *sentence fragments are almost never acceptable in written work.* You have already learned how to find a subject and a verb: a sentence fragment may be missing one or both of these parts; it may also be an unconnected phrase or subordinate clause.

✘ Miss Rumphius is a math teacher. Who inspires her students.

Unless "Who inspires her students" is a question, it is a sentence fragment. "Who," a word beginning with "wh-," signals the beginning of a dependent or subordinate clause, a group of words that cannot stand alone as a sentence. To correct the error, join the dependent clause "Who inspires her students" to the independent clause "Miss Rumphius is a math teacher."

✓ Miss Rumphius is a math teacher who inspires her students.

✘ That woman waiting for the bus.

The phrase "waiting for the bus" modifies the subject "that woman." A verb is needed to correct the error.

✓ That woman waiting for the bus is crying.

✗ Cats being by nature lazy.

"Being" is not a verb. A verb form ending in "-ing" cannot stand on its own. To correct the fragment, change "being" to "are."

✓ Cats are by nature lazy.

✗ Useless in every way.

This is a fragment because there is neither a subject nor a verb.

✓ These instructions are useless in every way.

EXERCISE 3-11

Identify and correct sentence fragments wherever they occur in the following exercises. Some of these are correct sentences.

1. Aside from her lack of money.

2. Being tired, he went home.

3. Because the movie is so much like the book.

4. Anyone who has a ticket should ask me.

5. Whoever works hard will be rewarded.

6. As usual, doing my homework.

7. Let's go out to eat.

8. The saying "A camel is a horse designed by a committee."

9. Whatever you say someone will oppose it.

10. The luge now being recognized in North America as a competitive sport.

EXERCISE 3-12

Identify and correct sentence fragments wherever they occur in the following exercises. Some of these are correct sentences.

1. Working day and night to maintain a meagre existence.

2. Looking forward to hearing from you soon.

3. Will he answer?

4. To place a long-distance call on someone else's telephone.

5. Anyone who believes such absurdities.

6. Everyone who works there is on strike.

7. The equestrian event scheduled to take place at noon.

8. Money talks.

9. If you read the newspapers faithfully every morning.

10. Gossiping incessantly to the neighbours being her chief method of passing the time.

EXERCISE 3-13

Identify and correct sentence fragments wherever they occur in the following exercises. Some of these are correct sentences.

1. Shut your mouth.

2. Let's never speak of it again.

3. Getting a regular haircut not considered important by teenagers in the 1960s.

4. The proverb, "A spoonful of sugar helps the medicine go down."

5. To win acceptance for his plan to promote nuclear disarmament and world peace?

6. Though I've never been to Vancouver before.

7. Whenever he runs into his ex-girlfriend in a movie theatre.

8. Before I started weight training and added some muscles to my puny frame.

9. While his mother-in-law droned on.

10. Making believe that he had supernatural powers seemed silly.

EXERCISE 3-14

Identify and correct sentence fragments wherever they occur in the following exercises. Some of these are correct sentences.

1. Unless you decide to come to your senses.

2. Leo Buscaglia speaking on the importance of love in human relationships.

3. Considering what he has to lose.

4. These days, the emphasis on telecommunications and technical advancements.

5. Because he had never seen a case of encephalitus, the diagnosis took some time.

6. Are you kidding?

7. Never again was she fooled by his apparent trustworthiness.

8. The title, *Puss in Boots*.

9. Because the clock just struck twelve.

10. The cat which slept at her feet.

EXERCISE 3-15

Identify and correct sentence fragments wherever they occur in the following exercises. Some of these are correct sentences.

1. Why she persists in refusing to look for a job.

2. Part-time students assembling to discuss tuition fees.

3. Animals which are abandoned are brought to this shelter in the hope that they will be adopted.

4. In rare cases, cruises beginning in July continue until September.

5. Which I knew about in the first place.

6. What I have always liked about it.

7. What are his chances of recovery?

8. Barring unforeseen complications, somewhere in the neighbourhood of six to eight weeks, if he's careful.

9. Whatever she does, wherever she goes, there are problems.

10. Repairing the roof was a costly and difficult job.

EXERCISE 3-16

Identify and correct sentence fragments wherever they occur in the following exercises. Some of these are correct sentences.

1. Whoever answers the summons.

2. When she starts to hear voices.

3. If they know what's good for them.

4. Before night starts to fall.

5. Even though you ought to know better.

6. Since the death of her favorite pet.

7. Because, after all, the children really disliked their new babysitter.

8. The terrier that growled at the intruder.

9. Suddenly, when you least expect it, you start to get wrinkles.

10. Which contestant are you cheering for?

EXERCISE 3-17

Identify and correct sentence fragments wherever they occur in the following exercises. Some of these are correct sentences.

1. Knowing how to give first aid can be one of the most important things you will ever learn.

2. Move over!

3. That doctor who offered the children lollipops.

4. Because the employee counselling program is provided free of charge.

5. Not only in the water, but also in the air.

6. When it stops raining.

7. Having come so far in such a short time.

8. Working towards a new theory of nuclear fission.

9. Who's the designated driver?

10. As long as you know what you're doing.

RUN-ONS AND COMMA SPLICES

The Run-On

As you have learned, a sentence must contain one independent clause or one main subject and verb. A run-on error occurs when two such independent clauses or sentences are joined together without any punctuation or connecting words. Such sentences are often almost impossible to understand. Here is an example:

✘ Some people like to talk too much they do not seem aware of their rudeness.

There are two independent clauses here.

$$\overset{\text{s}}{} \quad \overset{\text{v}}{}$$
Some people like to talk too much.

$$\overset{\text{s}}{} \qquad \overset{\text{v}}{}$$
they do not seem aware of their rudeness.

To correct the run-on, you could simply add a period after the first main clause.

✓ Some people like to talk too much. They do not seem aware of their rudeness.

Another example will show just how confusing a run-on sentence can be.

✘ Such people would rather not listen when someone else is talking they are easily bored.

In this example, the reader can't tell whether "when someone else is talking" is connected to the first independent clause or to the second one. There are two independent clauses joined without either punctuation or a proper connecting word.

$$\overset{\text{s}}{} \qquad\qquad \overset{\text{v}}{}$$
Such people would rather not listen (independent clause)

$$\overset{\text{s}}{} \qquad \overset{\text{v}}{}$$
they are easily bored (independent clause).

To correct this run-on, you could add one of these seven coordinating conjunctions (*and, or, nor, for, but, yet, so*) with a comma before it.

✓ Such people would rather not listen when someone else is talking, *for* they are easily bored.

(Note that "for" here is used in the sense of "because.")

95

The Comma Splice

Like the run-on, the comma splice is an error caused by a faulty connection between two independent clauses. It occurs when you try to join two sentences, two complete thoughts, with a comma. A comma itself is not strong enough to join two sentences or two independent clauses.

> ✘ Gossiping too much can be detrimental to your social life, listening is often a wiser idea.

In this example we have two main clauses separated only by a comma:

$$\text{Gossiping too much can be detrimental to your social life,}$$
S   V

$$\text{listening is often a wiser idea.}$$
S   V

To correct this comma splice error, you might make one of the independent clauses into a subordinate clause by using a subordinator. Consult the list of subordinators on p. 86.

> ✔ Because gossiping too much can be detrimental to your social life, listening is often a wiser idea.

Now because the first clause is dependent (since it begins with the subordinator "because"), the comma is acceptable.

Consider the next example:

> ✘ Talkative people prefer the sound of their own voices, however, their victims usually find them obnoxious.

In this instance, we again have two independent clauses.

$$\text{Talkative people prefer the sound of their own voices}$$
S   V

$$\text{however, their victims usually find them obnoxious.}$$
S   V

"However" is used as a connecting word here. But note that "however" is not listed among the coordinates. While "however" can sometimes be used as a subordinator, it is most often used to join two independent clauses, or sentences, as in the example above. When "however" is used to join two sentences, stronger punctuation than a comma is needed. To correct this comma splice, use a semicolon (;) before "however."

> ✔ Talkative people prefer the sound of their own voices; however, their victims usually find them obnoxious.

(Note that the comma after "however" is optional, though preferable.)

Methods of Correcting Run-Ons and Comma Splices: A Summary

Both run-ons and comma splices can be corrected using any one of the following techniques.

1. Insert a period before the beginning of the second independent clause.

2. Use a comma and one of these seven connecting words (and, or, nor, for, but, yet, so) to join the two independent clauses.

3. Add a subordinator to make one of the clauses dependent.

4. Use a semicolon before the beginning of the second clause, especially if the sentences are closely related in thought. (See the section on the semicolon for more information on this point.)

   ✗ Politicians talk too much, they are boring.

Corrections according to

Method 1 Politicians talk too much. They are boring.

Method 2 Politicians talk too much, and they are boring.

Method 3 Because politicians talk too much, they are boring.

Method 4 Politicians talk too much; they are boring.

EXERCISE 3-18

Correct all run-ons and comma splices. Keep in mind that not all of the sentences are incorrect.

1. Here is the plunger, I will unclog your toilet.

2. Jessye and Frank went to the First National Bank they wanted to make a withdrawal.

3. Going to Jamaica sounds wonderful, on the other hand, I don't have the money for air fare.

4. He loved video games, she preferred checkers.

5. His dentist reminded him of the dangers of gum disease, now he flosses daily.

6. Please be quiet, I'm very upset.

97

7. She objected to the price of the Porsche, nevertheless the salesperson insisted it was fair.

8. Some people who live in cold countries believe that fur coats are not a luxury, they're a necessity.

9. He hated having to mow the lawn, therefore he bought a flock of sheep.

10. Lotteries are extremely popular in Canada, those who like to gamble spend thousands of dollars a year on them.

EXERCISE 3-19

Correct all run-ons and comma splices. Keep in mind that not all of the sentences are incorrect.

1. The Beatles were originally called the Quarrymen, later they changed their name to the Silver Beetles.

2. Most people remember John, Paul, George, and Ringo, only a few people know that Pete Best was the group's first drummer.

3. Brian Epstein, who at the time worked in a record store, discovered the group in a small Liverpool nightclub called the Cavern, he became their manager.

4. At first, they were popular only in England and in Germany where they had performed when starting out, they became a hit in America in 1964.

5. The Beatles arrived in the U.S.A. in February 1964 they made their television debut on "The Ed Sullivan Show."

6. They had five best-selling singles in the top ten in March 1964 this record has never been equalled.

7. Two movies followed in 1964 and 1965, *A Hard Day's Night* and *Help,* these films were well received, consequently, the group met with increasing financial success.

8. About 100,000 people watched them perform at Shea Stadium in New York during their last tour in 1966, however they decided to give up live performances.

9. Many of the songs the group wrote and performed in the late sixties were considered controversial, for example, "Lucy in the Sky with Diamonds" was thought to be a song celebrating the use of LSD.

10. Despite their success, and to their fans' dismay, the Beatles disbanded in 1970, Paul McCartney sued the others in order to break their contract.

EXERCISE 3-20

The following exercise contains run-ons and comma splices. Correct whatever errors you find, keeping in mind that not all of the sentences are incorrect.

1. Elvis is alive and living in a trailer park in Red Deer, Alberta he now weighs 350 pounds.

2. If you hear it thunder, don't run under a tree, there will be pennies from heaven for you and me.

3. For the want of a nail, the battle was lost.

4. Harriet baked cookies in order to impress Mr. Elton, the new minister, unfortunately he got indigestion.

5. The filing cabinets toppled over and the copier exploded when the earthquake hit.

6. The painting caused a scandal when it was unveiled the artist was charged with creating a public nuisance.

7. The professor continued to lecture, unaware that his class was falling asleep, however the fire alarm woke them up.

8. Don't buy it however little it costs.

9. When she consulted the psychic, Belva discovered the ring was cursed nevertheless she decided to wear it.

10. Damian and Jojo were introduced to one another by a publisher subsequently they had successful writing careers and an unsuccessful marriage.

EXERCISE 3-21

The following exercise contains run-ons and comma splices. Correct whatever errors you find, keeping in mind that not all of the sentences are incorrect.

1. Run to the store buy some bandages.

2. Although this part of the jungle was supposedly undisturbed, Come-by-Chance Smith, the intrepid explorer, was surprised to find evidence of civilization near the waterfall he found Mars bar wrappers and an old *Chatelaine* magazine.

3. Boring as the television program was, it beat washing the dog.

4. Chess is an absorbing intellectual challenge it is nonetheless more interesting to play than to watch.

99

5. The sun will come up tomorrow, bet your bottom dollar that tomorrow there will be sun.

6. The return of spring had a noticeable effect on Sterling's mental outlook as a result he gave up smoking and drinking and became a priest.

7. After she fired her entire administrative staff, the director of the art gallery held a press conference to explain her managerial style, "A new broom sweeps clean," she said.

8. The proposed community centre, a combined concert hall and basketball court, was, in fact, rejected by the city council as being too expensive.

9. Don't cry for me Argentina the truth is I never left you.

10. By day Mrs. Luciani appeared to be the image of the traditional grandmother, by night she was "Grey Panther Woman," a tireless champion of senior citizens.

EXERCISE 3-22

Correct the comma splices and run-ons in the following student paragraphs, keeping in mind that not all of the sentences are incorrect. Remember that four different methods of correction are possible.

A. For decades we have sent terminally ill patients to the hospital to die. In hospitals, visiting was restricted, patients were isolated, a strict schedule was maintained these measures were often employed to prolong life even though everyone knew the patient would die anyway. Discussions about the patient's coming death were discouraged. Family members were cut off from their loved one, they had no one to help them cope with their grief. There is now a much-needed alternative to our traditional methods of caring for the terminally ill, it is called Palliative Care.

B. In a Palliative Care Unit, overall care is provided by a multi-disciplinary team, this team includes nursing staff, social workers, pharmacist, dietician, chaplain, occupational therapist, physiotherapist, speech pathologist, and trained volunteers, as well as physicians. When the patients arrive, they are welcomed by members of the staff they encourage the patients to call them by their first names. To make the patients feel at home, staff members encourage them to bring and use their personal belongings. Visiting is not restricted, family may help with day-to-day care, relatives often stay overnight especially when death is near, even pets are allowed to visit occasionally.

C. Most patients know they are going to die they become angry and upset when people attempt to hide this reality from them. Staff members in a Palliative Care Unit help patients to cope with the facts, patients are encouraged, but not forced, to talk about their feelings. PCU staff are trained to recognize signs that patients are ready and willing to talk to others, members of the family are also encouraged to lend support. Because patients are made aware of any changes in their condition, the family may help them work through their feelings as death comes closer.

D. Palliative Care offers us a far more satisfactory method of caring for the terminally ill than standard hospital treatment, patients and their families receive encouragement and support from the Palliative Care team. Patients are treated like contributing members of society, this treatment reduces or eliminates their feelings of alienation. Patients remain alert they are free of pain, they die with their families close by. The Palliative Care concept allows patients to die peacefully and with dignity it therefore provides us with a humane method of caring for the terminally ill.

REVIEW EXERCISES

REVIEW EXERCISE 1

Identify the parts of speech in these sentences, using the following code:
① Nouns   ② Verbs   ③ Adverbs   ④ Conjunctions
⑤ Pronouns   ⑥ Adjectives   ⑦ Prepositions   ⑧ Articles

1. To order this merchandise, call your local sales representative.

2. All sales are final.

3. Tailless amphibians from the family *Ranidae* are commonly called frogs.

4. When it freezes, water expands almost nine percent.

5. The Great Barrier Reef, off the northeast coast of Australia, is the largest coral reef in the world.

6. Proceed with caution.

7. Like the dodo, the great auk, a flightless seabird, has become extinct.

8. Obadiah went the way of all flesh.

9. The card game, Hearts, developed in the United States some time around the end of the nineteenth century.

10. He who laughs last laughs best.

REVIEW EXERCISE 2

Identify the parts of speech in these sentences, using the following code:

① Nouns   ② Verbs   ③ Adverbs   ④ Conjunctions
⑤ Pronouns   ⑥ Adjectives   ⑦ Prepositions   ⑧ Articles

1. Brian and Sarah gasped when they saw the book.

2. "Book him on a charge of disorderly conduct," said the officer.

3. Whatever you want is all right with me.

4. Home is where I hang my hat.

5. Picnicking is forbidden here, but swimming is permitted when a lifeguard is on duty.

6. With his hands in his pockets, the young man paced the length of the hospital corridor.

7. Through the night the fire raged.

8. Barely was the concert over when the audience burst into applause.

9. Crowded to the doors, the bus lurched to a halt.

10. Miss Persimmon asked all the nice-looking students to help her after class.

REVIEW EXERCISE 3

Underline the subjects and verbs in the following sentences. Use one line for subjects and two lines for verbs.

1. Swimming, cycling, and running are the components of most triathlons.

2. Triathlons are called "Ironman" competitions.

3. You have to be made of iron to survive one.

4. Usually held in places like Hawaii and California, Ironman meets attract more and more participants.

5. Many armchair athletes enjoy watching these contests on television.

6. Less strenuous ways of keeping fit, jogging, walking, and exercising, are more enjoyable than triathlons.

7. Following the lead of Jane Fonda, there are major industries devoted to fitness.

8. Special shoes, clothes, and equipment are required for each sports activity.

9. At some point each one of us has to decide whether or not we want to invest in fitness.

10. Of course, there is always the possibility of exercising your mind by watching triathlons on television.

REVIEW EXERCISE 4

Underline all the subjects and verbs in the following sentences. Use one line for subjects and two lines for verbs.

1. Looking at any of the popular dances of the twentieth century, many people would find it hard to believe that dancing began as religious ritual.

2. The early Christian church disapproved of dancing because it was considered pagan.

3. Not so different was the reaction of parents who saw their children doing the Charleston, the shimmy, and the twist.

4. In the late sixteenth century the sight of Elizabeth I being lifted off the floor and swung in the vigorous dance called the volta shocked the Spanish Ambassador.

5. Also considered improper when it was introduced was the waltz.

6. Because it meant that young unmarried people could hold each other familiarly, the waltz took a while to win social approval.

7. Associated now with sophistication and sensuality, the tango originated as a test of machismo in saloons in South America.

8. The Peppermint Lounge in New York was the birthplace of the most popular dance of the 1960s, the twist.

9. Derived from the twist were a number of other dances including the frug, the jerk, and the watusi.

10. With its spasmodic movements and separated partners, perhaps modern dancing is not so far removed from primitive man's religious rites.

REVIEW EXERCISE 5

Underline all the subjects and verbs in the following sentences. Use one line for subjects and two lines for verbs.

1. Through the centuries man has contrived different methods and devices to keep track of numbers.

2. Invented by the Chinese about 3000 B.C., the abacus is a calculating device that has been used all over the world.

3. The Peruvian Indians used the *quipu,* a simple system of knots on strings, to keep records of taxes and harvests.

4. The Aztecs told time on large round stone calendars, the most famous of which is on exhibition in Mexico's National Museum of Anthropology.

5. Around the Mediterranean Sea the merchants of ancient Rome drew markings in the sand and used pebbles to indicate numbers for their transactions.

6. The first digital calculator was invented by Blaise Pascal in France in 1644 to help his father, a tax collector.

7. Unfortunately, the device was too advanced for the technology of the time, and it frequently broke down.

8. Canada's first transistorized computer, called "Dirty Gertie," employed over 400 large circuit cards, each crammed with 50,000 resistors, transistors, capacitors, and other elements.

9. Today Gertie's capacity is equalled by that of a programmable pocket calculator.

10. A modern microchip less than 4.725 mm square can hold up to 50,000 circuit elements and contain 64,000 bits of information.

REVIEW EXERCISE 6

Identify and correct sentence fragments wherever they occur in the following exercises. Some of these are correct sentences.

1. Because he wanted to attend the rock concert.

2. Having lost her credit card.

3. The people who usually find fault with the government.

4. After he left the bar that fateful night of the assassination attempt.

5. Class cancelled due to lack of interest.

6. Wright Leaphart, formerly a censor with the CBC.

7. As far as I know.

8. Weather permitting, the trip will take place as scheduled.

9. Being by nature a loner, the prairie dog is an independent creature.

10. What profits it a man to gain the whole world and lose his own soul?

REVIEW EXERCISE 7

Identify and correct sentence fragments wherever they occur in the following exercises. Some of these are correct sentences.

1. Working too hard can cause heart attacks.

2. The police searching for the escaped convict.

3. Whether you win or lose.

4. Working in a bar, he hoped to meet interesting people.

5. Listening to a compact disc player.

6. Since she returned to Florida and he went on the wagon.

7. Going to meetings and listening to pointless speeches annoyed him.

8. Who cares?

9. Living alone being dull.

10. Unnecessary and offensive to say the least.

REVIEW EXERCISE 8

Rewrite the following student paragraphs eliminating the sentence fragments. Some rephrasing may be needed.

You are writing an important essay that is due tomorrow. You reach a point. At which you are unsure of which direction to proceed. Getting up from your desk and going to the refrigerator for a glass of milk while you ponder the problem. When you hear the hockey game on the television in the next room and you find yourself watching it for the rest of the night. Finally, your paper, submitted a week later, receiving a failing grade.

You're reading a murder mystery until 5 a.m. In order to find out whodunit. Even though you have an important business meeting in the morning.

If you find yourself in either of these situations. You may be a procrastinator. There are several types.

Despising the frequent criticism of his work. One procrastinator may terminate efforts to complete a project. Because he is afraid of failure and the resulting criticism. Similarly, another procrastinator avoids graduating from school. For fear of entering the cold, cruel world. Yet another may fear success because she believes she does not deserve it. Whatever the procrastinator's fear by never finishing the task at hand. He or she averts criticism but not failure.

REVIEW EXERCISE 9

The following exercise contains run-ons, comma splices, and sentence fragments. Correct whatever errors you find, keeping in mind that some sentences may be correct.

1. Kathy Dawn Lang, better known as k.d. lang, was raised in Consort, Alberta, which had a population of 714, the nearest city was over 200 miles away.

2. According to lang, Consort having "one TV channel, one radio station, no movie theatres, one bar, one drugstore, no police—and no swimming pool."

3. Her father bought her a motorcycle when she was nine and an electric guitar when she was in grade six.

4. The major inspiration for lang at the start of her career was Patsy Cline, killed in a plane crash in 1963, Cline was a famous country singer who had helped Loretta Lynn.

5. In recent years Cline's life has been the subject of two movies in *Sweet Dreams* Jessica Lange played Cline while in *Coal Miner's Daughter*, she was played by Beverly D'Angelo and Sissy Spacek played Loretta Lynn.

6. When she won the Juno Award for Most Promising Female Vocalist, lang's outfit including a wedding dress and veil, harlequin glasses and black boots.

7. Although she won a Grammy in 1989 for best country female vocalist, lang was never accepted by Nashville her original style of "cow punk" music was considered too unconventional.

8. Also her advocating of vegetarianism.

9. In spite of controversy, her popularity has increased her recording Ingenue was a "crossover" that broadened her appeal.

10. She has been compared to many different singers even Madonna has said, "Elvis is alive—and she is beautiful."

REVIEW EXERCISE 10

The following exercise contains run-ons, comma splices, and sentence fragments. Correct whatever errors you find, keeping in mind that some sentences may be correct.

1. What should you do when you find yourself coming down with the common cold? Hide in bed?

2. Most doctors recommend lots of fluids bed rest is also a good idea.

3. Common colds have some annoying symptoms, for instance, they stuff up your nose, make your muscles ache, and ruin your tastebuds.

4. Although you are advised to drink plenty of orange juice. You usually cannot taste it.

5. Even more irritating, TV commercials always try to sell you patent medicines that promise fast relief however they seldom work as well as you hope.

6. Your close friends generally try to avoid you, they beg you not to breathe near them it's discouraging.

7. Cures don't exist, but prevention is possible.

8. If you get adequate vitamin C, avoid chills and overexertion.

9. Of course, colds being contagious, you probably won't be able to avoid them entirely, moreover, it's not polite to avoid contact with family members, coworkers, and loved ones.

10. Colds are as unavoidable as air, if you ask me.

REVIEW EXERCISE 11

The following exercise contains run-ons, comma splices, and sentence fragments. Correct whatever errors you find, keeping in mind that some sentences may be correct.

1. Writing business letters can be easy if you remember a few basic principles.

2. Keep your audience and your purpose in mind you usually write a business letter to ask someone to do something specific.

3. There are several essential parts to the letter. The date, the inside address, the salutation, and the closing. All of which need special attention.

107

4. Your letter should be straightforward, don't waste words, don't waste your reader's time.

5. Language in a letter should be formal and polite. Avoiding slang and treating the receiver courteously at all times.

6. Begin the letter with an explanation of why you are writing. What you want to say.

7. Close the letter by making sure that the reader understands what you want him or her to do next, your main point should be clear.

8. You should always include any details that might help the reader understand the situation. File numbers and dates being especially important.

9. Proof-reading must be thorough, writers are often not careful enough.

10. Good letter writing presents a challenge, as a result, many bosses mistakenly believe they should leave the task to their secretaries, but whoever signs the letter should take responsibility for it.

REVIEW EXERCISE 12

The following exercise contains run-ons, comma splices, and sentence fragments. Correct whatever errors you find, keeping in mind that some sentences may be correct.

1. Horology is the art of measuring time, the name is derived from two Greek words meaning "time" and "telling."

2. The earliest device to measure time consisting of a stick placed in an upright position.

3. More sophisticated sundials were developed by the Egyptians, the Romans, and the Arabs the Egyptians also introduced the waterclock.

4. Dating from 1386, the oldest surviving clock at Salisbury Cathedral in England.

5. The best known British clock, however, is Big Ben at the Houses of Parliament practically all tourists in London take pictures of it.

6. Thought by many to be the most significant innovation in timekeeping, the quartz crystal was first used in clocks in 1929.

7. The Swiss watch industry began in the mid-eighteenth century a traveller showed his broken watch to a boy named Daniel Jean-Richard who became curious about how it worked.

8. After eighteen months, Daniel managed to build his own watch, he started a new industry and his five sons continued in it.

9. By 1900 the Swiss matched the English in the manufacture of watches because of their industry and inventiveness the Swiss were able to take over the market.

10. Today a watch is a necessary item for business and fashion many people have a watch for every occasion.

REVIEW EXERCISE 13

Correct the comma splices, run-ons, and sentence fragments in the following student paragraphs keeping in mind that not all of the sentences are incorrect. Remember that four different methods of correction are possible.

A. Pictographs have been found in every country in the world, across Canada, thousands of Rock Art sites have been discovered between British Columbia and Quebec. The largest concentration of Rock Art sites is located along the Canadian Shield in the Upper Great Lakes region. The Ojibwa Indians painted symbols and figures on the flat surfaces of rocks. These paintings telling stories about important events in the lives of the Ojibwa people. The number of pictographs at each site varies. At the Ojibwa site on the northeast coast of Lake Superior. There are dozens of pictographs, at the Gros Cap site in the same area, there are only five.

B. Rock Art in the Canadian Shield woodlands is found on the flat vertical surfaces of rocks. Which are located at the edge of the water. Surface features of the rocks are often incorporated into the pictograph, for example, occasionally, a patch of quartz on the surface of a rock is used for the specific painting of a mythical creature.

C. Sites located at the water's edge are kept clean by the actions of the waves and ice on the rock's surface, pictographs that are several feet above the present water level were painted when the water level of the lake was higher. Because the rocks are sometimes covered with lichen or stained with oxidized iron. Some Rock Art is difficult to find, the Ojibwa had a tendency to paint their pictographs in places that were not easily accessible. A large number of Rock Art sites which are located in remote areas they would not have been found without the assistance of local residents who gave researchers information about them.

D. Ojibwa pictographs being usually painted with red ochre, other common colours are white, yellow, and black. The pigment is difficult to scrape off the rocks. A fact which suggests that egg fluid was used as a binder. As long as the water did not touch the painting during the drying period, the pigment would remain on the rock.

E. The best information regarding a site's location comes from Native elders living in the area, there is often oral history associated with a particular site. An oral account of a historical battle is still told by the Ojibwa people near the Gros Cap site. This site having pictures of an animal track, a horned water spirit, a canoe, and two abstract forms, these symbols all being associated with the water realm of the Ojibwa universe. Dating procedures have established the age of the Gros Cap site at three to four hundred years, this date corresponds with the local legend that describes a battle between the Ojibwa and the Iroquois in 1662 at nearby Iroquois Point. This battle was also recorded in detail by Jesuit missionaries, local oral history and the Native belief in a resident water spirit in Whitefish Bay link the pictographs at Gros Cap to the Iroquois Point battle. The pictographs thus being meant to ward off evil spirits.

F. These Rock Art sites tell us something about the methods and materials the Ojibwa used to paint their pictures, when compared to local history, they also often demonstrate that the groups of figures and symbols tell a story. In instances where sufficient information about a site is available, we find that pictographs were used by the Ojibwa to relate stories about significant events in their lives.

Common Errors

VERBS

Tense

In English, verb forms indicate the time that an action occurs. The verb form itself changes to show these shifts in time, whether past, present, or future.

To form these tenses, you need to be able to recognize the four parts of the verb:

1. The **infinitive** or **base** form: (to) skip
   This form can stand alone or be combined with *can/could, may/might, shall/should, will/would, like, must.*

   > We *like to skip.* We *can skip.* We *might skip.*

2. The **simple past** form: skipped

   > Irving *skipped* lunch and lost twenty pounds.

3. The **present participle:** skipping
   This form is combined with the verb *to be* to indicate an ongoing action.

   > I *have been skipping* lunch for the past two years and haven't lost an ounce.

4. The **past participle:** skipped
   This form may be combined with the verb to *have:*

   > We *had skipped.*

   > They *have skipped.*

There are five ways of indicating **past** time:

> I skipped class yesterday. (simple past—action completed in the past)

> I was skipping class yesterday when I ran into my mother at the shopping mall. (continuous past—action going on in the past)

> I have skipped class three times this term. (present perfect—action that has happened more than once in the past)

Note that in the example above the tense is called the present perfect because the auxiliary verb "to have" is in the present tense. The perfect tense is used to indicate that an action is completed before another action. The present perfect shows that an action has just occurred.

> I had skipped class many times before I was caught. (past perfect—action completed before some other action occurred in the past)

Similarly in this example, the tense is called the past perfect because the auxiliary verb "to have" is in the past tense.

I had been skipping class for years before I was caught. (past perfect continuous—action that had been going on in the past before some other action occurred in the past)

There are three ways of indicating present time:

I skip classes on a regular basis. (simple present—action that occurs regularly or may occur immediately)

I am skipping class now. (present continuous—action occurring)

The present continuous can also indicate the future as in this example:

I am skipping class tomorrow.

I have been skipping classes all morning. (present perfect continuous—action going on in the present)

There are four other ways of indicating future time:

I will skip class tomorrow. (simple future—action to occur in the future)

I will be skipping class soon. (future continuous—action that is going on in the future)

I will have skipped class three times before the term is over. (future perfect—action to be completed before some other action will occur in the future)

I will have been skipping classes for two weeks tomorrow. (future perfect continuous—action that will be completed in the future before another future action occurs)

To summarize, the perfect tense is always formed with the auxiliary "to have" and the past participle:

PERFECT TENSE =	TO HAVE	+	PAST PARTICIPLE
	HAD		SKIPPED
	HAVE		SKIPPED
	WILL HAVE		SKIPPED

The continuous tense is formed with the auxiliary "to be" and the present participle:

CONTINUOUS TENSE =	TO BE	+	PRESENT PARTICIPLE
	WAS		SKIPPING
	AM		SKIPPING
	WILL BE		SKIPPING

Many verbs form the past tense by adding -ed as in the examples above. These are called **regular** verbs. The past tense and the past participle of regular verbs are the same.

Infinitive: to skip   **Past Tense:** skipped
Present Participle: skipping   **Past Participle:** skipped

Many common verbs, however, do not follow this form; they are called irregular verbs. Consider, for example, the verbs *to bring* and *to drink*, which take these forms: *bringing* (present participle), *brought* (past tense), *brought* (past participle); *drinking* (present participle), *drank* (past tense), *drunk* (past participle). If you don't know the correct forms of a verb or whether it is regular or not, check a dictionary. It will list any irregular verb forms.

Here is a list of the most common irregular verbs:

INFINITIVE	PAST TENSE	PAST PARTICIPLE
be	was, were	been
begin	began	begun
bite	bit	bitten
build	built	built
burst	burst	burst
choose	chose	chosen
do	did	done
draw	drew	drawn
eat	ate	eaten
fall	fell	fallen
forget	forgot	forgotten
freeze	froze	frozen
get	got	got, gotten
go	went	gone
hang (a person)	hanged	hanged
hang (an object)	hung	hung
know	knew	known
meet	met	met
prove	proved	proved, proven
ride	rode	ridden

run	ran	run
see	saw	seen
shine	shined, shone	shined, shone
show	showed	showed, shown
sink	sank	sunk, sunken
speak	spoke	spoken
steal	stole	stolen
swim	swam	swum
take	took	taken
teach	taught	taught
throw	threw	thrown
wake	woke, waked	woke, waked
wear	wore	worn
wring	wrung	wrung
write	wrote	written

Auxiliary Verbs

Besides TO HAVE and TO BE, and WILL and SHALL (used to form the future tense), seven other auxiliary verbs are used to indicate different meanings. These verbs are fixed in form, meaning that when you use them, you don't have to change the verb ending. These verbs are

can   could   should   would   may   might   must

CAN shows ability:

John can program computers.

COULD is the past tense of can:

My grandfather could build canoes.

COULD also shows possibility:

I could build canoes if I had the tools.

SHOULD shows responsibility:

I should know when to quit.

WOULD is the past tense of will:

My dog would hide under the bed during a thunderstorm.

117

MAY shows permission:

> You may borrow my typewriter.

MIGHT shows possibility:

> I might go to the party if I finish my work.

MUST shows necessity:

> This report must reach Medicine Hat by 5:00 p.m.

Some Special Cases

Two pairs of verbs which are often confused are *lie* and *lay*, *sit* and *set*. The forms of the verb *(to) lie*, meaning *to recline* are *lie, lying, lay, lain*.

> Jeanette *was lying* on the bearskin rug.

> She *had lain* there all evening.

Do not confuse this verb with *(to) lay*, meaning to put or place. The forms of the verb are *lay, laying, laid, laid.*

> The riverboat gambler *laid* his cards on the table.

> The whippoorwill *is laying* an egg.

Note that the verb *to lay* always takes an object.

> The forms of the verb *(to) sit* are *sit, sitting, sat, sat.*

> Mrs. Martinello *sat* up until two waiting for her daughters to come home.

> The mother bird *is sitting* on the egg.

The forms of the verb to set, usually meaning *to put an object down*, are *set, setting, set, set.*

> Anton *set* the teacups on the table.

Here, as in the case of *(to) lay*, the verb *(to) set* takes an object.

EXERCISE 4-1

Fill in the blanks with either the past tense or the past participle (as appropriate) of the given verb.

1. (dive) With a final flick of his tail, Flipper _____ beneath the waves.

2. (forget) I have _____ his address.

3. (choose) The contestants _____ among the three mystery doors and a cash prize.

4. (bite) Too late they discovered that they had been _____ by Dracula.

5. (rise) By the time she finished her paper route, the sun had _____.

6. (shrink) The cotton shirt _____ a whole size when I washed it.

7. (hang) The curator _____ the pictures in the new gallery.

8. (ride) Having _____ all day, the cowboy was exhausted.

9. (give) Richard had to borrow a subway token because he had _____ all his spare change to a bag lady.

10. (ring) The bell had already _____ when the instructor stumbled into class.

EXERCISE 4-2

Fill in the blanks with either the past tense or the past participle (as appropriate) of the given verb.

1. (pay) The hospital bill has been _____ in full.

2. (prove) The crown attorney had _____ beyond all doubt that the accused was guilty.

3. (tear) The wind _____ the scarf out of her hands.

4. (write) I had just _____ to her when the telegram came.

5. (shake) That cocktail should be _____, not stirred.

6. (see) By tomorrow I will have _____ all the available property.

7. (dig) Mr. Falbo should have discovered where the power lines were before he _____ his pool.

8. (freeze) These vegetables are not fresh; they have been _____.

9. (light) They _____ a fire upon arrival at the cabin.

10. (spring) It was not until he was in the middle of the lake that Martin realized his boat had _____ a leak.

EXERCISE 4-3

Fill in the blanks with either the past tense or the past participle (as appropriate) of the given verbs.

1. (take) The unsuspecting couple was _____ for a ride by the gangster.

2. (speak) Victorian children _____ only when they were _____ to.

3. (sell) Let me show you the sculpture that I _____ at the art sale.

4. (lose) If you _____ the directions to the cottage, we will undoubtedly become _____.

5. (rise) I _____ from my bed six hours after the sun had _____.

6. (slink) After making a fool of himself in front of all the guests, Mr. Pancks _____ out of the room.

7. (drag) The energetic sheepdog _____ his tiny owner down the street.

8. (eat, drink) Because we had _____ taco chips with salsa, we _____ gallons of water for the rest of the evening.

9. (blow) The ship was _____ way off course.

10. (throw, slide) After the pitcher _____ the ball, Ted _____ into second base.

Verb Tense Shifts

It is important that, in your writing, your verbs be consistent. If you begin a discussion in the present tense, you should not change tenses unnecessarily, or you will confuse the reader. Here is a passage in which the verb tenses are confused:

> Every morning it *is* a race between me and the dog to see who gets the paper. If I *won*, I *get* to read the paper. On the days when the dog *wins*, the paper *was torn* to bits and *scattered* all over the front lawn. I *read* the paper so seldom these days that I *think* the paperboy *was* in league with the dog.

Here is the corrected passage:

> Every morning it *is* a race between me and the dog to see who *gets* the paper. If I *win*, I *get* to read the paper. On the days when the dog *wins*, the paper *is torn* to bits and *scattered* all over the front lawn. I *read* the paper so seldom these days that I *think* the paperboy is in league with the dog.

EXERCISE 4-4

Correct the verb tenses in the following sentences, making sure they are consistently in the past.

1. First, my parents leave me home alone for the weekend, and the next thing I know, the light bulb burns out in the basement.

2. Because Ardath believed that fibre was good for her health, she eats baked beans and bran flakes every morning for breakfast.

3. Christine's speech became confused as she tries to explain how to use the fire extinguisher.

4. After Cecil searched through the entire playground, he realizes that Muffy is playing hide-and-seek under the slide.

5. The instructor starts by asking us a question to which she didn't know the answer herself.

6. If you ask me nicely what I think, I would tell you.

7. Mrs. Wirewater had to learn to keep her wits about her if she is to avoid problems during the blackout.

8. Janice kept calling Elias in an effort to collect the money he owed her, but he doesn't answer the phone.

9. The clock was just striking three when Marlon and his friends pull into the driveway.

10. While her husband was sleeping on the futon, Amanda goes quietly down to the convenience store and buys a package of breath mints, but he wakes up as soon as he heard the door shut.

EXERCISE 4-5

Put the words in these sentences in the past tense, making sure to check for consistency.

1. Fiona is waiting on tables for the last three weeks; she has made over $200 in tips.

2. Fifi receives the highest marks in obedience school; her owner could make her jump through a hoop on command.

3. Bernard gasps as he opened Daisy's gift; she bought him a new pair of trousers.

4. After Polly puts the kettle on, we all have tea.

5. When the traffic lights turn yellow, the pedestrians made a run for it.

6. Josh is too weak to get out of bed and finish painting the car as his mother tells him to do.

7. Jeremiah gets very upset when I told him that he was paid too much and that he's lacking in education.

8. Stanley yells at Stella, but they made up almost immediately and decide to go bowling.

9. Roger is considered to be a gifted musician by his friends; he could play "Turkey in the Straw" on the guitar, the piano, and the spoons.

10. Shelley can eat breakfast only if she doesn't stay up to watch David Letterman and all-night music videos.

More about Tense Sequence

The verb tense used in a main clause generally influences the verb tense in the subordinate clause. Although a main verb in the present or future may be followed by any tense, a main verb in the past tense is usually followed by some form of the past tense.

> Linda *knew* that he was divorced. (same time)
>
> Linda *knew* that he had been divorced. (time before)
>
> Linda *knew* that he would be divorced. (time after)

Note that occasionally the past tense may be followed by the present tense if the subordinate clause describes a repeated action, a comparison, or a general statement.

> Grandma *said* that she always *sleeps* with a shotgun handy.
>
> Mark *had* a larger collection of Mickey Mouse Club memorabilia than I *have*.
>
> Irene *said* that Club Med *offers* a variety of interesting holiday packages.

EXERCISE 4-6

Change the verb in the main clause to the past tense, making sure that the verb in the subordinate clause is also correct.

1. Albertine says that she doesn't care for Odette.

2. The marketing committee asks if I agree to the proposal.

3. Reba reveals that she knows who her father is.

4. Alberto believes that the boss pays him better than he pays me.

5. The art instructor claims that "Beauty is Truth; Truth Beauty."

6. Mr. Feeley, the lawyer, asserts that his partner is responsible for the mess.

7. The gardeners will have finished by dusk if you have kept out of their way.

8. Mrs. Wiggins asks me where her cat is.

9. The repairman assures me that the bill will arrive tomorrow.

10. I wonder whether it will rain when we have our picnic.

EXERCISE 4-7

Change the verb in the main clause to the past tense, making sure that the verb in the subordinate clause is also correct.

1. The chaperones hope that the students behave themselves at the dance.

2. The Siamese twins expect to be separated when they go into the hospital.

3. Scientists report that the ozone layer is as thin over Toronto as it is over Antarctica.

4. After the fire drill is completed, the children return to their classes.

5. Because his waterbed leaks, Colin wrings out his pyjamas every morning.

6. I am so confused that I don't know what to do.

7. Although Pat enjoys salmon-fishing, his family finds it a great bore.

8. Wendy and Ron are obsessed with picking out wallpaper and doorknobs because they have just decided to build their dream house.

9. This exercise video is so strenuous that even Jane Fonda can't do it.

10. Alec's skin reacts so violently to the sun that when he gets a sunburn he looks like a leper.

ACTIVE AND PASSIVE VOICE

Some verbs have two voices: active and passive. In the active voice, the sentence proceeds in the normal order: performer of the action, action, receiver of the action. Here is a sentence in the active voice:

The swans chased intruders away from the nest.

Here we have a subject, verb and object in the usual order. Sometimes, however, we invert the order of the sentence to change the emphasis from the performer of the action to the receiver of the action. The same sentence in the passive voice would read like this:

Intruders were chased away from the nest by the swans.

Here the object and the subject of the previous sentence are reversed, and the focus is now on the intruders.

Any verb that takes an object, in others words a transitive verb, can be made passive.

> Tom and Nicole played the game.
>
> The game was played by Tom and Nicole.

Note that passive verbs can be formed in any verb tense, past present, or future.

> Missionaries are eaten by cannibals. (present)
>
> Missionaries have been eaten by cannibals. (past)
>
> Missionaries will be eaten by cannibals. (future)

A passive verb always consists of two parts, some form of the verb "to be" and a participle.

> Exceptions are always being made to the rules.

While passives are often considered wordy and awkward, they are especially useful when the performer of the action is unknown or is not the focal point of the sentence.

> The Mirvish family built the Princess of Wales Theatre for the Canadian premiere production of *Miss Saigon.*
>
> The Princess of Wales Theatre was built in Toronto for the Canadian premiere production of *Miss Saigon.*

The information about who did the building is not the focal point of the sentence.

> The school windows were soaped on Hallowe'en. (passive)
>
> Someone soaped the school windows on Hallowe'en. (active)

In this example, the active voice really adds nothing to the meaning of the sentence.

EXERCISE 4-8

Identify the voice of the verbs in the following sentences.

1. The autograph seekers were turned away at the door.

2. Attention must be paid.

3. The stockings were hung by the chimney with care.

4. People are talking about you.

5. The hot air balloon sailed by my window.

6. Whales can be seen off the coast of New Brunswick.

7. The fate of the Franklin expedition in the Northwest Territories was only ascertained ten years after.

8. Donna has been receiving money for doing nothing.

9. The retirement party was a disappointment.

10. Roma's secretary was fired for general incompetence.

EXERCISE 4-9

Identify the voice of the verbs in the following sentences.

1. Clive's spirits were dashed by the news of the recent cutbacks.

2. Peanut butter has been smeared on the chair in the hall.

3. The groceries have arrived.

4. The groundhog that was seen in the garden has been eliminated.

5. I always discover something new on my computer after Thomas has visited.

6. These strawberries have not been washed.

7. The farmer takes a wife.

8. There are more than 16 million portable videocameras in North America.

9. The project was finished only two hours before it was due.

10. Morris never expected to become a father at forty-two.

EXERCISE 4-10

Change the verbs in the following sentences from passive voice to active voice. Some rewording may be necessary. Some sentences may be fine as they stand.

1. Cathy's arm was broken by a fall from her bicycle.

2. Marietta's baby was given a bath by its godmother after the ball game was over.

3. Mara's knee was injured by a fall, and it was operated on by a team of orthopedic surgeons.

4. Dave's sinuses were clogged by the respiratory infection.

125

5. The beach was crowded with noisy, eager tourists whose hotel bills were being paid by the conference's sponsor.

6. The photographs were taken by a friend of the family whose works were displayed throughout the house.

7. The photocopying was done by the work-study student whose wages were paid by the government.

8. The workshop was conducted by a trained psychologist whose autographed collected works were available in the bookstore for $150 plus tax.

9. The amber necklace was purchased by Fiona who had been encouraged to buy jewellery by her father.

10. The Heimlich manoeuvre was performed on the choking dinner guest by a registered nurse who had luckily also been invited to the reception.

EXERCISE 4-11

Change the verbs in the following sentences from passive voice to active voice. Some rewording may be necessary. Some sentences may be fine as they are.

1. The nursing home was owned and managed by Patsy's brother Charles.

2. Rebecca's dog Fluffy was pleased with the freedom she was allowed by her owner when they spent a week at the cottage.

3. The sandwiches were prepared by the women of the community for the meeting that was planned by the council on Monday.

4. The department was axed when the news was relayed that several officials had been lining their pockets.

5. The bus trip was cancelled when the folk singers' performance was put off for two months.

6. The husky was sprayed by the skunk and was given a bath in tomato juice by its owner.

7. The moosehead, a trophy from Vern's garage sale, was mounted ostentatiously above the bar.

8. The chicken was stuffed with breadcrumbs and fruit by Garcia.

9. When they were tidying up the room, the doll was laid on the bed by the children.

10. As a finishing touch, the lightbulbs were screwed in by the electrician.

SUBJECT AND VERB AGREEMENT

Make sure the verb agrees in number with the subject (even when words come between).

1. Subjects joined by *and* take a plural verb.

   > Wanda *and* Alphonse are getting married.

2. Some phrases are not part of the subject. They are prepositional phrases and therefore do not affect the agreement between subject and verb. These include *together with, such as, as well as, in addition to, with, along with, like,* and *including.*

   > Wanda, *together with* her fiance's sister, is making out the invitations.

3. Singular subjects joined by *or* or *nor* take singular verbs. However, if a singular subject and a plural subject are linked by *or* or *nor*, make the verb agree with the subject closest to it.

   > *Neither* Edna *nor* her mother wants to accept the invitation.

   > *Neither* Edna *nor* her parents are coming to the reception.

4. *Each, either, neither,* and words ending in *one, thing,* and *body* all take singular verbs.

   > Each of Wanda's sisters is hoping to catch the bouquet.

   > *Anyone* with guts and determination is welcome to try.

5. Note that when the phrase one of those ... *who* (or *that*) is used in the subject the verb that follows is plural. In this case the verb agrees with the antecedent of the pronoun.

   > Zelda is *one of those* girls *who* use a lot of hairspray.

   However, when the sentence reads *the only one of those ... who* (or *that*), the verb that follows is singular.

   > Scott is the *only* one of those columnists *who* dislikes Andrew Lloyd Webber's musicals.

6. Collective nouns are words that treat a group of people or things as a unit: *jury, committee, class, orchestra.* If you are referring to the group as a single unit, use a singular verb.

   > The *orchestra* is playing at the concert on Saturday.

   > The *public* is invited to attend.

127

If you are referring to the individuals who make up the group, use a plural verb.

The *orchestra* are tuning up their instruments now. (Each member of the orchestra is tuning up his or her particular instrument; they are not all tuning up one instrument.)

The *public* are requested to remain in their seats until the governor-general has departed. (Each member of the public has his or her own seat.)

EXERCISE 4-12

Choose the verb form that agrees with the subject.

1. Amy, along with Frieda and Del, (attend/attends) a self-defense course on Tuesday nights.

2. Neither the Fergusons nor the rest of the neighbourhood (want/wants) the shopping mall to expand.

3. One of these support groups (is/are) probably going to lose its government subsidy.

4. Each of my sister's friends (hope/hopes) to appear on "Much Music."

5. Monica and her sisters, together with their parents, (plan/plans) a camping holiday every August.

6. (Is/Are) Jesse or Fredo going to drive you to the airport?

7. Chocolate or chips (form/forms) the basis of his diet.

8. The members of the Board of Control, in addition to the mayor, (has/have) approved the new zoning by-laws.

9. Neither Billy nor any of his brothers (like/likes) brussel sprouts.

10. Dennis is the only one of my friends who still (smoke/smokes).

EXERCISE 4-13

Choose the verb form that agrees with the subject.

1. Either one or the other of those two witnesses (has/have) lied under oath.

2. The proceeds from the house tour, as well as a telephone campaign, (provides/provide) most of the money for the orchestra members' salaries.

3. (Has/Have) anybody here seen Patrick?

4. There (is/are) no such fish as sardines; fish only (becomes/become) sardines during the canning process.

5. Once you have decided to buy a new car, there (remain/remains) the questions of colour, size, and price.

6. Holes in Swiss cheese (is/are) caused by a special bacterium that (help/helps) ripen the cheese and (create/creates) its flavour.

7. In contrast to popular belief, the eyesight of cats (is/are) worse than that of humans; no breed of cats (sees/see) anything in the dark.

8. This envelope, together with these packages, (need/needs) to be sent immediately.

9. Marian, like me, (hate/hates) having to use the photocopier.

10. The leopard, in addition to other species of wild animals, (smell/smells) fear.

EXERCISE 4-14

Choose the verb form that agrees with the subject.

1. (Does/Do) any of these flavours of ice cream appeal to you?

2. Over the couch there (is/are) a painting, two ceramic masks, and a small curio cabinet.

3. Liberty, equality, and fraternity (was/were) the battle cry of the French Revolution.

4. Here (lies/lie) the bodies of Romeo and Juliet.

5. On the dessert table (was/were) several bowls of jello, three layer cakes, a trifle, and a rhubarb pie.

6. My family (is/are) very eccentric; each of its members (go/goes) its own way.

7. A series of sad events (have/has) led to Pat's appearance at the employment insurance commission today.

8. Kate, along with Bianca, (attend/attends) the sock hop every Friday night.

9. There (is/are) a petition as well as a letter of protest being circulated by the women's group.

10. Not Richard's mother but all his screaming, misbehaving brothers and sisters (was/were) what upset me.

EXERCISE 4-15

Choose the verb form that agrees with the subject.

1. Cash, free tickets, or a bonus gift (is/are) given to the lucky winner.

2. The shoddy work Blake does, not to mention his bad habit of talking with his mouth full, (make/makes) him an unlikely choice for company president.

3. The grammarian, like other English teachers, (has/have) a sadistic streak.

4. You will be shocked to hear that neither the plumbing nor the electricity (functions/function) in this establishment.

5. Nobody in the world, not even the Supremes, (sing/sings) like she can.

6. The girls' soccer team (is/are) collecting money for new uniforms to wear at the provincial playoffs.

7. Neither Rambo nor I (is/am) the least bit interested in the assertiveness training course you mentioned.

8. Deloris' best friend and favourite handyman (was/were) her boyfriend Elmo.

9. The polar bears, and not the gorilla, (was/were) the most popular attraction at the zoo.

10. Its record number of Emmys (make/makes) "The Wonderful World of Disney" the most honoured show on television.

EXERCISE 4-16

Correct the faulty subject and verb agreements in the following sentences.

1. Either Elaine or Mrs. Robinson are going to have to give up her claims on Benjamin.

2. The reason for Mrs. Robinson's marriage to her husband were the events that took place in an old Ford after a drive-in movie.

3. Mr. Robinson, as well as Benjamin's parents, were outraged by Benjamin's affair with a respected friend of the family.

4. Why do the group of people on the bus stare at the young couple running from the church?

5. Disagreements about infidelity cause many divorces.

6. Plastics, Benjamin is told, is the best way to make money after graduation.

7. Each of the women want to keep Benjamin for herself.

8. Anyone who associates with seductive older women like Mrs. Robinson are in danger of encountering family troubles.

9. Corruption, treachery, and adultery is what characterizes the older generation, according to that movie.

10. In 1967, every one of the filmgoers who saw *The Graduate* had to be over eighteen: these days, no one in the audience have to have proof of age.

EXERCISE 4-17

Correct the alignments between subject and verb in the following sentences.

1. Even though the number of upwardly mobile citizens are small in this city, a lot of BMWs are sold here.

2. The Senate Review Board meet next week to discuss the student's petition.

3. The student body of the community college were referred to as funding units by the administration.

4. What offended some censors were the obvious primary sexual characteristics of the child in Maurice Sendak's *In the Night Kitchen*.

5. The handbell choir are scheduled to perform at the Christmas service.

6. Everybody we see at the beauty salon feel safe in that hairdresser's hands.

7. The greater part of his conversation concern his fear of crazed weasels and his low self-esteem.

8. Do any one of the Fellini films remind you of a party you've attended lately?

9. A closed door and a "Do Not Disturb" sign means that the gossip columnist is slandering someone and needs her privacy.

10. There is several reasons for having your make-up done professionally: it soothes dry skin, it improves your circulation, and it provides a wonderful ego massage.

EXERCISE 4-18

Choose the verb that agrees with the subject.

1. Although a mammal, the Canadian grey seal, like the whale, (sleep/sleeps) on the ocean floor; during sleep it occasionally (rise/rises) to the surface to breathe without waking.

2. Neither the church bazaar nor the Boy Scouts (wants/want) your old clothes.

3. The students' council, along with the Student Health Service, (sponsor/sponsors) a health education seminar every fall.

4. Each of these potatoes (is/are) rotten.

5. Either Albertine or the Murphys (bring/brings) the refreshments for after the meeting.

6. Somebody, no one knows who, always (leave/leaves) the seat up.

7. Newfoundland is the only one of the provinces that (interest/interests) me.

8. There (is/are) much money to be made these days teaching investment strategies.

9. Any one of these hobby kits (take/takes) a great deal of time and patience to assemble properly.

10. Rebuilding old cars and roller-skating (offer/offers) hours of fun.

EXERCISE 4-19

Choose the verb form that agrees with the subject.

1. Any one of you answering the description (is/are) to report to the police station as soon as possible.

2. Everybody we meet lately (talk/talks) about insider trading.

3. The rate of student dropouts in these programs (is/are) increasing in proportion to the amount of homework that the instructors (has/have) assigned.

4. At this school the only available food (consist/consists) of overpriced sandwiches, soggy salads, and candy bars.

5. Since she quit school, the number of Gertie's hobbies (has/have) increased dramatically: she now makes stained glass, collects stamps, and cuts out paper dolls.

6. The reason that parents dread the thought of their children becoming teenagers (is/are) premarital sex, drugs, and financial ruin.

7. Neither the instructor nor the class (accept/accepts) the administration's proposal that six more weeks be added to the term.

8. Penny's attitude about the scuba diving classes (was/were) that they (was/were) too expensive: the class (is/are) taking a cruise to Venezuela.

9. Every one of the houses that we looked at with the real estate agent (has/have) serious drawbacks.

10. Neither rain nor snow (stands/stand) in the way of the mail carrier on his or her appointed rounds.

EXERCISE 4-20

Choose the verb form that agrees with the subject.

1. The whole clan, with the exception of the family pet, Dino, (is/are) vegetarian.

2. Either beer or iced tea (taste/tastes) good on a hot day.

3. Everything he promised me last night (seem/seems) unethical today.

4. (Have/Has) either of you ever been to sea?

5. The combination of aspirin and soda pop (is/are) disgusting, if not dangerous.

6. The variety of TV stations (overwhelms/overwhelm) the subscriber, but each of them (offer/offers) nothing more than the reruns of "MASH."

7. When there (is/are) no table of contents, you can't find the page numbers quickly.

8. Until the rock concert begins, the audience (scream/screams) its encouragement to the performers backstage.

9. The public (wants/want) something that it can sink its teeth into.

10. (Are/Is) the company going bankrupt, or (is/are) the board of directors just skinflints?

EXERCISE 4-21

Make up sentences using verbs in the present tense with these words as subjects.

1. nobody

2. Susy Jacuzzi and the Hot Tubs

3. one of those jackets that I saw at the sale

4. neither fish nor fowl

5. the team

6. one of those books

7. each of the volunteer firefighters

8. Mr. Dweeb together with his pet squirrel Fernando

9. his family

10. either rowing or gymnastics

PRONOUN AGREEMENT, REFERENCE, AND CASE

What is a **pronoun**? A pronoun replaces or refers to a specific noun or phrase in a sentence.

> The bite of the vampire bat is dangerous because *it* can cause rabies.

> Vampires can be discovered by *their* avoidance of mirrors, garlic, crosses, and daylight.

> Dracula, the most famous vampire of all, is based on a fifteenth-century figure *who* was known as a bloodthirsty warrior.

Pronoun Agreement

1. A pronoun must agree with the noun it represents in **person**. These are the pronouns used to identify person: *I, you, he, she, we, they.* In addition, some indefinite pronouns can be used to identify person: *anyone, anybody, everyone, everybody, nobody, someone, all, some, many.* Most errors in person occur through misuse of the pronoun you.

   ✗ If anyone has information concerning the robbery, you should contact the police.

   ✓ If anyone has information concerning the robbery, he or she should contact the police.

2. A pronoun must agree with the noun it represents in **gender**, whether feminine or masculine. To avoid antagonizing your reader, where appropriate, use language that includes both male and female references.

   Each choir member should bring *his* or *her* pencil to every rehearsal.

   All choir members should bring *their* own pencils to every rehearsal.

The second version avoids the potentially awkward *his or her* construction by using a plural subject.

3. A pronoun must agree with the noun it represents in **number**, whether singular or plural. The following constructions, which can be troublesome, always require singular pronouns:

anybody	no one	either (of)
anyone	somebody	neither (of)
everybody	someone	every one (of)
everyone	each (of)	one (of)
nobody		

    ✗ *Someone* left *their* bikini in the locker room.

    ✓ *Someone* left *her* bikini in the locker room.

Collective nouns (which we have already looked at on page 127), like *team, company, union, orchestra,* or *family,* represent groups of people but can take either singular or plural pronouns depending on the context of the sentence.

> After several days in a locked hotel room, the *jury* still could not reach *its* verdict.

Here *the jury* acts as a single unit.

> The *jury,* after several days of hotel food, relished *their* hamburgers.

Here *the jury* refers to each individual separately.

> The *class* is having *its* picnic today.

Here *the class* acts as a single unit.

> The *class* are getting *their* report cards today.

Here *the class* refers to each individual separately.

EXERCISE 4-22

Choose the correct pronouns in the following sentences. Note that the verbs may also need adjustment.

1. Everyone who rides in a car should use (his or her/their) air bag or (his or her/their) seat belt to ensure safety.

2. Each of the sisters know how to operate the jackhammer (herself/themselves).

3. No one with any sense wants to see (herself or himself/themselves) gain forty pounds.

4. Unless you stop cracking your knuckles, no one will get (his or her/their) necessary hours of sleep.

5. None of the awards shows on television is ever entertaining in (itself/themselves); though such programs celebrate excellence, (it/they) bore me to tears.

6. All TV evangelists swear that (his or her/their) programs are dedicated to saving souls rather than to making money.

7. Everyone must ask (himself/herself/themselves) if (he/she/they) really wants to buy an ant farm or if (he/she/they) is just succumbing to peer pressure.

8. The child who reads *Winnie the Pooh* will learn the importance of playing by (himself/itself/themselves).

9. Business and economics were valuable even though (it/they) demanded a great deal of work from students deficient in mathematics.

10. Everyone who goes scuba diving should make sure (their/his or her) oxygen tank is securely fastened and (their/his or her) life insurance is paid up.

EXERCISE 4-23

Correct the pronoun errors in these sentences.

1. The master chef showed the apprentice cooks the oyster shells and explained how they shuck them.

2. The front runner knew every member of the community and was counting on their vote to win the election.

3. Do you think any one of these respected citizens will admit that they saw a UFO after the New Year's party?

4. Every man, woman, and child who prefers this brand of popcorn is cordially invited to attend the film festival in his or her honour.

5. Everybody living in Canada secretly wishes they could move to California during the winter months.

6. The survey reported that each of the animals in the taste test preferred their usual brand of cat food to Brand X.

7. No one watching that soap opera really believes that their favorite character will not recover from amnesia.

8. One or other of the brothers always insists on showing everyone their tattoo.

9. Anybody who eats lunch regularly in the school cafeteria will find that their health suffers from a lack of the four basic food groups.

10. One of the boys had a mosquito bite on their elbow.

Pronoun Reference

Pronoun references must be as clear and unambiguous as possible.

1. Make sure the pronoun refers to a word or phrase that actually appears earlier in the sentence or in the previous sentence.

   ✗ In the tabloid, they said that Satan has been seen in Charlottetown, P.E.I.

   Who are *they*?

   ✓ The tabloid said that Satan has been seen in Charlottetown, P.E.I.

2. Make sure that there is no possible confusion about which noun or phrase the pronoun refers to.

   ✗ *Hildy* told *her* sister that *her* car had a flat tire.

   Whose car has the flat tire?

   ✓ Hildy told her sister, "My car has the flat tire."

3. A pronoun should act as a substitute for a noun. That noun, in formal writing, should be clearly identifiable in the sentence. Even though we tend to be more relaxed in our speech, when we write *this* and *which* should refer to specific nouns rather than to the whole sentence. You will encounter some writers who do use *this* and *which* to refer to a general idea, but references to the sense of a clause or sentence or paragraph should be used carefully and sparingly.

4. There is one distinction that should be maintained between *that* and *which*. Good writers use *that* when the clause that follows is restrictive and *which* when it is non-restrictive.

   The dog that she chose was the runt. (restrictive)

   Her dog, which was the smallest of five in the litter, was white. (non-restrictive)

In the first sentence, the clause "that she chose" identifies which dog, so it restricts the meaning to that dog. In the second sentence, the dog is already

137

identified by the pronoun "her" and the clause "which was the smallest in the litter" simply offers additional information.

EXERCISE 4-24

Correct errors in pronoun reference in the following sentences.

1. One irate woman told Yvette to stay away from her husband.

2. Eating too much salt leads to hypertension, kidney problems, and heart disease, and we should control this.

3. Millicent asked the woman if she thought she should divorce her husband because of his chronic fits of temper.

4. On Delbert's report card, it said that he never paid attention in class.

5. The supervisor in the exam room said that if any cheating was discovered, the school would demand their suspension, no matter what their excuse might be.

6. In the second chapter of this book, it discusses the formation of a thesis statement.

7. In the crowded department store, they play soothing Muzak to prevent riots from breaking out during special sales.

8. Herbert sat beside his four-year-old brother and sucked his thumb.

9. We fed the jujubes to the monkeys which we had been snacking on throughout the field trip.

10. Mark thought that his gym teacher was a good coach, but he never did get the hang of the parallel bars.

EXERCISE 4-25

Correct the pronoun errors in the following sentences.

1. Christie told Jaclyn that she had dandruff.

2. Whenever her mother makes lunch for Queenie, she eats too much.

3. When Alain patted the horse's mane, it kicked him.

4. Elwy loves to go to movies and does it a lot.

5. I have always liked nursing sick animals, and after a year at veterinary school, I'm going to be one.

6. In the first chapter of the book on basic car maintenance, it tells how to do a lube job.

7. When the baby hit its head, it screamed.

8. Whenever Yuri and Sergei play monopoly, he cheats shamelessly.

9. When Farley and Gore finally step into the ring, he'll hit him below the belt until the referee has to step in.

10. The night-shift workers rallied for wage parity because they all believed theirs should be higher.

Pronoun Case

Personal pronouns can function three ways in a sentence. They can indicate the subject, the object, or the possessive. (See the discussion of pronouns in chapter 3.) While you may not be conscious of these labels, you use pronouns in these ways every day.

For the most part, choosing the correct form of the pronoun is not difficult. There are, however, some special cases:

1. Pronouns in compound subjects and objects

    ✗ Michel and her tried Japanese food for the first time.

Here we have a compound subject. If you leave out the noun part (Michel), the sentence would read, "Her tried Japanese food for the first time," which is obviously wrong. When in doubt about which pronoun to use, try leaving out the noun part of the compound construction.

    Try another example:

    ✓ The clown at the birthday party was hired by Yolanda and *I*.

This is a very common mistake. Here you have a compound object. You can test for the proper form by again leaving out the noun part of the compound. You would never say, "The clown at the birthday party was hired by *I*."

One compound construction that often causes problems is *between you and me*. The correct form is always "between you and me" because *between* is a preposition and takes the object form of the pronoun.

2. The pronouns *who* and *whoever*, are used to indicate subjects in sentences; *whom* and *whomever* indicate objects.

    Who is the fairest of them all?

In this sentence *who* is the subject of the verb *is*.

139

Ask not for *whom* the bell tolls.

In this sentence *whom* is the object of the preposition *for.*

Pedro will reward *whoever* finds his wallet.

In this sentence *whoever* is the subject of the verb *finds.*

In his will, Alastair will leave his money to *whomever* he likes.

In this sentence *whomever* is the object of the verb *likes.*

3. Pronouns in comparisons using *as/than*

Olaf likes me more *than* she.

Olaf likes me more *than* her.

Although these two sentences look similar, because of the difference in pronouns, they have different meanings. The first means that Olaf likes me more than she does; the second means that Olaf likes me more than he likes her. In the first case, a verb is implied after the pronoun. If you can logically add a verb after the pronoun, then you must use the subject form.

✗ Susan has lost more books *than me.*

✓ Susan has lost more books *than I* (have).

✗ Rodney has as many freckles *as her.*

✓ Rodney has as many freckles *as she* (does).

4. Pronouns with nouns ending in *-ing*

Use the possessive form of the pronoun with a noun ending in *-ing.*

✗ Madelena hated *him* talking all the time.

✓ Madelena hated *his* talking all the time.

Since *talking* is a noun here, it takes the possessive pronoun.

EXERCISE 4-26

Improve the pronoun usage in the following sentences if necessary.

1. The dinner guests who she served flatly refused to eat hearts of palm because, in their opinion, they looked like popsicle sticks.

2. The agency asked specifically for the model who she recommended, not the one who had thick ankles.

3. My brother purchased Frieda, a red-haired doll, for my mother and myself.

4. I know who you are speaking of.

5. Frederick gave the canned goods and the money for the food bank to she and I.

6. The Petersons have a dog that is as big as me.

7. We always believe that other people are happier, richer, and thinner than us.

8. They presented the award to he and I.

9. Jim and me usually eat too many doughnuts when we get together.

10. To whom is her most recent book dedicated?

EXERCISE 4-27

Improve the pronoun usage in the following sentences if necessary.

1. Tina gets more out of the aerobics class than them.

2. The boss will give the raise to whomever is most competent.

3. At who did Francine throw the bouquet?

4. Miss Fishbane didn't like me working on the assignment in class.

5. The bears asked whom had been sleeping in their beds.

6. Between you and I, his life is a mess.

7. After work, Norton and him left for the fishing trip.

8. Mr. Weller disapproved of them playing loud music late at night.

9. Al and we will organize the company soccer team tomorrow.

10. The change in the hiring policy will affect you more than she.

MODIFIERS

The modifiers which cause writers the most difficulty are actually verbal phrases; that is, they are forms of the verb that function in different ways in a sentence. There are three kinds of verbal phrases: infinitives, participles, and gerunds.

Infinitives: Infinitives (to lose, to compete, to live, to win) can function as nouns, adjectives, or adverbs.

141

To lose one parent may be regarded as a misfortune; *to lose* both looks like carelessness. (noun, subject)

Ivan loved to *compete* in dance marathons. (noun, object)

You have only one life to *live*. (like an adjective, modifies "life")

To *win* the Governor General's Award for Fiction, you need talent, luck, and a good press agent. (like an adverb, modifies the main clause)

Participles: Participles (building, tired, seen) used as part of verbal phrases (building on her success with the students' council, tired of his career as a cosmetic industry spokesperson, seen on late night TV) function as adjectives.

Building on her success with the students' council, Eloise joined a public relations firm.

Fabio sailed away to the south seas, *tired* of his career as a cosmetics industry spokesperson.

Talk show hosts, *seen* on late night TV, seem much alike to me.

Gerunds: Gerunds (running, lying, advertising, singing) and gerund phrases (running with the wrong crowd, lying in the sun, advertising, singing opera) function as noun phrases.

Running with the wrong crowd can get you into trouble. (subject)

Puffball, my cat, loves *lying* in the sun. (object)

These days newspapers allot more space for *advertising* than for news. (object of the preposition)

Maria Callas's grand passion was *singing* opera. (complement)

We often use verbal phrases to avoid lengthy subordinate clauses. Look at the following examples:

Talking on the phone all night, Gretchen was sleepy but well informed the next morning.

This sentence could also perhaps read this way:

Because Gretchen talked on the phone all night, she was sleepy but well informed the next morning.

Written in a hurry, the essay seemed incoherent when he reread it.

The lengthier version might look like this:

Because the essay was written in a hurry, it seemed incoherent when he reread it.

The Chief Inspector called in Miss Marple *to investigate the murder.*

The lengthier version might look like this:

> The Chief Inspector called in Miss Marple because he wanted to investigate the murder.

MISPLACED AND DANGLING MODIFIERS

> *Wallowing happily in the mud,* Clay watched the newborn piglets.
>
> His mother taught him to read, *while still wearing diapers.*

The sentences, though laughable, don't make much sense. The first implies that Clay is wallowing happily in the mud; the second, that his mother was still in diapers when she taught him to read. The italicized portion of each sentence is called a **modifier** since it is used to describe another word in the sentence; *wallowing happily in the mud* describes the piglets, and *while still wearing diapers* describes him. Modifiers or modifying phrases must be used carefully to avoid confusing your readers. The following rules will help you handle problems with modifiers.

1. Make sure modifiers are close to the subject to which they refer.

   ✗ *Just like animals,* my parents knew that children make a lot of noise.

   Who is "just like animals"?

   ✓ My parents knew that children, *just like animals,* make a lot of noise.

2. Often, troublesome modifiers end in *-ing* or in *-ed.* Often, too, they are used with words like *in, by, when* or (as in the example above) with *while.*

   ✗ *Calmly chewing her cud,* Melissa gazed at the cow.

   Ask who or what was chewing. Then rewrite the sentence.

   ✓ Melissa gazed at the cow *that was calmly chewing her cud.*

   ✗ His mother taught him to read *while still wearing diapers.*

   Ask who or what was still wearing diapers. Since *him* cannot serve as the subject—you wouldn't say "Him was wearing diapers"—the sentence needs revision.

   ✓ *While still wearing diapers,* he was taught to read by his mother.

3. Make sure that modifiers that describe verbs are close to the verbs.

   ✗ The students told their instructor that they *wanted* to learn to write *badly.*

   ✓ The students told their instructor that they *badly wanted* to learn to write.

143

The adverb *badly* needs to precede the verb it modifies.

   ✗ Brenda broke up with Jeff, who is currently dating Robin, *last summer.*

   ✓ *Last summer* Brenda broke up with Jeff, who is currently dating Robin.

4. Words such as *only, hardly, just, nearly, almost,* and *even* limit the words that follow them, so position them carefully.

   ✗ Jess *almost* ate the whole thing.

   ✓ Jess ate *almost* the whole thing.

You cannot *almost* eat anything.

5. Make sure that a modifier refers clearly to its subject. If there is no subject for it to refer to, it is called a dangling modifier.

   ✗ To *write* good reports, *research* is necessary.

Ask who or what writes good reports. The answer *research* doesn't make sense. Add an appropriate subject for the infinitive form to *write* so that this modifier is no longer dangling.

   ✓ To *write* good reports, you need *research.*

Now we know that *you* is the subject of the modifier *to write.*

   ✗ *Staying awake* all last night, *class* was difficult today.

Ask who or what was staying awake. Since it isn't class, a proper subject must be added.

   ✓ *Having stayed awake* all last night, *I* found class difficult today.

You could also correct this dangling modifier by replacing it with a dependent clause.

   ✓ *Because I stayed awake* all last night, *I* found class difficult today.

To correct problems with misplaced or dangling modifiers, remember the following steps:

A. Ask yourself, "Who or what is being described in the modifying phrase?"

B. Make sure that there is a word *in the sentence* to serve as the subject for the modifier.

C. Put the modifier close to the word or phrase which it describes.

EXERCISE 4-28

Correct the misplaced modifiers in the following sentences. Note that some of the sentences may be correct.

1. The nurse who attended the elderly gentleman only was working during the night shift.

2. My astrologer predicted in September that I would become rich and famous.

3. From the last row of the orchestra, they watched Mr. Roffey's Amazing Canine Friends on stage using their opera glasses.

4. There on the doorstep was a tiny newborn baby wrapped in newspaper, screaming at the top of its lungs.

5. Dolly had worked for years before becoming the owner and manager of Vancouver's best restaurant as a short-order cook.

6. She has a fur coat in her closet with a hood.

7. The hostess warned us not to smoke immediately.

8. What did you say to that woman with such a nasty sneer?

9. They almost got run over by an ice cream truck on their way to the orthodontist.

10. Unless they're on sale, they have no intention of buying those blue jeans.

EXERCISE 4-29

Correct the misplaced modifiers in the following sentences. Note that some of the sentences may be correct.

1. Rocko was lying on the couch all the time his mother was visiting lazily.

2. The customers just wait a minute before they are served with their hamburgers and french fries.

3. The teller gave the one hundred dollars to the robber in a plain brown bag.

4. Some people are paid to make demands, such as union leaders.

5. That actress has a terrible case of stage fright; she nearly loses her nerve before every single performance.

6. The troubled patient told her counsellor that she wanted to talk to someone secretly.

7. He couldn't believe that he almost drank the whole case of beer himself.

8. Hanging from the ceiling, the parlour maid spotted the cobweb.

9. The bankrupt couple did their best to pay their overdue bills, taking on odd jobs.

10. The German shepherd woke up the neighbourhood barking at passing cars.

EXERCISE 4-30

Correct the dangling modifiers in the following sentences, taken from student paragraphs.

1. After having moved several times over the past eight years, my knowledge of the process is extensive.

2. During my last relocation, taking inventory of what I had to move, lots of heavy books and cumbersome possessions were discovered.

3. Preparing for the move, my new home seemed threatened by the loads of debris I had accumulated over the years.

4. Resolving never again to keep cards and letters for sentimental reasons, the contents of my desk drawers were destroyed before leaving my old apartment.

5. Deciding what is no longer needed, it is time either to throw things out or to find people who can use them.

6. Discarding items that no longer seem important is an essential task to maintain order in a household.

7. When packing fragile items, it is convenient to use boxes with lids to prevent breakage, soiling, and invasion of your privacy.

8. To avoid excessive moving costs, your friends can be bribed into helping you in return for a case of beer or a meal.

9. If moving gradually into your new place, everything but the bare necessities should be packed.

10. Having accomplished the task painlessly, a larger, cheaper, and nicer apartment than your new one is advertised in the paper the following week.

EXERCISE 4-31

Correct the dangling modifiers in these sentences, also drawn from student paragraphs.

1. When attending classes, it can be seen that there are two kinds of people enrolled in any educational institution: students and pupils.

2. To distinguish between the two groups, a student is someone who studies various subjects, whereas a pupil is merely registered in courses.

3. Differing from the pupil, not only in academic pursuits, but in social disposition, hard work and dedication are important to the student.

4. When walking through the library, the student can be seen sitting quietly in a corner reading a lab manual.

5. Finding pupils is not so difficult. Listening to the sounds of chatter, it is possible to hear Biff and Bob talking to Betty and Buffy, rather than studying biology.

6. After going for a coffee, a pupil's main occupation is gossiping.

7. Taking a cigarette break, signs of restlessness are exhibited in the pupil.

8. Writing essays in a single night, it often seems that getting a diploma is easy.

9. Cramming for exams, a reward for the pupil's academic efforts is often massive amounts of alcohol.

10. Rewarding themselves differently, real students might allow themselves to read a book not related to their course of study.

EXERCISE 4-32

Correct the dangling modifiers in the following sentences by supplying a subject for them to apply to. Some sentences may be correct.

1. Eating a chocolate bar, his tooth broke.

2. The house should be cleaned before giving a party.

3. Ralph knows that, being a forgiving woman, he can count on Trixie's sympathy even when he doesn't deserve it.

4. Watching television, the picture suddenly became cloudy.

5. We were instructed to stay inside the lines by our teacher learning to write.

6. Realizing that she couldn't help it, her hacking cough didn't distract me during my talk.

7. Hoping to win, the ski pole slipped out of her hand in her nervousness and cost her a medal.

8. After calling me names, I was asked to leave.

9. Aiming his camera, the panda seemed to pose for the tourist's picture.

10. As a track and field runner, my feet need special care.

EXERCISE 4-33

Correct the dangling modifiers in the following sentences by supplying a subject for them to apply to. Some sentences may be correct.

1. Admiring the football star, his weak academic record didn't matter to the cheerleader.

2. Her mother complained about her laziness after refusing to help with the dishes three nights in a row.

3. Slaving over the stove all day, her lasagne was devoured in five minutes.

4. Withdrawing so much money, the bank manager refused to grant my request for a loan.

5. When comparing these animal acts, both the trained penguins and the gorilla are excellent, but the pit bull terrier is more exciting.

6. Believed to be dangerous, an old lady was accosted on the street, and her purse was stolen by an escaped convict.

7. Not wanting to offend anyone, they kept their opinions to themselves.

8. Battling the elements for days, it snowed as the crew reached the North Pole.

9. Writing home, her letter begged her parents for extra money to finance her trip to Barbados.

10. When eating, your hands should be clean.

EXERCISE 4-34

Correct the sentences in Exercise 4-32, this time replacing the modifier with a subordinate or dependent clause.

> Modifying phrase: After receiving a good grade in English, his problems with mathematics didn't bother Feodor anymore.

> Subordinate clause: After he received a good grade in English, Feodor didn't get upset about his problems in mathematics anymore.

EXERCISE 4-35

Correct the sentences in Exercise 4-33, this time replacing the modifier with a dependent clause.

EXERCISE 4-36

The following sentences contain both misplaced and dangling modifiers. Make corrections where necessary.

1. As a health-conscious senior citizen, bran and prune juice are important to Mr. Littlejohn.

2. After allowing it originally, smoking was banned by the students' council.

3. Blushing furiously, the audience laughed at the game-show host who lost his pants.

4. It is important to make a will while being of sound mind and body.

5. Trapped in the basement, the sun could not be seen by the political prisoner.

6. A duck-billed platypus was seen by the Canadian tourists while creeping through the swamp.

7. At the age of three months his father changed Michael's diaper for the first time.

8. I see that a national election is going to be held in *The Globe and Mail.*

9. After accusing me of cheating, my exam paper was torn up.

10. When using my credit card, price is of minor importance.

EXERCISE 4-37

The following sentences contain both misplaced and dangling modifiers. Make corrections where necessary.

1. The acting dean of the library school was accused of incompetency before she could defend her actions in the press.

2. The feminist group asserted that, being women, civil servants at the Unemployment Insurance Commission were biassed against them.

3. Licking his face affectionately, David knew that the cocker spaniel was grateful for his new toy.

4. Suffering from a highly contagious social disease, his friends have stopped visiting him in the hospital.

5. A lobster dinner was served at the gynecologists' convention, broiled in butter and eaten with béchamel sauce.

6. As a home owner, the high rates for property taxes in this area seem to me unjustified.

7. To succeed in life, responsibility must be accepted.

8. Wanting to see her old flame one more time, the other guests were invited merely as camouflage.

9. In order to win the game, a strategy must be planned.

10. As a meat eater, vegetarians have always seemed to me pale, thin, and undernourished.

REVIEW EXERCISES

REVIEW EXERCISE 1

Fill in the blanks with either the past tense or the past participle (as appropriate) of the given verbs.

1. (fling) As the teacher approached the door of the classroom, Rita _____ the pie at him.

2. (swim) After suntanning on the beach for an hour, Vera _____ across the river with Chuck and Dave.

3. (arise) Maxwell _____ in the morning, quite oblivious to his obnoxious behaviour the night before.

4. (lie, fall) When he had finished reading the novel, Jake _____ down and asleep.

5. (break, shake) After the dryer _____ down, Laura always _____ her clothes out before hanging them on the line.

6. (swear) My former secretary usually _____ in French so that our English clients would not understand what she was saying.

7. (lend) I should never have _____ her the top of my thermos flask.

8. (lead) The old witch _____ Hansel and Gretel to the cages behind the gingerbread house.

9. (think, be) Cecily and Gwendolyn _____ that Ernest _____ a charming name for a prospective husband.

10. (steal) She _____ these towels from the Shady Rest Hotel.

REVIEW EXERCISE 2

Fill in the blanks with either the past tense or the past participle.

1. (pay) Annie _____ her telephone bill, but the electric company is about to turn off the lights.

2. (hang) The collectors _____ the picture in the living room even though an art critic claimed that the artist should have been _____ for producing such a monstrosity.

3. (set) George _____ the bowling trophy on the mantelpiece.

4. (hurt, dive) Jill _____ her head when she _____ into the shallow end of the pool.

5. (leave) After the swallows have _____ Capistrano, it will be time to return.

6. (speed) The car _____ up when the light turned yellow.

7. (strike, feel) When the miners _____ gold, they _____ vindicated in their determination.

8. (write) My aunt finally _____ her will after a lawyer convinced her that she should have _____ it years ago.

9. (choose, find) Hilda generally _____ soft-centred chocolates; I, on the other hand, always _____ hard centres and nuts to be more appetizing.

10. (know, see) I have never _____ what Lolita _____ in her first husband.

151

REVIEW EXERCISE 3

Eliminate problems in tense agreement in the following sentences.

1. Dominic is a teacher in a boys' private school that was located not far from a major city and found in the late nineteenth century.

2. The school was noted for its strict disciplinary measures; for instance, teachers are still allowed to cane unruly students.

3. In addition, teachers were known to shortsheet beds and had sent students to bed without their suppers.

4. The model for the school's regimen is taken from Dickens's *Oliver Twist*, except that there was less food for individual boarders.

5. Doing the laundry at this establishment was a real chore; he has to wrestle the students three falls out of five for the use of the dryers.

6. As well as teaching, currently Dominic was coaching the debating team and monitored the library.

7. Several of the boys are grounded last week for smoking in the locker room.

8. One senior class, famous in the school's history, is confined to the grounds for an entire term; no one is able to discover what happens.

9. Despite the school's reputation and the hard work, Dominic will have been enjoying his job.

10. He is saying his memoirs would make a great bestseller and eventually a movie or a TV miniseries.

REVIEW EXERCISE 4

Select the correct tense of the verb in parentheses to complete these sentences.

1. Dawson City in the Yukon Territory (found) in 1896 by a man named Joe Ladue.

2. During the first years of the Klondike Gold Rush over forty thousand people (pour) into Dawson City; it (become) the largest western city north of San Francisco.

3. The gold boom (start) at a place called Bonanza Creek; Grand Forks, the town that (spring) up almost overnight there, (vanished) now.

4. The greatest year for the discovery of gold (to be) 1900 when prospectors (mine) twenty-two million dollars worth.

5. After 1900 the boom (go) bust, and the prosperity of the town steadily (decline).

6. Today Dawson City (base) a third of its economy on tourism, and Parks Canada (develop) it as a historic area.

7. Tourists (be able) attend the Gaslight Follies, a 1900 vaudeville show, or they (be able) visit the Keno, a restored paddle wheeler; on Labour Day weekend they (be able) see the popular outhouse race.

8. The tourist season, when Dawson City's population (rise) from one thousand residents to anywhere between thirty and fifty thousand, (be limited) to about one hundred days from thaw to freeze-up.

9. In the early twentieth century Robert Service and Jack London (recreate) the excitement and atmosphere of life in the Gold Rush in their writing.

10. Many eccentric characters like Willie the Weasel who (be known) as "the Most Arrested Man in Canada" and Madame Zoom who (wear) a different hat every week and (allow) her suitors to roll dice to win her in marriage (live) on in the stories told nowadays in Dawson City.

REVIEW EXERCISE 5

Make up sentences using verbs in the present tense with these words as subjects.

1. a package of toys

2. one of his shoes

3. none of the food

4. litter

5. two thirds of the work

6. the Chief Executive Officer as well as the General Manager

7. the flock of sheep

8. rice or potatoes

9. a large number of employees

10. the committee

153

REVIEW EXERCISE 6

Choose the verb form that agrees with the subject.

1. Leprosy is one of those diseases which (has/have) been dreaded since antiquity.

2. Although it is a debilitating disease, neither its incidence nor its contagiousness (is/are) as alarming as one might think.

3. These days the existence of leper colonies (is/are) generally confined to Asia, Africa, and Central and South America.

4. Man, as well as the mouse, (are/is) known to be susceptible to the disease.

5. Neither is the cause of this bacterial infection known, nor does any cure (exist/exists); the only effective treatments (are/is) the drug sulfone, together with isolation in a colony to prevent the spread of infection among families.

6. The sufferers of leprosy rarely (die/dies) of the disease; all the stages of the condition (leads/lead) to gradual disability, as each victim (loses/lose) feeling in and control of some part of the body.

7. Leprosy, along with many similar diseases, now (seems/seem) to occur only in tropical climates.

8. The tropical climate, such as that found in the countries where leprosy is still prevalent, (do/does) not cause the disease; it used to occur in temperate climates as well.

9. Anyone in tropical villages who (contracts/contract) leprosy (is/are) obliged to leave to avoid spreading the contagion.

10. Medical research, together with current statistics, (point/points) to squalid living conditions as the cause of the disease.

REVIEW EXERCISE 7

Make up sentences using verbs in the present tense with these words as subjects.

1. Dr. Wilbrod and Mrs. Tangelo

2. Camille Paglia along with Naomi Wolf

3. *The Birds* (the film)

4. Ten thousand dollars

5. Both those women

6. My brother Marco together with his girlfriend Pepa

7. A slide rule and a calculator

8. Only one Canadian in four

9. A batch of brownies

10. Not one of those pieces of furniture

REVIEW EXERCISE 8

Rewrite these sentences according to the model.

> Potato chips are one food low in nutritional value.
>
> One food low in nutritional value is potato chips.

1. What Dwight needs is a hot bath and a few choice words from his mother.

2. Terry's downfall is watching horror movies and doing his calculus homework at the same time.

3. Something that always makes me laugh is his trouser legs hanging down over his shoes.

4. Tea, rice, and sisal are what constitute the main exports of the Hunan province of China.

5. One reason that Jamaica was declared a disaster after the hurricane was the torrential rains that destroyed the crops.

6. Dody's best feature was her twinkling eyes.

7. Bloodshot eyes, dry mouth, and a blinding headache often result from drinking too many margaritas.

8. Cigarettes are his passion.

9. What the job requires is a cool head, a steady hand, and immaculate table manners.

10. One thing that always baffled me was Jeannie's supernatural powers.

REVIEW EXERCISE 9

Choose the verb form that agrees with the subject.

1. A pair of shoes that (hurt/hurts) can be tormenting to the wearer.

2. A litter of pigs (make/makes) a frightful amount of noise.

3. My best brooch, along with my bifocals, (was/were) missing after your great-aunt's visit.

4. The whole set of wine glasses (was/were) covered with unsightly spots.

5. Neither Ali Baba nor the forty thieves ever (eat/eats) in steak houses.

6. Neither this herd of cows nor those (graze/grazes) in that field.

7. Either the children or the babysitter (lose/loses) control when the parakeet gets loose.

8. None of this group (know/knows) what it means to have indoor plumbing.

9. Together with the band, Sting (perform/performs) to raise money to preserve the Brazilian rain forest.

10. In the far corner of the photograph (stand/stands) Alannah in the company of her intended.

REVIEW EXERCISE 10

Correct the pronoun errors in the following sentences.

1. Emmylou refused to go to the crisis centre because she insisted that she wasn't having one.

2. When it snows late in the spring, it is usually bad new for the farmers.

3. Ralph and Alice spend most of their money on baseball cards because it is a fascinating pastime.

4. I bought a tight-fitting formal outfit to attend his wedding which was uncomfortable.

5. Martha longs to be a dancer, but her mother doesn't approve of it.

6. Because exercise shows are so popular on television right now, many people do it on a regular basis.

7. In the censorship report, it says that game shows should be banned for contributing to an increase in the seven deadly sins.

8. In Alice Munro's *Lives of Girls and Women*, she writes about a young woman growing up in small-town Ontario.

9. After using an ice pick for many years, I have come to find it easy.

10. When I offered cigarettes to the public health nurse, it was not appreciated.

REVIEW EXERCISE 11

Correct any errors in pronoun agreement, reference, and case in the following sentences.

1. Only superstitious people check their horoscopes every morning; reasonable people like you and me read them only for their entertainment value.

2. Ivana had never seen a real gold mine, but she said she had always wondered about them.

3. After living in a retirement village for three years, I no longer find them boring.

4. Jennifer left the hockey rink scornfully when she was told that girls were not permitted to play it.

5. In this movie review, they say that the director's latest release is mindless, sick, and sure to be a raging success at the box office.

6. Speaking in public makes me sick to my stomach, and this has stood in the way of my political career.

7. The anchorman refused to wear a jacket and tie which is why they fired him.

8. None of the large yellow sweaters were purchased because every customer feared they would look like Big Bird in them.

9. Each of you must ask themselves if you want to wear a perfume made from the secretions of goat glands.

10. If one attempts to make this recipe by hand instead of with an electric beater, you will end up with a leaden rather than a marble cheesecake.

REVIEW EXERCISE 12

Correct any errors in pronoun agreement, reference, and case in the following sentences.

1. Even though the average woman approves of orthopedic shoes in principle, they refuse to wear them, regardless of pain, if they are to be seen in public.

2. After hearing your plan to make turkey pies for the new neighbours, I do not think it is a good idea.

3. The nutritionist made this suggestion: "One should take vitamins when preparing for exams. You may still fail, but at least you'll be able to smash your desk to pieces before you leave the exam room."

4. Jacqueline spends a lot of time on her rock collection because it is her favorite hobby.

5. Neither of the women were pleased with their husband's behaviour at the bowling tournament.

6. I got a compact disc player for Christmas, which has a random access memory.

7. We asked about our refund for the tickets, but they did not give us any information.

8. In the latest issue of *Equinox*, it says that we are not alone in the galaxy.

9. When it rained last week, it was caused by a low pressure area off the east coast.

10. I called the fire department and asked them to get my cat out of the tree.

REVIEW EXERCISE 13

Correct any errors in pronoun agreement, reference, and case in the following sentences.

1. Every ambitious young student today dreams of getting their degree in Business Administration.

2. When Henrietta asked the speaker to support her opening statement, it was met with loud hissing from the audience.

3. Murray sat down beside Lewis and ate his sandwich.

4. We stayed up all night writing the proposal, which was not appreciated by our boss, who thought that we should not have been late for work.

5. After working behind a counter for ten years, Gisela had grown to dislike it.

6. Us teachers never get the recognition we deserve.

7. Although Abe studied dentistry in university, he flatly refuses to become one.

8. One should avoid alienating their employers if they expect a good letter of reference.

9. Whoever you talk to will tell you that Elsie is a cow.

10. After a truck hit the gopher, it crawled to the side of the road.

REVIEW EXERCISE 14

The following sentences contain both misplaced and dangling modifiers. Make corrections where necessary.

1. In a dark room, hanging upside down, tourists observed the vampire bat.

2. Firmly attached to a chain, the key could not be lost by the security guard.

3. To operate the coffee maker, eight cups of water and eight scoops of coffee should be added.

4. Having spent years in fitness classes, weight training came naturally to Zelda.

5. Of forty-eight students, everyone almost passed.

6. The patient was cared for by an intern in an oxygen tent.

7. Removing the money from the cash register, the policeman arrested the robber.

8. Swinging from a tree, we noticed the old tire that the children used to play with.

9. Sneaking quietly into the kitchen, a frying pan narrowly missed his head.

10. Sleeping in the old mansion, nightmares kept him awake.

REVIEW EXERCISE 15

The following sentences contain both misplaced and dangling modifiers. Make corrections where necessary.

1. Completely stuffed, the chef put the chicken in the roasting pan.

2. When expecting a baby, downhill skiing is forbidden to the mother-to-be.

3. While sipping my tequila, the goldfish in the aquarium swam before my eyes.

4. A bib is a good idea when eating spaghetti.

5. Looking under the bed, many dustbunnies were seen.

6. To leave home and settle in a big city, both financial and emotional independence are required.

7. Having usually gotten to work by eight o'clock, the traffic jam on the expressway was especially vexing today.

8. By writing a trumped-up résumé, Homer almost persuaded the public relations firm to hire him.

9. Stopped along the side of the road, a passing motorist nearly sideswiped us.

10. Overwhelmed with gratitude, the social worker accepted the award as volunteer of the year.

REVIEW EXERCISE 16

Add a main clause to each of the following modifiers. Make sure that no dangling or misplaced modifiers result.

> Playing bingo every day
>
> Playing bingo every day, *she won a lot of money.*

1. To win an argument

2. Seizing the opportunity

3. Gone to lunch

4. Sneezing violently

5. To attract attention

6. Speeding up

7. Fired from the committee

8. Covering her eyes

9. Dragging his feet

10. To cut his wire

REVIEW EXERCISE 17

Add an appropriate modifier to the following main clauses. Try using a variety of "-ing," "-ed," and infinitive forms.

_____, she called the travel agent.

Planning a vacation, she called the travel agent.

1. _____, her father insisted that she should not quit school.

2. _____, the photographer spotted Bigfoot.

3. _____, scalpers tried to sell tickets to the eager fans.

4. _____, the gorilla watched the tourists through the bars of his cage.

5. _____, the mechanic tuned up the engine.

6. _____, he did the laundry.

7. _____, Bobby gave his sister a new tape deck for Christmas.

8. _____, bats sleep in the daytime.

9. _____, the couple was holding hands.

10. _____, the building was scheduled to be demolished.

REVIEW EXERCISE 18

Combine these pairs of sentences by making one of them into a modifier. Make sure the subject is close to the modifier in each case.

1. She worked the whole day.
   A great deal was accomplished.

2. We decided to enjoy the beautiful weather.
   We had a picnic on the beach.

3. We witnessed a serious accident on the main street.
   We called the ambulance.

4. Roxy returned from Florida.
   She knew that if she had a tan the other students would be bitterly envious.

5. The rich couple bought a Jaguar.
   They did not fear the car payments.

6. The skater got good marks for artistic impression.
She did not worry about technical merit.

7. Nell is going on a diet tomorrow.
She can eat anything she wants tonight.

8. Catriona smeared chocolate cake all over her face.
She enjoyed her sixth birthday party.

9. Trudy failed to leave the premises.
The police fined her $53.75.

10. He hated the ballet.
He bought tickets to *The Nutcracker* only to impress his girlfriend.

Punctuation

FINAL STOPS

The Period

1. The period indicates the end of the sentence, whether the sentence is a statement or a command.

   Struggling with the trout, the fisherman lost his hip waders.

   Feed the elephant before cleaning the monkey cage.

2. Polite commands, though in the form of a question, are punctuated with a period.

   Would you mind closing the door when you leave.

   May we ask you to circulate this memo.

3. The period indicates the end of a sentence fragment which is being used for dialogue or emphasis.

   "When will the volcano erupt?" "Any minute now."

4. The period is used after many abbreviations.

   Mrs.   p.m.   B.Sc.   etc.   Dr.   i.e.   Ltd.

   However, the trend is toward the omission of periods in abbreviations, especially those that form words (commonly called acronyms).

   NATO CBC AIDS RCMP UNESCO NDP NASA

5. Three spaced periods (...), called an ellipsis, are used to indicate that something has been left out of the material quoted in a sentence.

   As George Bernard Shaw said, "This is the true joy in life, the being used for a purpose recognized by yourself as a mighty one ... the being a force of nature instead of a feverish selfish little clod of ailments and grievances complaining that the world will not devote itself to making you happy."

The Question Mark

1. The question mark is used after a direct question.

   Do you want one lump or two?

   Will that be cash or credit card?

2. Indirect questions are punctuated with a period.

   I wonder who's kissing her now.

   Lorraine asked what the instructor wanted her to do next.

The Exclamation Mark

1. The exclamation mark is used to indicate emphasis or surprise in a statement.

   "Reach for the sky!" said Bugsy as he entered the bank.

   Mind your own business!

2. For best effect, the exclamation mark should be used sparingly.

EXERCISE 5-1

Add the proper punctuation to the following sentences.

1. Heather wondered if she could sue for defamation of character

2. "What do you mean by 'tragic business loss' " the tax auditor inquired

3. Wipe your feet before walking on my white carpet

4. The mechanics rioted when they saw the final examination

5. Would you bring two coffees and a danish when you come back

6. When will I be eligible to collect unemployment insurance

7. The manager was insulted by his employees' lack of attention to him at his retirement party

8. Look at that

9. What colour do you want your office painted

10. For his project on black history, John asked what conditions on slave ships were like

EXERCISE 5-2

Add the proper punctuation to the following sentences.

1. During the interview, the celebrated author was asked why none of her friends spoke to her anymore

2. Which do you prefer: brains or money

3. Where would you like your temperature taken

4. Thank you for not smoking

5. "I can't believe I've been charged with careless driving" shouted Renato angrily

6. Did the murder take place in the conservatory or in the billiard room

7. The policewoman wondered if the subject knew where his family was

8. Ms Banerjee, a radiologist from the U S, is now living in Edmonton, Alta, and working for I B M

9. When keyboarding, leave two spaces after a period

10. Are you hoping to win "Cash for Life"

COMMAS

1. Use a comma with a coordinating conjunction to join two independent clauses that could stand as complete sentences. The coordinating conjunctions are *and, or, nor, for, but, yet,* and *so.*

> They married in haste, but they repented at leisure.

> Some people believe in UFOs, yet most scientists remain sceptical about the possibility of life on other planets.

Make certain that when you use *and, or, nor, for, but, yet, so,* that the conjunction joins two complete sentences. If the conjunction links two words or phrases, do not separate them with a comma. Notice in the following sentences that there is no comma because the two elements connected by the conjunction are not independent clauses.

> He accepted the wine but refused the cigarette.

> The joggers ran once around the track and then through the gates.

> Should we buy the refrigerator or the jacuzzi?

2. Use a comma to separate items in a series.

> Jennifer, Bruce, Arthur, and Brenda were all implicated in the court case.

> Two marriages broke up, a child was conceived, and the guest of honour dropped dead at the party.

> Having a successful garden demands that you dig, water, weed, and pray.

3. Use a comma to separate two or more adjectives when they modify the same noun or pronoun. Because they have a similar function in modifying the same word, these are called coordinate adjectives. If they really are coordinate adjectives, you should be able to change their order, replace the commas with *and,* and still have an intelligible sentence.

> Ross wore a shabby, patched tweed sports coat with blue-checked polyester pants.

> The model in the shampoo commercial had thick, lustrous, wavy red hair.

4. Use commas to isolate any word or group of words that has the same meaning as the preceding noun phrase. Words or phrases use in this way are called appositives. The appositive provides incidental information; it can be used interchangeably with the noun or noun phrase.

> Margaretha Zella Macleod, alias Mata Hari, was a famous dancer and spy during the First World War. Although the extent of her spying career is unknown, Mata Hari, Malay for "eye of the dawn," was shot by the French on October 1, 1917.

Make sure that your meaning is clearly indicated by the use of the commas. Compare these two sentences:

> My sister Sarah is coming for a visit.

> My sister, Sarah, is coming for a visit.

The first sentence indicates that the writer has more than one sister and must specify which sister is coming to visit. The second sentence indicates that the writer has only one sister; her name could be deleted from the sentence, and the reader would still understand who was coming to visit.

5. Use commas to set off non-restrictive modifying phrases or clauses. A phrase or clause is restrictive if it is used to identify or limit the noun preceding it.

Restrictive: The woman who drove the getaway car was never apprehended. (WHICH woman? The restrictive clause identifies her as the one "who drove the getaway car.")

Non-restrictive: Betty-Jo Calhoun, who drove the getaway car, was never apprehended. (The non-restrictive clause that follows provides additional, but not essential, information.)

Restrictive: Students who don't work fail.

Non-restrictive: That furrier in Toronto, who opened his store illegally on Sunday, was given a heavy fine.

Restrictive: The bicycle salesman who owns the store on Park Street is also a marathon runner.

Non-restrictive: Timothy Findley, who won the Governor-General's Award for his novel *The Wars*, has also written *Famous Last Words, Not Wanted on the Voyage, The Telling of Lies* and *Headhunter*.

6. Use commas to isolate words or phrases that describe the entire sentence.

> Generally, it is not a good idea to sit in the sun too long.

> He discovered, moreover, that water does go down the drain counter-clockwise in the southern hemisphere.

> The price of gasoline did not go down, however.

"Moreover," "generally," and words like these are sentence modifiers. You can move them around in the sentence without changing the meaning of the sentence.

7. Use a comma after a long phrase or clause that introduces the subject and verb.

> When learning to ride a horse, keep both feet in the stirrups.
>
> After Chrissie left her husband and moved to Winnipeg, she became a blocker on a Roller Derby team.
>
> While she was eating, the baby was fretful.

In this last example the comma is also used to prevent confusion of meaning. Consider how the sentence would read without the comma.

If the subject-verb order is inverted, as in the next sentence, this rule does not apply:

> After many a summer dies the swan.

8. Use commas to set off names in direct address and interjected words.

> No, you are not invited to the wedding.
>
> Frankly, Scarlett, I don't give a damn.
>
> That's a lovely dress you're wearing today, Mrs. Cleaver.

9. Do not use a comma to separate the main elements of a sentence; do not use it between subject and verb, between verb and object, or between verb and complement.

> ✗ Lester Pearson won the Nobel Peace Prize, in 1957.
>
> ✓ Lester Pearson won the Nobel Peace Prize in 1957.
>
> ✗ He became, leader of the Liberal party in 1958, and prime minister in 1963.
>
> ✓ He became leader of the Liberal party in 1958 and prime minister in 1963.

EXERCISE 5-3

Add commas wherever necessary.

1. For his vacation Alex was trying to decide among skiing big game hunting bodysurfing and watching television.

2. The tall dark handsome stranger was disappointed; Jane was looking for a famous short blond millionaire.

3. At the concert the choir performed difficult unmelodic modern music; unfortunately the audience was more in the mood for the familiar old standards.

4. The restaurant has paid the hospital bills and offered a cash settlement so there will be no need for a lawsuit.

5. Betting on the horses buying lottery tickets and playing bingo are effective ways to spend extra cash.

6. Those expensive shoes look wonderful yet they are very uncomfortable.

7. Today you are successful if you have a job are able to meet your mortgage payments go to aerobics at least once a week and keep your sanity.

8. This calls for a tall cold glass of chocolate milk.

9. The drones in a beehive make neither honey nor wax.

10. The first meeting of the joint committee proceeded smoothly but there are hidden agendas to be considered and personality conflicts to be resolved before the merger can be declared a success.

EXERCISE 5-4

Add commas wherever necessary.

1. He refused to drink at the party for he was the designated driver.

2. A really good vacation would mean no emergencies no phone calls no calories in the food and no bills waiting at home.

3. That ugly old vase was the only one of its kind.

4. Merv and Bernice are coming for a visit; they will want to see Ethel and Bill Paul and Nancy and Lucy and Desi.

5. The very last piece of that delicious low-calorie strawberry cheesecake was sold ten minutes ago.

6. He took a swing at the ball and he missed.

7. Loreena McKennitt a singer has released a number of albums including *Elemental Parallel Dreams To Drive the Cold Winter Away* and *The Visit*.

8. When writing an ad for the newspaper remember to be as precise as possible for the fewer words you use the lower the cost.

9. Mary-Lou will gain extra points for every new customer and she will soon have enough to qualify for the car.

10. Tuponia Cabotia Hochelaga Borealia and Transatlantica were names that were not chosen when in 1867 the four colonies joined in Confederation.

EXERCISE 5-5

Add commas wherever necessary.

1. That is why my fellow Canadians I am asking for your vote in the up-coming election.

2. The real Laura Secord a heroine of the War of 1812 bears little or no resemblance to the woman on the boxes of chocolate.

3. Obviously you can't give them that for a wedding present!

4. Whatever do you mean Mr. Johnson?

5. For example it is still possible in some parts of the country to be fined for leaving your horse unattended for too long a time.

6. My white angora cat Mrs. Bates has just devoured an entire box of After Eights a present I intended to give to Marion.

7. Weather permitting the balloon launch should take place at the usual time.

8. In order to buy the outfit that she wore to the christening she had to sell the silver tea service.

9. Bellowing and waving the newspaper the enraged businessman strode into the editor's office.

10. Mrs. White who used to be a cook now runs the Clue Detective Agency in partnership with Professor Plum.

EXERCISE 5-6

Add commas wherever necessary.

1. On the contrary I'm sure Susan doesn't mind paying her own way when she goes out on a date with you.

2. Anyone who hopes to win a million in a lottery must buy a lot of tickets each week.

3. Zabaglione a dessert made of eggs and sugar stirred over high heat is difficult to make; if you make one wrong move you have something for breakfast scrambled eggs.

4. Yes I think you should apologize to the neighbours for what you did to their plants during their absence.

5. After the storm comes the sunshine.

6. To be perfectly honest I don't think that complete candour is advisable or healthy.

7. As a matter of fact I don't think that black leather spiked hair and heavy mascara are appropriate for a primary school teacher.

8. In spite of the terrific view and the up-to-date recreational facilities the rent for this apartment is still too high.

9. Sally I would like you to meet the most notorious and most often photographed member of my family my cousin Scarface.

10. Sydney Biddle Barrows who was the Mayflower Madam now appears on TV talk shows discussing business management.

EXERCISE 5-7

Add commas wherever necessary.

1. Mackenzie King was without a doubt the only Canadian prime minister to govern by crystal ball.

2. Following the revolution the dictator and his wife opened a Burger King franchise.

3. That is the correct answer and you win a million dollars.

4. In order to compete with the novelty of television in the late 1950s and early 1960s Hollywood filmmakers had to resort to some gimmicks of their own including an increased screen size called Cinerama a technique which released smells into the theatre called Odorama and a process called 3-D that created the illusion that certain objects emerged from the screen.

5. When the students arrived for the class they found the classroom door locked and the instructor pacing in the hall.

6. The vice-principal naturally made all the necessary arrangements to ensure the school picnic would be a success; he has purchased large quantities of hot dogs ice cream lemonade and shark repellent.

7. If the chips are down it's best to pass the dice to the next player.

8. Jennifer will eat anything except lima beans squash bread pudding and Big Macs.

9. A Mercedes a Rolls-Royce and a BMW are among his most valued possessions.

10. The couple lost everything in the tornado but their washer and dryer.

EXERCISE 5-8

Add commas wherever necessary.

1. Mountain biking wall climbing and roller blading are strenuous ways to keep fit.

2. When filming a scene a director can use a long shot a medium shot a close-up or an overhead shot.

3. To play baseball well you need to be able to hit the ball out of the park to catch it on the fly to run like hell and to slide on your stomach in the dirt.

4. Although some people think that hard work perseverance and talent will get them to the top others believe that connections and a complete lack of morals will get them there sooner.

5. Money can't buy health and happiness but there are compensations.

6. Schoolwork used to be confined to reading writing and arithmetic; now advanced calculus pottery and restaurant management can be found on the curriculum.

7. Before we can close up the cottage we will have to put on the storm windows and repair the screens.

8. Unfortunately John was the only one who remembered to bring the insect repellent.

9. Working out with weights is an effective way to relax after school build up your body and meet new friends.

10. Although he searched through all the documents at least those he could find he was never able to discover with any certainty who his father was.

EXERCISE 5-9

Add commas wherever necessary.

1. Many popular movie stars these days get their acting experience on daytime TV soaps sitcoms and commercials.

2. Despite their apparent happiness their marriage to my knowledge anyway is based on mutual infidelity and greed.

3. James despite his success with women has never met one who is willing to marry him.

4. If I were you Fred I would look for a less dangerous not to say exposed profession than hang-gliding.

5. At her shower Lisa was according to rumour given three coffee makers four pairs of towels one toaster and a complete set of Tupperware.

6. He is an expert so he claims at solving computer crimes.

7. About seventy-five percent of the foods we eat contain chemical additives yet many people remain unaware of this fact.

8. Lying on the couch Judith recounted her dream to the analyst including her sense of liberation as she flew around St. Paul's Cathedral with a doughnut in her mouth.

9. Although Emily says she is a careful driver she has been involved in five minor accidents in the past six months and her insurance premiums have risen dramatically.

10. You can have the strawberry mousse or you can have the pumpkin cheesecake.

EXERCISE 5-10

Determine which clauses and phrases in the following sentences are restrictive and non-restrictive. Punctuate accordingly.

1. His only living relative who used to be a movie star is coming to visit him.

2. Lulu's cat which just got its shots last week is safe from the threat of rabies.

3. Her dinner which consisted of three leaves of lettuce, a tomato, and a few carrots was intended to help her lose weight.

4. People like my neighbours ought to be taught to respect the privacy of others.

5. His previous wife Myrtle had written a book about the time they spent together.

6. Students who have never taken a language course will find the advanced section of this course too difficult.

7. Those who expect too much will be disappointed.

8. Aristotle gave the corsage to that woman over there wearing the green evening dress.

9. The tenants in this apartment building who are, for the most part, students are protesting the latest increase in rent.

10. Two of her sisters Emily and Charlotte preferred sports to reading.

THE SEMICOLON AND COLON

The Semicolon

1. Use a semicolon between two independent clauses, if they are closely related in thought.

> Man proposes; God disposes.

> Seven-year-old Alicia likes to see the snow arrive; her parents dread it.

2. Use the semicolon between items in a list if those items contain commas.

> The letters of complaint were sent to Joe Lyons, the editor of the local newspaper; Jackie McPherson, the president of the board; Khiet Tse, the executive secretary; Ron Ferrier, the head of the finance committee; and the volunteers, Maxine, Patty, and Laverne.

3. Use a semicolon to join two independent clauses linked by one of the following conjunctive adverbs: consequently, accordingly, nevertheless, however, hence, indeed, moreover, therefore, thus, as a result, for example.

> The rain poured down on the field; however, the fans stayed and the game continued.

> Doris entered the room; consequently, I left.

Note that *however* is not always used to link two independent clauses. When it appears in one sentence, only commas are needed to set it off.

> The rain, however, dampened the enthusiasm of the players.

EXERCISE 5-11

Adjust the punctuation, adding semicolons where necessary.

1. The Corvette was travelling along the highway at great speed it failed to negotiate a turn.

2. Knowledge comes wisdom lingers.

3. At the staff party, all the men gathered in the den to watch the hockey game the women sat in the living room.

4. The baker mixed the ingredients of the cake then he turned the batter into the pans.

5. When the teacher came down the hall, the students hid in the stairway they didn't want to be caught.

6. Nancy and Harold just bought a new car consequently they sent their daughters out to work.

7. Writing letters is a chore still it is the only way to prevent losing your friends or paying large phone bills.

8. To make the most of her new swimming pool, Betty has recently acquired new lawn furniture, purchased at Canadian Tire a cordless phone, on sale at Radio Shack and a string bikini found in the lingerie department at Kmart.

9. He got his tax rebate today therefore he's having a party tomorrow.

10. The celebration was cancelled however when he discovered the cheque had been sent to the wrong address.

EXERCISE 5-12

Adjust the punctuation, adding semicolons where necessary.

1. The newcomers entered the auditorium noisily they were unaware that they were late for the recital.

2. A good artist must paint the subject and, at the same time, show his or her reaction to it while the first is easy, the second is unusually difficult.

3. Going to the hairstylist is hard on my nerves I'm afraid I'll wind up looking like something the cat dragged in.

4. Often the stylist will show you pictures of the latest cuts however these are always worn by handsome men and glamorous women who would look good bald.

5. Nevertheless no one, least of all me, ends up looking like the person in the illustration.

6. Usually the next day my hair stands straight up worse it may develop a cowlick.

7. You know that your haircut is not a success when your friends make no comment, instead they greet you with looks of startled surprise.

8. Maintaining a style is frequently a challenge however if you use enough mousse, gel, and spray your hair should stay put for about a week though it will be as hard as a football helmet.

9. If you really want a change, you can tint or streak your hair, using a wide range of colours, many of them not found in nature.

10. The ideal stylist has to have the patience of Job, in order to deal with the public the invention of Leonardo da Vinci, to adapt unsuitable cuts for demanding clients and the acting talent of Greta Garbo, to be able to say "You look great!" whatever happens.

EXERCISE 5-13

Adjust the punctuation, adding semicolons where necessary.

1. Cookbooks have become an important mainstay of the publishing industry each year many different books appear presenting a variety of new ways to prepare food.

2. One of the earliest ones to survive to the present is called *The Learned Banquet* it was written by a Greek gourmet in the second century B.C.

3. We may think that cheesecake is a recent discovery however *The Learned Banquet* contains several recipes for it.

4. Apicius, a Roman merchant who lived during the first century A.D., held enormous parties whose cost eventually led him to bankruptcy and suicide although his cookbook has been preserved it is not recommended to people on budgets.

5. Medieval cookbooks contain many recipes that appeal more to the curious than the hungry as they call for ingredients like snails and frogs.

6. Cooking was revolutionized by the printing press as a result of this invention cookbooks were widely available for the first time.

7. The first printed cookbook was written in Italian and appeared in 1485 it says a lot about the human appetite that the majority of the recipes in this book were for candy and sweets.

8. One of the most successful and popular books, *The Boston Cooking-School Cook Book*, was originally published in 1896 it has however been reprinted many times since.

9. Its editor was Fannie Farmer she was the first to standardize her recipes, guaranteeing reliable results to her readers.

10. Today you can find a cookbook on any subject there are vegetarian ones with instructions on how to prepare tofu there are Cajun ones that show how to cook squirrel and possum and there are even "natural" ones with hints on how to harvest edible mushrooms and flowers.

The Colon

Use a colon to introduce something, whether a word, a list, a sentence, or a quotation. Unlike the semicolon, it does not need to be followed by an independent clause. Whatever follows the colon explains or amplifies the meaning of the first independent clause. Remember that a colon can only be used after a complete sentence:

> Among Canada's notable prime ministers have been the following: John A. MacDonald, Wilfrid Laurier, Mackenzie King, and Pierre Trudeau.

> In his essay, Alfonso quoted these lines: "Hope springs eternal in the human breast/Man never is, but always to be, blest."

> His scholastic career could be summed up in one word: dud.

> As Margaret Atwood says, "A divorce is like an amputation: you survive, but there's less of you."

Note that in the last example the quotation is introduced by a comma because "As Margaret Atwood says" is not a complete sentence; it is a subordinate clause that cannot stand by itself.

> Canadian humorist Eric Nicol has made this observation: "A man should preserve his integrity, though he must sell his soul to do it."

In this example the quotation is preceded by a colon because it is introduced by a complete sentence.

EXERCISE 5-14

Adjust the punctuation, adding or deleting colons where necessary.

1. At her divorce settlement, Brenda thought of the words of the old philosopher "God is love—but get it in writing."

2. For their new apartment, Chip, Robbie, and Ernie made up a list of necessities candles, TV dinners, toilet paper, and a roach motel.

3. Pat lived for one thing salmon fishing.

4. Larry and Liz are getting a divorce: he's decided he can't stand her perfume anymore.

5. Although foreign travel is not new, the modern travel industry was really invented in the nineteenth century by one man Thomas Cook.

6. In 1841 he persuaded the Midland Counties Railway Company to run a special train to take passengers to a temperance meeting it was the first excursion train in England.

7. Later in his career he expanded the business to include: conducting tours to France and Europe, selling tickets for local and overseas travel, and organizing military transport for the British army.

8. Today Thomas Cook offices throughout the world provide assistance at any one of these offices harried tourists can cash their travellers cheques.

9. It has been said that travel is broadening: which is especially true if you go on a cruise which offers nine meals a day.

10. If you want a holiday and can't afford it right now, take comfort from the traveller who said, "The more I see of other countries the more I love my own."

EXERCISE 5-15

Adjust the punctuation, adding or deleting colons where necessary.

1. Before his job interview Rico was so nervous that he forgot what he ordered for lunch a donut and a coffee.

2. Edward knew his insurance rates would go up after the accident he was a single male driver under thirty-five and the owner of a brand new sports car.

3. Delores guessed correctly and won the game; the murder was committed by Colonel Mustard in the conservatory with the wrench.

4. Without butter, popcorn is actually good for you: it is a food high in carbohydrates, said to reduce stress.

5. If you plan to sit on the committee for student government: you will need patience, determination, and Tylenol.

6. The two things Lucy wants in life are: real estate and Schroeder.

7. Gamblers suffer from a hopeless addiction: whether they win or lose.

8. I'll never forget you, mother, you gave away my dog.

9. Mark Twain was cynical about journalists, he once made this comment on the practice of reporting, "Get your facts first, and then you can distort 'em as much as you please."

10. Snapper's favorite parts of the newspaper are the TV guide, the comics, and the want ads.

EXERCISE 5-16

Adjust the punctuation, adding or deleting colons and semicolons where necessary.

1. *The Origin of Intelligence in Children* and *The Early Growth of Logic* are books written by: Jean Piaget.

2. According to Piaget there are: four stages in the development of the child.

3. First the child learns from experience, this stage lasts approximately two years.

4. Next, at the pre-operational stage, the child experiments with words; in the same way as he or she at first learned about concrete objects, this stage occurs from ages two to seven.

5. In stage three, children's logic continues to develop they learn to classify and compare objects.

6. In the final stage, children learn formal logical operations; a stage which continues into adulthood.

7. All of Piaget's major research was conducted at the Sorbonne while he was there he initiated a study of the failure of children's reasoning powers.

8. Piaget himself was a child prodigy, did you know, for example, that he wrote his first article at the age of ten?

9. Like Jean Piaget, Maria Montessori believed in "periods of sensitivity" ages at which children are best suited to acquire certain kinds of know edge.

10. In her schools, Montessori stressed a curriculum based on her research: physical freedom for students, early reading and writing skills, and individual self-instruction.

EXERCISE 5-17

Adjust the punctuation, adding or deleting colons and semicolons where necessary.

1. The qualities of a good prizefight are: action, an enthusiastic crowd, and lots of blood.

2. The guests ate the meal quickly, then they left the hostess without offering to wash the dishes.

3. The Blue Jays are my favorite team therefore I always buy season tickets.

4. He won a year's free subscription to: *Big Pecs*, a magazine devoted to body building.

5. The only thing that this candidate lacks is: brains.

6. Unless you commit perjury: your brother will be sent to the slammer.

7. Snakes deserve a much better reputation than they have, for example, they help keep the frog and rat populations down.

8. Despite the hardships of winter, many Canadians take consolation in one thing, a trip to Florida is cheap.

9. Writer and publisher Robert Fulford once expressed this sentiment "My own observation is that there is no Canadian community which is as dull as the newspaper it reads."

10. The party was successful; there are two gaping holes in the plaster, there's nothing left to eat in the house, the host is still sleeping in the bathtub.

DASHES AND PARENTHESES

Dashes

A dash is used as a stylistic device. It can be used to replace a pair of commas or a colon, although the dash is always slightly informal in tone. Remember that you should use dashes sparingly.

1. Use a dash to indicate a sharp break in thought:

> Someone—was it Voltaire?—once called Canada "a few acres of snow."

In this example, the dashes are used to set off part of the sentence, as a pair of commas might do.

2. Use a dash to indicate special emphasis:

> Pierre Berton claims that a Canadian is somebody who knows how to make love—in a canoe.

In this example, the dash introduces a startling element and thus replaces a colon.

Parentheses

Parentheses, like dashes, should be used with care. The function of parentheses is to give the reader some necessary information, in an understated way. Too much dependence on parentheses will have the opposite effect.

1. Use parentheses to enclose material (words, phrases, dates, or numbers) not essential to the sentence.

> On the way to her execution, Mata Hari (1876–1917) exclaimed, "All these people! What a success!"

2. Use parentheses to enclose a brief definition necessary to the reader's understanding.

> Marquetry (the creation of intricate patterns on furniture using pieces of wood) is an art developed in France in the late sixteenth century and almost entirely lost today.

EXERCISE 5-18

Add dashes and parentheses where needed in the following sentences.

1. Country and western music, the Roller Derby, and burritos these are Lance's least favorite things.

2. AIDS Acquired Immune Deficiency Syndrome is of international concern to the health-care profession.

3. A week ago or was it two my bird, Mr. Biddle, died.

4. Abraham Lincoln once said of an incompetent general, "Sending men to that army is shoveling fleas across a barnyard not half of them get there."

5. My favorite nineteenth-century authors of children's literature are Louisa May Alcott 1832–88 and Lewis Carroll 1832–98.

6. To many historians, the sinking of the Titanic April 15, 1912 signals the start of the twentieth century.

7. Vern, how nice to see you after your trip to Paris or was it Rome?

8. Rosalita Feldman née Gonzalez is the new office manager at my bank.

9. Our get-rich-quick system is foolproof you pay us money and we get rich quick.

10. The Association of Canadian Television and Radio Artists ACTRA is hosting its annual awards next week.

EXERCISE 5-19

Add dashes and parentheses where needed in the following sentences.

1. Stupidity that's what's wrong with the world today.

2. Several pieces of the new bedroom suite bed, chest of drawers, and mirrors arrived in damaged condition.

3. Many environmental factors for example, holes in the ozone layer are thought to be causes of the "greenhouse effect."

4. The rising costs of production and advertising see Exhibits A and B are responsible for the decline in profits Table 1.

5. Mary Anne Evans a.k.a. George Eliot shocked Victorian society by living for many years with a married man.

6. His theory doubtless many will disagree is that a woman's place is in the home.

7. The epitaph of Dorothy Parker 1893–1967 reads, "Pardon my dust."

8. Some of the players' parents disapprove of the violence in junior hockey or for that matter in all sports.

9. Utilitarianism the theory that happiness lies in the greatest good for the greatest number was first developed by Jeremy Bentham.

10. Mrs. Larsen I think she's the oldest woman in the city celebrated her 105th birthday on Tuesday.

THE APOSTROPHE

The apostrophe is used mainly to indicate contraction and possession.

Contraction

1. Use an apostrophe to indicate a missing letter or letters when you contract two words into one.

we are	we're	is not	isn't	she has	she's
they are	they're	do not	don't	they would have	they would've
let us	let's	can not	can't	you would	you'd
Note the change:		will not	won't		

EXERCISE 5-20

Form contractions of the words in parentheses.

1. Nutritional food (is not) necessarily boring: just because (it is) good for you (does not) mean (you will) hate it.

2. Although some people believe that only brussel sprouts, lima beans, and skim milk constitute healthy food, (they are) wrong: (there is) as much nutritional value in a dish of ice cream, for example, as in a glass of skim milk.

3. (There is) one difference, of course; if (you are) one of those people who must watch their weight, the skim milk may well be your choice.

4. Nevertheless, it (is not) a bad idea for people to learn something about the nutritional value of their foods, so that (they will) be free to enjoy many of the things they like.

5. (It is) never advisable to go on a diet that obliges you to eat cottage cheese and melba toast if these foods are unappetizing to you; (you would) do better eating smaller portions of your usual foods.

6. If your weight or a sluggish energy level indicates that a change of diet is called for, (you will) be most successful if you (do not) attempt to diet too drastically.

7. A diet (will not) necessarily be rigorous: (it will) just demand an adjustment in your daily habits.

8. Admittedly, some people are spared the necessity of dieting: (they are) able to eat anything without gaining a pound; if you (are not) so lucky, (do not) despair.

9. (There is) some hope if you keep these rules in mind: (do not) expect miracles and (do not) cheat even if the diet (does not) show results immediately.

10. (Here is) one more bit of advice: if you (cannot) stop eating too much, ask your dentist if (he is) willing to wire your jaws shut.

EXERCISE 5-21

Add apostrophes to form contractions where necessary in the following sentences.

1. Its often frightening for people to discover that theyre in need of dental work.

2. Whenever Ive had to go to the dentist Ive always tried to trick myself into thinking that it wont hurt.

3. Once shes got the drill in her hand, however, its almost impossible to feel that youre safe.

4. Whats most annoying is the way that dentists often ask questions of you just as youre incapable of answering them.

5. Dentists arent really sadistic, though, theyre just trying to do their job.

6. Nevertheless, if youve had any bad experiences with them, youll find yourself shivering whenever you hear the words, "Spit and rinse."

7. Im not really sure why my fear of pain never seems to inspire me to use the dental floss that shes recommended.

8. Wouldnt it make sense, after all, for me to take care of my teeth as Ive been instructed to do?

9. Whats your excuse for not brushing your teeth regularly?

10. Whos going to suffer for your negligence? Its not a problem for dentists: theyll go on charging you for cleaning and fillings regardless.

Possession

Use an apostrophe to indicate ownership.

1. Add 's after a singular noun to show possession.

dog's breakfast (the breakfast of the dog)

month's rent (the rent of the month)

Derek's car (the car belonging to Derek)

2. Add only an apostrophe after a plural noun (except for some nouns that form a plural without adding s).

> the nuns' chorus (the chorus of the nuns)
>
> the bankers' convention (the convention of bankers)

men	men's
women	women's
children	children's
media	media's

Another possibility is to add 's where the *s* is sounded. Add only the apostrophe if the *s* is not sounded. If the following word begins with an *s* or *z* sound, the apostrophe alone is preferable. Make sure, though, that the possessive form is really required; a word that ends in *s* may just be plural, and not possessive.

> the class's president
>
> the class' schedules

3. Note that there are some words that indicate possession, even though they do not require apostrophes. They are called possessive pronouns.

my, mine	its
your, yours	our, ours
his	their, theirs
her, hers	whose

> He pursued his prey.

Its, the possessive pronoun, and *it's*, the contraction, are often confused. Look at the following examples:

> The cheetah pursued its prey.

Note that *its* functions like *his* or *her* and therefore does not need an apostrophe.

> It's known for its speed and ferocity.

Here *It's* is a contraction for *it is*, which requires an apostrophe to show the omission of a letter.

Note that the same distinction applies to *whose* and *who's*, their and *they're*, your and *you're*. In each case the first forms are the possessives (*whose, their, your*), while the second are contractions (*who is, they are, you are*).

Whose overshoes are these?

Who's been sleeping in my bed?

EXERCISE 5-22

Make the following words possessive. Then write a sentence for each new form.

1. Thursday
2. Kathleen
3. turtle
4. everyone
5. briefcase

6. saleswomen
7. hero
8. dress
9. cutlass
10. elephants

EXERCISE 5-23

Make the following words possessive. Then write a sentence for each new form.

1. weekend
2. tomorrow
3. Emily
4. Camrose
5. seamstresses

6. somebody
7. Dickens
8. their
9. who
10. Honduras

QUOTATION MARKS

1. Use quotation marks around the exact words that someone has written or spoken. Use a colon to introduce a quotation after a complete sentence. If the sentence is incomplete, only a comma is needed.

> Dick Beddoes has said, "The sportswriting confraternity is burdened with hacks who make tin-can gods out of cast-iron jerks."

> Queen Elizabeth II is reported to have said, "I know the song and I can make all those noises at home."

All direct quotations should begin with a capital letter. If the quotation is interrupted or if the quotation is necessary to make the clause complete, the second part is not capitalized unless it is the start of a new sentence.

> "The promises of yesterday," Mackenzie King said, "are the taxes of today."

> "It makes little difference," said Madame de Pompadour, on learning of the fall of Quebec in 1759. "Canada is useful only to provide me with furs."

> She said that "while the cat's away the mice will play."

Indirect or paraphrased speech does not need quotation marks.

> Pierre Trudeau said that he had never been president and wondered what it would be like.

2. Use quotation marks around the titles of poems, short stories, songs, TV and radio programs, and essays or articles in magazines, books, or newspapers.

> Before going to Beaver Lumber, Paula studied the article, "How to Upgrade Your Basement," in the April issue of *Chatelaine*.

> Titles of books, magazines (like *Chatelaine* in the sentence above), movies, and newspapers are underlined or italicized.

3. Use quotation marks around proverbs and individual words when you want to refer to the words as words.

> A number of words, "hopefully," "parameters," and "disinterested," to name just a few, are often used incorrectly in writing and speech.

Generally, you should avoid placing quotation marks around slang or colloquial expressions.

4. There are some special rules about punctuation to remember when you use quotation marks. Commas and periods appear inside the closing quotation mark; semicolons and colons appear outside the final mark.

> "I think I could be a good woman," says Becky Sharp in Thackeray's novel *Vanity Fair*, "if I had five thousand a year."

> She thinks that "the way to a man's heart is through his stomach"; he has the shape to prove it.

Question and exclamation marks appear inside the closing quotation mark when they apply to the quotation itself, outside when they apply to the whole sentence.

> Sophie, the high-powered executive, snapped to her secretary, "Get me my lawyer!"

> Do you really believe that "there's no fool like an old fool"?

EXERCISE 5-24

Add quotation marks and punctuation where necessary.

1. What was that they cried in amazement.

2. How many of you are coming on the trip the instructor asked.

3. Alva inquired if I had seen her new article, Adventures in a Canoe, in *Equinox*.

4. Politics Lester Pearson said is the skilled use of blunt objects.

5. Bob Hope made the following comment about Toronto You're going to have a great town here if you ever get it finished.

6. If you are moving at the speed of light you're already there Marshall McLuhan has noted.

7. In the film *Broadway Danny Rose* one character reminds another that you can't ride two horses with one behind.

8. On reaching sixty, Coco Chanel said cut off my head and I'm thirteen.

9. In *Casablanca* Dooley Wilson plays As Time Goes By for Ingrid Bergman, not for Humphrey Bogart as everybody thinks.

10. After reading *Carrie,* Heidi told Conrad I don't want to go to the prom.

EXERCISE 5-25

Add quotation marks and punctuation where necessary.

1. Every woman needs one man in her life who is strong and responsible in the view of social critic Richard Needham. Given this security, she can proceed to do what she really wants to do—fall in love with men who are weak and irresponsible.

2. The Red Queen yelled off with her head.

3. About her own profession Joan Didion has commented that writers are always selling somebody out.

4. Jack Kerouac dubbed his peers the beat generation.

5. In spite of everything Anne Frank writes at the end of *The Diary of a Young Girl* I still believe that people are really good at heart.

6. Oh brother sighed Jodie Here comes Gino in his sportscar.

7. Joey Smallwood has called Newfoundland this poor bald rock.

8. Explaining why he had not hired her for the job, he said that many are called but few are chosen; she was not amused and called the Human Rights Commission.

9. Don't call us: we'll call you is what most job applicants hear at the end of an interview.

10. Sue refused to be a scab during the strike; she didn't feel that the cleaning staff was paid enough.

CAPITALIZATION

1. Always capitalize the first word of a sentence:

> The power drill Rhonda bought at Sears was useful for building her bookcase.

2. Capitalize the first word of a direct quotation:

> Lily Tomlin has said, "The trouble with the rat race is that even if you win, you're still a rat."

If the quotation is interrupted, you don't need to capitalize the first word of the second part unless it is the start of a new sentence:

> "Depend upon it, sir," Dr. Johnson said, "when a man knows that he is to be hanged in a fortnight, it concentrates his mind wonderfully."

3. Always capitalize the proper or specific names of people, places, and things:

Dr. Jarvik	**but not** the doctor
Uncle Ted	**but not** my uncle
Centennial College	**but not** the community college
Employment Canada	

Capitalize days of the week and months of the year but not seasons:

Tuesday, September 12	**but not** the fall

Capitalize names of specific courses but not the general subjects, except for languages:

> I am taking Communications 102 this term; I studied Italian and business last term.

4. Always capitalize the important words in titles of books, films, magazine articles, and so on. As a rule, you should capitalize the first and last words of the title and all significant words, except short prepositions and articles.

The Diary of a Country Priest
I've Heard the Mermaids Singing

EXERCISE 5-26

Add capital letters where appropriate.

1. the doctor worked for the ministry of health after graduating from medical school at the university of western ontario in london.

2. this year christmas falls on the third sunday in december.

3. mr. and mrs. sheepshanks are going camping in algonquin park either in the spring or in july.

4. professor erickson will present a lecture entitled "taking your money seriously" on monday, november 13, in room 253 of the social sciences building.

5. "to die will be an awfully big adventure," said peter pan.

6. the counsellor wanted me to take business 200 and english, but i'm taking chemistry instead.

7. her uncle floyd and aunt eppie are taking joanne to kalamazoo to visit her cousins.

8. on her summer vacation, karen read something i've been meaning to tell you by alice munro, the closing of the american mind, and remembrance of things past in the original french.

9. "i would never put my money in that bank," said the reverend peabody, "because it still has investments in south africa."

10. this week the ambassador from the netherlands will be conferring with the prime minister in ottawa and touring the maritimes.

EXERCISE 5-27

Add capital letters where appropriate.

1. captain preston of the royal canadian mounted police came to r.b. bennett high school to recruit for the force.

2. when i was younger, a variety show hosted by juliette would follow "hockey night in canada" on television.

3. the blessed virgin mary appeared to bernadette soubirous at lourdes in france in the mid-nineteenth century.

4. this semester i'm taking comparative religion 310; we have read parts of the koran, the talmud, and the teachings of buddha.

5. the progressive conservative party will be holdings its annual convention at the banff springs hotel in april.

6. doctors haycock and toth are chairing the fundraising campaign for the hospital for sick children in toronto.

7. most of the songs on the beatles' *sergeant pepper's lonely hearts club band* album are pop classics, especially "with a little help from my friends," "she's leaving home," and "when i'm sixty-four."

8. when you are out in british columbia, make sure you visit stanley park.

9. the opening sentence of daphne du maurier's novel *rebecca* is "last night i dreamed i went to manderley again."

10. for his uncle's fiftieth birthday party, dick is renting *a day at the races* with the marx brothers, woody allen's *everything you always wanted to know about sex but were afraid to ask*, and *casablanca* with bogart and bergman.

REVIEW EXERCISES

REVIEW EXERCISE 1

Add commas wherever necessary.

1. This new portable computer weighs less than fifteen pounds has two disk drives and has three times the character definition of previous models so it is a bargain at that price.

2. Hockey is but one of the many sports that is overexposed on television.

3. The tour brochure lists many attractive features but I'm suspicious about the price and the reference to "sleeping under the stars."

4. Despite his ambition Phil will never be elected to public office for by now everyone has heard about the Christmas party.

5. The celebrity leading the fitness class was to take part in a photo session and he was therefore instructed to participate only in exercises that would not make him sweat.

6. He dreaded becoming a father since he feared responsibility diaper changes early-morning feedings and the possibility that his children would one day sue him for mental cruelty.

7. Fortunately June a talkative individual fell in love with Ward a man with little to say.

8. Dr. Williams the chairman of the department was in favour of the part-time staff those who worked less than fifteen hours a week taking jobs on the side.

9. While Mrs. Anderson is a kindly and well-meaning soul she doesn't have the sense the good Lord gave to fish.

10. Unhappily we cannot accept your first novel a thousand-page chronicle of family life in primitive North America for the public is not sufficiently interested in the Stone Age.

REVIEW EXERCISE 2

Add commas wherever necessary.

1. Andrew a bright small-town boy came to the big city for the first time when he entered university.

2. Despite the misgivings of his parents he majored in English a field with great potential but few real job prospects.

3. Now he works in Don Mills outside Toronto for a large greeting card company trying to figure out new ways to say "Happy Birthday" and "Best Wishes on Your New Arrival."

4. While many of the people interviewed particularly in the seniors category were not in favour of reinstating capital punishment they did suggest the return of the pillory and the cat-of-nine-tails.

5. Realizing that the police were following him the burglar fled over the roof leaving behind his sack which contained jewellery cash a small oil painting and gourmet coffee.

6. After all who would have suspected the butler?

7. There is no doubt a perfectly good reason for the length of the phone bill for last month when I was away on vacation but I do not intend to pay it.

8. Those people in the crowd who were environmentalists were not im-

pressed by the cabinet minister's decision to replace the bird sanctuary with a parking lot.

9. When camping in the woods we were reassured to know that the attacks of grizzly bears which are played up in the newspapers are actually very rare.

10. At Expo '67 Mauritius an island off Africa in the Indian Ocean had the smallest pavilion which was in the shape of a grass hut and displayed the skeleton of a dodo an extinct bird.

REVIEW EXERCISE 3

Add commas wherever necessary.

1. People who want it all deserve it all.

2. I suggest that instead of crying over it you clean up that spilled milk.

3. Morris dancers perpetuate an ancient tradition in British culture but despite their venerability they have sometimes been disparagingly described as the "shriners of folk culture" because of their spirited conviviality and their tendency to drink.

4. Blowing through the town the tornado picked up the roof of a house several chickens a small rowboat and Miss Gulch on her bicycle.

5. Jonathan Swift concludes with some irony that "happiness is the perpetual possession of being well-deceived."

6. When a woman is in mourning the proper fur to wear according to books of etiquette is sable.

7. It was not yet dawn so he gathered up his fishing tackle and bait and quietly made his way down to the dock hoping that as an early bird he would get more than worms.

8. Protective vinyl trim which you can apply yourself will cover the scratches small dents and chipped paint that develop along the side of a car and will prevent more damage from occurring.

9. When he bought her a tall cherry-topped chocolate ice cream soda Anne knew Gilbert was serious perhaps even intending to propose that afternoon.

10. I have realized as I get older that most occasions for gift giving involve thanking people I don't like for something I didn't want.

REVIEW EXERCISE 4

Add commas wherever necessary to this passage from *Lady Oracle** by Margaret Atwood.

CHAPTER
5

I made it to Tivoli without accidents then down the long hill to the plain. Rome hovered in the distance. The closer I came to it the more raw earth there was the more huge pipes and pieces of red blue and orange machinery lay strewn like dinosaur bones beside the highway. Men were digging excavating tearing down abandoning; it was beginning to look like North America like any big junk city. The road was now crowded with trucks small ones and large ones with trailers carrying more pipes more machines in and out but I couldn't tell whether it was evidence of growth or of decay. For all I knew the country was teetering on the edge of chaos and it would be plunged into famine and revolt next week. But I couldn't read the newspapers and the disasters of this landscape were invisible to me despite the pipes and machines; I floated along serenely as through a movie travelog the sky was blue and the light golden. Huge blockish apartment buildings lined the road to Rome their balconies festooned with washing but I couldn't guess what kind of life went on inside them. In my own country I would have known but here I was deaf and dumb.

REVIEW EXERCISE 5

Add commas wherever necessary to this passage from *Generation X* by Douglas Coupland.

Fifteen years ago on what remains as possibly the most unhip day of my life my entire family all nine of us went to have our group portrait taken at a local photo salon. As a result of that hot and endless sitting the nine of us spent the next fifteen years trying bravely to live up to the corn-fed optimism the cheerful waves of shampoo and the air-brushed teeth-beams that the resultant photo is still capable of emitting to this day. We may look dated in this photo but we look *perfect* too. In it we're beaming earnestly to the right off toward what seems to be the future but which was actually Mr. Leonard the photographer and a lonely old widower with hair implants holding something mysterious in his left hand and yelling "Fromage!"

When the photo first came home it rested gloriously for maybe one hour on top of the fireplace placed there guilelessly by my father who was shortly thereafter pressured by a forest fire of shrill teenage voices fearful of peer mockery to remove it immediately. It was subsequently moved to a never-sat-in portion of his den where it hangs to this day like a forgotten pet gerbil

*Used by permission of the Canadian Publishers, McClelland and Stewart, Toronto.

dying of starvation. It is visited only rarely but deliberately by any one of the nine of us in between our ups and downs in life when we need a good dose of "but we were all so innocent once" to add that decisive literary note of melodrama to our sorrows.

Again that was fifteen years ago. This year however was the year everyone in the family finally decided to stop trying to live up to the bloody photo and the shimmering but untrue promise it made to us. This is the year we decided to call it quits normality-wise the year we went the way families just do the year everyone finally decided to be themselves and to hell with it. The year no one came home for Christmas. Just me and Tyler Mom and Dad.

REVIEW EXERCISE 6

Write out the comma rules in your own words and make up one or two sentences to illustrate each one.

REVIEW EXERCISE 7

Correct the punctuation in the following sentences.

1. Henry Ford made the automobile affordable for the average American family his famous cars were products of his revolutionary money-saving assembly line method of production.

2. The Ford Motor Company was launched in 1903, by 1908, it was manufacturing the Model T, in 1927, it began producing the Model A.

3. Ford had a reputation as a pioneer of industry, for example, he paid salaries approximately 15 percent higher than those of his contemporaries.

4. As a captain of his industry for over forty years, Ford made many advances he standardized manufacturing methods, he built assembly plants at various locations he marketed his product at a reduced cost and with a high volume of sales.

5. Ford was a typical man of the nineteenth century in his fatherly approach to business he enforced principles of sobriety in his plants he also forbade smoking.

6. He was deeply concerned for the welfare of workers, nevertheless, he opposed unions wholeheartedly for many years.

7. He is in many ways a paradoxical character he is known for his innovation in the auto industry, but he resisted the developments of the hydraulic brake and the six- or eight-cylinder engine he also produced his cars only in black.

8. Ford rose from a mechanic's apprentice to the head of his own company however he still enjoyed making repairs on cars.

9. He was a profoundly respected capitalist who "put America on wheels" he is nonetheless remembered for one major mistake the Edsel.

10. The Edsel, named after Henry Ford's only child, was touted as a great American classic it was despite much promotion a dismal failure.

REVIEW EXERCISE 8

Correct the punctuation in the following sentences.

1. Chocolate comes from beans grown on cacao trees, they are found in the West Indies, Africa, South and Central America, among other places.

2. A tropical plant, the cacao tree is difficult to grow it requires good soil and protection from harsh weather conditions.

3. Cacao beans, roasted and crushed, are processed to manufacture two products cocoa butter and cocoa powder.

4. Although chocolate is considered expensive today; the Aztecs and the Mayans valued it so highly that they used it as currency.

5. Check the label carefully, the best chocolates are made without preservatives they also contain more chocolate than sugar.

6. If the chocolate content is high; the price will be high too.

7. Be sure to store chocolates away from heat and moisture they start to sweat at temperatures above 24°C.

8. Chocolates should also be eaten soon after they are opened: since they have a short shelf life.

9. It has been proven scientifically that chocolate makes you feel happy it contains the chemical phenylethylamine, also produced naturally in the brains of people in love.

10. In exclusive shops, for example, you can find chocolates in many shapes, such as: golf balls, tennis rackets, small cars, and teddy bears.

REVIEW EXERCISE 9

Correct the punctuation in the following sentences.

1. A stiff neck used to be an omen among many people in Europe it meant the sufferer was going to be hanged later in life.

2. In England it is good fortune to discover a nail in the road; because since Roman times when iron was a sacred metal, nails have been considered a protection against evil.

3. Green has long been thought of as an unlucky colour in Great Britain it is the colour of the "little people" who will abduct anyone who wears it however in the rest of Europe it is lucky because of its association with trees and growing plants.

4. Because of their resemblances to horseshoes, wishbones are good luck if two people hold the ends and snap the bone whoever holds the larger piece will have a wish come true.

5. It is a bad omen to see the new moon through a window or through any glass to have good luck you should look at it outside and over your right shoulder.

6. In Europe and North America newly married couples are showered with rice and old shoes are attached to the bumper of their car these are rituals meant to ensure fertility.

7. According to Germanic folklore Thursday is the unluckiest day marriages should not be performed, no important business should be transacted, children should not be sent to school for the first time.

8. It is an English tradition that those people born at sunrise will be intelligent and quick-thinking while those born at sunset will be idle and slow.

9. In an old rhyme cutlery reveals what will happen "Knife falls, gentleman calls fork falls, lady calls spoon falls, baby squalls."

10. Superstition says it is lucky to put on clothing inside out however it is bad fortune to button anything up wrongly.

REVIEW EXERCISE 10

Correct the punctuation in the following sentences.

1. Archaeologists can show that gambling existed about 40,000 years ago they have found artifacts called astragali; bones that were tossed in a sport something like horseshoes.

2. Early gambling might have been a form of divination, the Bible refers frequently to the casting of lots.

3. It is believed that certain strict religions decry gambling; because it leads to too great an emotional involvement with the things of this world.

4. Many ancient folktales about gambling come from Asia; where stories are related of men using their female relatives as stakes.

5. Gambling is most common today in China and in Southeast Asian countries, by contrast, Spain, and Switzerland, outlaw some forms, like casino gambling.

6. In America, only half the states permit horse racing, however, in Nevada all common forms of gambling have been legalized.

7. Gambling; otherwise known as gaming; was once frowned on by the church: since it led to idleness, cursing, and cheating.

8. These days gambling is not illegal; as long as the state gets some of the take.

9. Lotteries are now state-legislated and widespread; offering as they do a way to get rich quick; both for the state and the individual.

10. Some questions about gambling remain: whether governments should sanction it by legalization; or whether gambling can lead to addiction.

REVIEW EXERCISE 11

Correct the punctuation in the following sentences.

1. Charles' friends deserted him; when he lost his job, his money, and Diana.

2. The time to deal with one's doubts, fears, and reservations is: afterwards.

3. I detest: television commercials featuring drooling babies; fluffy animals: or smart-mouthed children.

4. Only one thing persuaded the police not to storm the house where the hostages were held their captors were armed with machine guns.

5. Writing teachers secretly enjoy inventing confusing rules, making fun of student errors, and assigning extravagant amounts of homework.

6. Having a bank account is teaching me the importance of maintaining a proper balance the deposits must at least equal the withdrawals.

7. Totsy's favorite breakfast consists of: peanut butter and bananas on toast, lemon-lime soda pop, and a big bowl of porridge.

8. Julia Child insists that only two things are needed to produce a magnificent souffle courage and a lot of hot air.

9. Lord Byron did not want a divorce from his wife he wished her dead.

10. According to Descartes, we think therefore we are.

REVIEW EXERCISE 12

Correct the punctuation in the following sentences.

1. There are thirty-one flavours of ice cream to choose from however all of them are fattening.

2. The dentist filled all six cavities with lead therefore he cautioned her against the dangers of going swimming.

3. Phillip disliked his in-laws intensely nevertheless to please his wife he assiduously practised the art of social hypocrisy.

4. Lucy Maud Montgomery's novels are set on Prince Edward Island and seem to represent Canadian experience nevertheless they are inexplicably popular in Japan.

5. At the express counter, Hester paid for the following items a pack of filter-tipped cigarettes an economy-sized box of laundry detergent meant for cold-water washes two frozen pepperoni pizzas some catfood in gourmet and seafood flavours and a *Cosmopolitan* magazine.

6. The bank manager offered some good advice to any client with financial problems pay bills on time never let cheques bounce and destroy credit cards before it's too late.

7. Swimmers off the Florida coast were nervous they knew that the sharks in the area had sharp pointy teeth.

8. When reporting some court cases, journalists insist on the public's right to know however presiding judges will sometimes order a media blackout to ensure that justice is served.

9. Lorne's instructor warned him of a potential danger "You have a first-rate mind operating in a second-rate way."

10. For his twenty-first birthday, Emmet received the following gifts from his mother, six pairs of underwear from his father, a snorkel and fins and from his girlfriend, a year's supply of strawberry twizzlers.

REVIEW EXERCISE 13

Add apostrophes to indicate contraction or possession where necessary in the following sentences. Note that some may be correct as they stand.

1. Whose house is this, anyway?

2. None of us knows the answer to that question, but when Fred suggests, "Lets go trick or treating to find out," there arent any objections.

3. Perhaps were silent because were always wanted to know whose property it is.

4. "Whos there?" answers a strange voice in response to Freds loud rapping.

5. Its a pity that none of us are brave enough to open our mouths.

6. All of us lose our nerve easily: I guess we couldnt really face our fears. Would you have been able to face yours?

7. If youre going to go out on Halloween, its probably wise to confine your visits to familiar neighbourhoods.

8. At least, thats what we concluded after a frightening evenings experience.

9. Well probably never meet the "haunted houses" owner.

10. Had we stayed, however, wed most likely have discovered that the owner is a kindly woman, whos by no means a wicked witch.

REVIEW EXERCISE 14

Add or omit apostrophes to indicate contraction or possession, making any necessary spelling changes. Note that some sentences may be correct as they stand.

1. If your looking for safe thrills in the comfort of you're living room, why do not you try murder mysteries?

2. They're are many different kinds, such as Nicholas Freelings police procedurals, James M. Cains hard-boiled thrillers, and Agatha Christies traditional English body-in-the-library style.

3. Christies books arent as gory as the others', but like the detective you have to rely more on you're powers of deduction. Hercule Poirots "little grey cells" and Miss Marples stories' of life in St. Mary Mead are the basis for their crime stories solutions.

4. You can learn a lot reading the novels of Dorothy Sayers's: she was a writer who's subjects included advertising, bell-ringing, trains, and history.

5. Sayers novels, *Strong Poison, Have His Carcase, Gaudy Night*, and *Busmans Honeymoon*, all deal with Lord Peter Wimsey and Harriet Vanes courtship and marriage.

6. P.D. James most unusual work is called *Innocent Blood*; its about a man whose planning to kill the woman accused of being his daughters murderer.

7. Ruth Rendells works are much different from her predecessors. Hers' are violent, contemporary in tone, and often short: you can read one in about two hours time.

8. A comic detective is found in John Mortimers *Rumpoles Last Case*.

9. Robert Parkers Spenser and Joseph Hansens Dave Brandstetter are descendents of Raymond Chandlers Philip Marlowe and Dashiell Hammetts Sam Spade.

10. Spades been played in the movies by Humphrey Bogart; Chandlers heroes have been played by Dick Powell, Robert Montgomery, and Elliot Gould.

REVIEW EXERCISE 15

Add quotation marks and punctuation where necessary.

1. Ernestine calmly told the angry customer You owe us $23.50. You can't argue with the phone company. We are omnipotent.

2. Who said You're only as young as you feel?

3. Holy cow! cried Lester I can exchange my trading stamps for this wonderful battery-operated golf ball washer.

4. I'm working on a new chapter for my book on leisure activities. It's called How to Get a Great Tan Without Third-Degree Burns.

5. The zookeeper shouted Keep your hands out of the alligators' cage! They haven't been fed yet.

6. Pee-Wee announced I have terrible news. The Saturday morning cartoons have been cancelled so that we can bring you this message from the Prime Minister's office.

7. Kathleen claimed that we all could get ahead if we were willing to scratch, bite, and kick people into submission.

8. While acceptable in ordinary conversation, phrases like you know, like, sort of, kind of, and sounds like um and ah do not make a positive impression when quoted in print.

9. A nation said a prominent Canadian historian is a body of people who have done things together in the past and who hope to do great things together in the future.

10. Equal pay for equal work and A fair wage read the placards carried by the protesters.

REVIEW EXERCISE 16

In the following passage of dialogue, taken from Robertson's Davies' *The Rebel Angels**, add quotation marks and punctuation where appropriate.

You don't understand he would say when I protested. Publishers are always buying books they haven't seen in a completed form. They can tell from a chapter or so whether the thing is any good or not. You constantly read in the papers about huge advances they have paid to somebody on the promise or mere sketch of a work.

I don't believe all I read in the papers. But I have published two or three books myself.

Academic stuff. Quite a different matter. Nobody expects a book of yours to sell widely. But this will be a sensation and I am confident that if it is brought out in the right way with the right sort of publicity it will make a fortune.

Have you offered it to anybody in the States?

No. That will come later. I insist on Canadian publication first because I want it read by those who are most involved before it reaches a wider public.

Those who are most involved?

Certainly. It's a *roman à clef* as well as a *roman philosophique*. There will be some red faces when it comes out I can tell you.

Aren't you worried about libel?

People won't be in a hurry to claim that they are the originals of most of the characters. Other people will do that for them. And of course I'm not such a fool as to record and transcribe doings and conversations that are too easily identified. But they'll know don't you worry. And in time everybody else will know as well.

*From *Rebel Angels* by Robertson Davies ©1981 Reprinted by permission of Macmillan Canada

It's a revenge novel then?

Sim you know me better than that! There's nothing small about it. Not a revenge novel. Perhaps a justice novel.

Justice for you?

Justice for me.

REVIEW EXERCISE 17

Add quotation marks and correct the punctuation where necessary in these sentences.

1. Pardon me said Nathan I didn't know this room was occupied. Could you direct me to the Men's Room.

2. The posters called it The Greatest Show on Earth; however, to us it wasn't even The Greatest Show in Medicine Hat.

3. Who wrote Men seldom make passes at girls who wear glasses asked Agnes puzzledly.

4. You needn't thank me retorted Beatrice I am here against my will. I'd rather be home watching The Simpsons or reading The Cremation of Sam McGee.

5. When I asked him about his meeting with his future in-laws, Brian said that it was lousy.

6. If you are keyboarding in a hurry, don't confuse personal with personnel.

7. Alley-oop cried the acrobats as they suddenly hoisted Babette onto their shoulders.

8. I asked Winston if he knew which play by Shakespeare refers to the whirligig of time.

9. The licence bureau warned me if you don't pay the thirty-five dollars for Bunny's new tag, he will be impounded.

10. It is always a mistake not to close one's eyes said the old philosopher whether to forgive or to look better into oneself; if we follow this advice, some of us will spend a lot of time walking into walls.

Sentence Patterns
and Variety

SENTENCE PATTERNS

There are four sentence patterns: simple, compound, complex, and compound-complex.

Simple

A **simple** sentence has one main clause, that is, one subject and one verb.

> The pub closed.
>
> At one o'clock, the pub closed.

The second example above is still a simple sentence, even though it begins with a prepositional phrase.

> The beer having run out, the pub closed.

Since the only complete verb is *closed,* there is only one clause in this sentence. Although it may look like a clause, *The beer having run out* is only a phrase and cannot stand alone, so the sentence is still simple.

> The pub, a popular student hang-out, closed.

In this example, *a popular student hang-out* is an appositive, a word or phrase that renames the subject of the sentence. Since there are still only one subject and one verb, the sentence is simple.

Compound

A **compound** sentence is made up of two main independent clauses (or simple sentences) joined by a coordinating conjunction, *and, or, nor, but, yet, for or, so,* or by a semicolon.

> Neil liked Mary, Flo, and Diana. They reminded him of his sisters. (Two simple sentences)
>
> Neil liked Mary, Flo, and Diana, for they reminded him of his sisters. (Two main clauses linked by the coordinating conjunction *for*)
>
> The pub closed, but some of the students stayed to clean up.
>
> The pub closed; most of the students went home.

Note that you usually need a comma before a coordinating conjunction that connects two main clauses; see the discussion on the comma in chapter 5.

Complex

A **complex** sentence has one main clause and one or more subordinate clauses. When you subordinate, you join two clauses together by making one of them dependent on the other. (For a list of subordinators, see p. 86.)

Most people instinctively avoid too many simple sentences (*See Jane run. See Spot run.*), but many writers need to watch their overuse of compounds as well. They need to develop skills in subordination.

> When the pub closed, some of the students stayed to clean up.

The subordinator *when* indicates that the first clause *when the pub closed* is dependent on the main clause *some of the students stayed to clean up.*

Compound-Complex

A **compound-complex** sentence has two main clauses joined by a coordinating conjunction (or a semicolon) plus at least one subordinate clause.

> When the beer ran out, the pub closed, and some of the students stayed to clean up.

The subordinate clause *when the beer ran out,* is dependent on the two main clauses: (1) *the pub closed* and (2) *some of the students stayed to clean up.*

EXERCISE 6-1

Classify each of these sentences as either simple, compound, complex, or compound-complex.

1. Either you leave now, or you will have to wait until tomorrow for the next train. C D

2. Marlene presented a new and controversial marketing campaign, but when her co-workers objected, she was forced to modify it. C D CX

3. No one will be allowed in that class unless he or she has registered in advance for it. Complex

4. Don't forget to put out fresh food and water for the dog.   S

5. On Tuesday, the Websters painted the porch, watered their lawn, and bought new summer furniture.

6. Greg is articulate but very immature.

7. I don't care what you say; this book is boring.

8. If you cannot send the program to the mainframe, all your hard work will be wasted.

9. Evangeline was hard at work in her garden which demanded most of her time and energy.

10. In the meantime, let us take a straw vote before he returns.

EXERCISE 6-2

Classify each of the sentences in the following paragraphs as either simple, compound, complex, or compound-complex.

(1) Once upon a time, there was a man who was very rich and who had a blue beard. (2) Although frightful in appearance, he eventually persuaded a poor woman to give him her daughter in marriage. (3) Their honeymoon completed, he brought his bride to the castle. (4) Giving his ring of keys to his wife, he explained that she might open all the doors in the castle except for one. (5) If she opened the forbidden door and looked in, he would punish her. (6) One day the bride's sister, Anne, came for a visit. (7) The bride showed her all the rooms in the castle, and finally they came to the forbidden door. (8) Not heeding her husband's warning, the bride unlocked the door and opened it, disclosing the bloody corpses of Bluebeard's former wives.

(9) So terrified was she that she dropped the key in the blood on the floor and discovered to her horror that the blood would not come off. (10) At this moment, Bluebeard appeared. (11) When he saw the key, he realized that she had opened the forbidden door, and he swore that she too would take her place among the dead wives. (12) She begged for some time, so she could say her prayers. (13) She then sent her sister to the highest tower of the castle to look for help. (14) After a short time, she called out to her. (15) "Anne, sister Anne, do you see anyone coming?" (16) She asked this question repeatedly, but each time the sister's reply was that she saw nothing.

(17) Bluebeard sharpened his sword, and, yelling for his wife, began to approach her chamber. (18) Just then, Anne, in the tower, cried out that she saw their brothers approaching. (19) As Bluebeard was about to strike his wife's head off, her brothers entered the castle and slew him. (20) Bluebeard's widow gave her sister half the wealth she inherited, and they all lived happily ever after.

EXERCISE 6-3

Form compound sentences by combining the following simple sentences. Use the method of coordination that indicates the relationship between the two sentences most effectively, and punctuate correctly.

1. Kent does not smoke. He does not drink either.

2. The students listened to the teacher with complete indifference. Undaunted, he continued to speak.

3. Myrna was hardworking and gifted. She practised the piano every day, never complaining about the difficulty of the exercises.

4. The dog slept on the landing of the stairs. The cat prowled through the house all night.

5. Jean-Paul worked at McDonald's during the day and Arby's at night. He needed the money.

6. The progress report must be on my desk tomorrow at nine. Heads will roll.

7. Most of the people at the party ate scallops. The guest of honour was allergic to shellfish and ate perogies instead.

8. Mr. and Mrs. Osbourne didn't holiday in the Caribbean. They didn't cruise the Mediterranean.

9. Leigh-Anne looked directly at me. I pretended not to notice.

10. Elvira claimed not to be offended by his silly remarks. She never came to another of his parties.

EXERCISE 6-4

Rewrite each of these pairs of simple sentences to form a complex sentence.

1. We were led into the theatre by an usher. He was showing people to their seats in the balcony.

2. The sports fans entered the stadium. A lot of noise came from it.

3. Melody went directly to the toy department. She stopped there to look over the dump trucks.

4. The firemen returned to the station house. They had been called away by a false alarm.

5. Malcolm's pet aardvark had a wicked disposition. None of his friends were warned about it.

6. There was a YMCA in the town. The unemployed often stayed there.

7. The boss walked over to the podium. The text of her speech was resting on it.

8. Cornelia, the debutante, toyed with her beads jadedly. She was waiting for her chauffeur.

9. The bartender introduced a husky man to the bar patrons. He had just been hired as the bouncer.

10. The Continis put the personal notice back in the paper. They had removed it two weeks before.

EXERCISE 6-5

Rewrite each of these pairs of simple sentences to form a complex sentence.

1. There is a rose bush climbing up our trellis. It has huge thorns growing on it.

2. Joan and Sandy wandered along the beach. There they saw driftwood, some broken shells, and the remains of an old pirate ship.

3. Luther picked up the lint idly. It was lying on the carpet.

4. Charlie Brown thought of another scheme. By it he hoped to capture the attention of the little red-haired girl once and for all.

5. Angelica discovered what was in the bouquet sent by her unknown admirer. She let go of it quickly.

6. The police officer gave a ticket to the driver of the green Corvette. He had been speeding.

7. The phantom of the murdered duke appears regularly in the upper hall of the castle. It seeks vengeance.

8. We tried to talk to the hotel clerk. We did not speak his language.

9. Rupert accidentally broke his aunt's favorite china figure. He hid the fragments under the cushions of the sofa.

10. The travellers lost their map and their bearings. They wandered in the forest aimlessly for several hours.

SENTENCE VARIETY

There are many ways of creating and holding a reader's interest in your writing. If you use a variety of simple, complex, compound, and compound-complex sentences in your letters and reports, they will appeal to your reader more than if you always use the same sentence pattern. There are also other ways to add vitality to your sentence structure.

1. Join two sentences by condensing one of them into a single word.

    The man smoked a cigar. He was fat.

    The *fat* man smoked a cigar.

    David and Joanne argued with their editor. Their editor was picky.

    David and Joanne argued with their *picky* editor.

2. Join two sentences by condensing one of them into a prepositional phrase.

    The fat man smoked a cigar. He stood in front of the drugstore.

    The fat man smoked a cigar *in front of the drugstore.*

3. Join two sentences by using an appositive.

    Morris was formerly the owner of a snake farm. He is now president of our local Humane Society.

    Morris, *formerly the owner of a snake farm,* is now the president of our local Humane Society.

4. Join two sentences by forming a compound verb. Make sure that both the sentences have the same subject.

    The fat man snored. He moved restlessly in bed.

    The fat man *snored and moved restlessly in bed.*

5. Join two sentences by using -ing and -ed modifiers (with regular verbs) or the correct past participle (with irregular verbs).

    The singer continued her recital. She ignored the hissing in the audience.

    Ignoring the hissing in the audience, the singer continued her recital.

    Marcelle was disgusted by Jake's habit of talking with his mouth full. She stopped dating him.

    Disgusted by Jake's habit of talking with his mouth full, Marcelle stopped dating him.

    Ian was hung over from the night before. He couldn't get out of bed.

    Hung over from the night before, Ian couldn't get out of bed.

Note that *hung* in the last sentence, while neither an -ing or an -ed modifier, is the past participle of the irregular verb, *to hang* and can be used as a modifier.

EXERCISE 6-6

Combine the following sentences, by using appositives.

1. Geoffrey had been a teacher for many years. He did not think it was appropriate to wear shorts to class.

2. Lizzie Borden's house is an ordinary-looking building located in Fall River. It has become a tourist attraction for those with a macabre curiosity.

3. This grammar book is the product of many months of hard work. It will be largely unappreciated by the students who use it.

4. Janet Gaynor was one of the first to win the Oscar for best actress. She played the lead in the film *A Star is Born*.

5. Tanya's father was a minister. He disapproved of her tattoos.

6. The squirrels ran from one corner of the cage to the other. They were new patients at the veterinary clinic.

7. Frederica hated her new glasses. They were pink-tinted granny glasses.

8. Mel trained as a pilot with the Canadian Armed Forces. He wants to open his own flying school after retiring.

9. Lima beans and squash are actually her favorite vegetables. I hate them.

10. *Kiss of the Spider Woman* is a musical about the friendship between two prison inmates. It won the Tony award for Best Musical in 1993.

EXERCISE 6-7

Join the following pairs of sentences together, using the appropriate coordinating conjunction (and, or, nor, for, but, yet, so) to make one sentence with a compound verb.

1. The elephant roared. It sprayed the spectators with water.

2. The twins ran away from home. They were found next door.

3. You may wish to order off the menu. You may prefer to choose à la carte.

4. The band played a free concert in the park. Later it was interviewed on a local television show.

5. The columnist printed the letter. He chose to delete the writer's name.

6. The coven enlisted new members because it needed thirteen for spell-casting. It also had a spare broom.

7. Every morning Brandon jogs five kilometres before work. He rides his bicycle after work.

8. Cotton is a cool, comfortable natural fabric. It needs to be ironed if it is to look attractive.

9. The hiring committee offered the job to an American. It passed over five local applicants.

CHAPTER
6

10. The nurse came in to take my temperature. She also intended to take my blood pressure.

EXERCISE 6-8

Join the following pairs of sentences together, using the appropriate coordinating conjunction (and, or, nor, for, but, yet, so) to make one sentence with a compound verb or to make a compound sentence.

1. The criminal mastermind scooped up the defense plans. He hid them in his trench coat.

2. The stranger swung open the doors of the saloon. She entered with guns blazing.

3. Answer the phone. The caller will think you're not home.

4. The toddler burst into tears. His mother had forgotten to change him.

5. At the end of the performance, the skater picked the flowers off the ice. She proceeded to skate into the boards.

6. Leaping to her feet, Barbarella grabbed the electro-synergetic laser. She could draw the enemy's fire and cover the princess's escape.

7. With only minutes to spare, Dr. Who ran to the Tardis. The Daleks were there before.

8. Hal the computer cut off the life-support system to the rest of the spacecraft. He jettisoned the escape vehicles.

215

9. The incident occurred at 2:45 p.m. The nurse forgot to mark it on the patient's chart.

10. Searching for dinner, the shark cruised through the shallow waters close to the beach. The bathers did not see it.

EXERCISE 6-9

Join these pairs of sentences, condensing one sentence into a phrase introduced by an -ing modifier.

1. The boys approached the old house cautiously. They were searching for monsters.

2. Jason and Norm opened the front door. They glanced over their shoulders nervously all the time.

3. They peered into the entrance hall which was large and filled with ominous shadows. They paused on the threshold.

4. The boys looked to the left and to the right. They could see many rooms crowded with furniture which was covered in sheets.

5. Suddenly they both heard a noise like a low moan. They froze instantly in their tracks.

Now complete the story with five more sentences which follow the same pattern.

EXERCISE 6-10

Join these pairs of sentences by turning one of them into a phrase introduced by an -ing or -ed modifier or an irregular past participle. Beware of creating dangling modifiers.

1. Minh went out to dinner with her friends. She forgot to set the VCR timer.

2. The survivor was delirious. He was found at the scene of the crash.

3. The suspect thought he was in the clear. He tried to leave town but was apprehended at the airport.

4. Debbie was encouraged by the response to her new album. She signed a contract for a thirty-six week tour of North America and Europe.

5. The dandelion seeds were borne by the wind. They blew all over the field.

6. Jennifer was fed up with Kurt's wisecracks. She threw a mug of beer in his face.

7. The member of Parliament spoke in favour of the motion. She then began the filibuster.

8. The hiker tripped over the fallen log. He sprained his ankle.

9. The child and the dog ran to answer the doorbell. They tore down the stairs.

10. The archaeological team excavated the site. They hoped to find the remains of the ancient settlement.

EXERCISE 6-11

Join these pairs of sentences by turning one of them into a phrase introduced by an -ing or -ed modifier or an irregular past participle. Beware of creating dangling modifiers.

1. The detective drank coffee and ate doughnuts to stay awake during the stakeout. He waited in his car outside the apartment building.

2. A shadowy figure crept close to the car. It was hidden by the fog.

3. The figure took aim carefully. It fired a revolver at the unsuspecting victim.

4. The murder weapon was thrown into the bay. It sank without a trace.

5. The detective was murdered by an unknown assailant. He was found the next day slumped over the steering wheel of his car.

6. His widow swore to track down her husband's killer herself. She was angered by the lack of police cooperation.

7. She followed a lead provided by an anonymous phone call. She discovered that someone had been embezzling from the firm and cooking the books.

8. She gathered the incriminating evidence. She confronted her husband's partner and tricked him into a confession.

9. He realized that he had spilled the beans into a tape recorder. The killer tried to escape, but the police were waiting for him.

10. She was pleased at her success. The widow decided to keep the detective agency open and run it herself.

PARALLELISM

Examine the following sentence:

> Martha likes eating candy, drinking soda pop, and movies.

This sentence would be clearer if the items listed were parallel in structure:

eating	candy
drinking	soda pop
_____	movies

If you supplied a word with the same grammatical form, the sentence would be improved.

> Martha likes eating candy, drinking soda pop, and watching movies.

Let's look at another example:

> A boy scout is cheerful, kind, and has good manners.

Try to picture these items in a list:

> A boy scout is cheerful
>
> kind
>
> has good manners.

The sentence is not parallel because in the list the first two elements are adjectives and the third is a verb with a noun phrase. Change the sentence to make the items parallel. There are two possible answers.

A boy scout is cheerful	**OR**	A boy scout is cheerful
is kind and		kind and
has good manners.		polite.

The second sounds better, but both are parallel now and hence correct. As you can see, parallel construction ensures easy reading and clear understanding of your sentences. There are several basic rules that will help you avoid faulty parallelism.

1. Watch for the connecting words *and, or, nor, for, but, yet,* and *so* and make sure that they are used to link matching grammatical elements.

   ✘ The locker room is dirty, chilly, and there is always the odour of perspiration in the air.

   ✓ The locker room looks dirty, feels chilly, and smells sweaty.

   ✘ Nikki works out every morning and in the evening.

   ✓ Nikki works out every morning and every evening.

    ✗ Charlotte likes swimming and to go to baseball games.

    ✓ Charlotte likes swimming and going to baseball games.

2. Check to make sure that parallel structure is used with the following pairs of words: *either/or, neither/nor, not only/but also, both/and.*

    ✗ Ramon wanted either to take up ballroom dancing or karate.

What follows *either* is an infinitive phrase; what follows *or* is a noun. In this case, we will change them both to nouns.

    ✓ Ramon wanted to take up either ballroom dancing or karate.

    ✗ Peggy's academic career was not only troubled, but also was unprofitable.

What follows *not only* is an adjective; what follows *but also* is a verb and an adjectival phrase. In this case, we will change them both to adjectival forms.

    ✓ Peggy's academic career was not only troubled, but also unprofitable.

3. Make sure that items in a series are all of the same grammatical form.

    ✗ Emmeline chose that college because of its proximity to her home, its fine academic reputation, and it offered many opportunities to mingle with the rich and famous.

    ✓ Emmeline chose that college because it was close to her home, it had a fine academic reputation, and it offered many opportunities to mingle with the rich and famous.

    ✗ Her teacher advised her to stay home at nights, doing her homework regularly, and stop asking fellow students for autographs.

    ✓ Her teacher advised her to stay home at nights, to do her homework regularly, and to stop asking fellow students for autographs.

4. Make sure not to unbalance sentences by leaving out necessary words.

    ✗ Siegfried always has and always will eat supper in front of the television set.

    ✓ Siegfried always has eaten and always will eat supper in front of the television set.

    ✗ I have never and I will never deny that I am a compulsive liar.

    ✓ I have never denied and I will never deny that I am a compulsive liar.

5. Make sure that constructions using *like* or as are parallel grammatically.

    ✗ A janitor's salary should not be larger than a teacher.

    ✓ A janitor's salary should not be larger than a teacher's (OR: than that of a teacher).

CHAPTER

6

219

✗ His research is as valid as Freud.

✓ His research is as valid as Freud's (OR: as that of Freud).

EXERCISE 6-12

Correct the faulty parallelism in the following sentences.

1. This van may seat eight people comfortably or twenty people may sit in it uncomfortably.

2. Angrily, bitterly, and with tears in his eyes, the child filed a lawsuit against his parents.

3. This summer he visited New York, the Rockies, and he also went to his mother's house in Toronto.

4. If Dolly was given the choice of doing the laundry or a movie, she would choose the laundry.

5. Babs not only enjoys eating snails, she enjoys eating squid as well.

6. Cricket is more popular in England than Canada.

7. The instructor advised the members of the class to work diligently and that they should not ask for extensions.

8. Elton either works at a library or a car wash after school each day.

9. Matilda believes and is an advocate of women's rights.

10. Bill and Hillary not only have high-paying professions, but also they are the proud parents of some perfectly awful children.

EXERCISE 6-13

Correct the faulty parallelism in the following sentences.

1. Phil is neither working nor is he attending college.

2. Ferdinand the Bull is shy, peaceful, and he likes to smell the daisies.

3. Al and Peg are basically compatible, considering that they fight all the time, their problems with children, and their different attitudes towards money.

4. Make sure all prospective employees are polite, hard working and that they don't have a criminal record.

5. Rousseau's theory of perception is as valid as Dewey.

6. He will either have to give up a promising career as a movie director, or he will fail his freshman courses.

7. You can pass the time in the bus station with a magazine, by striking up a conversation with other people who are waiting, or you could loiter in the coffee shop.

8. I would be willing to contribute to the construction fund in order to get a tax deduction or if the college would agree to name a building in my honour.

9. The marriage ceremony has changed its wording: wives swear to love and honour their husbands, and obedience is disregarded.

10. The rising birth rate among unwed teenage mothers can be attributed to a lack of knowledge of contraceptive devices, and there is more parental tolerance of promiscuous behaviour.

EXERCISE 6-14

Correct the parallelism in the following sentences. Some may be fine as they are.

1. Not only did he lose the match but also his chances of winning a medal.

2. A job search involves finding an appropriate opening, writing an effective letter of application, and you have to create the right impression at an interview.

3. Either that perfumes goes, or I go.

4. Her jokes are often much funnier than Waldo.

5. I wanted to find a man with Paul's looks, the charm of Tim, and with intelligence like that of Keith.

6. The travel agent will want to know whether you want to go to Tahiti or Finland.

7. The revealing stories printed in the tabloids lost her both her hopes of marrying a millionaire and her Miss Canada title.

8. Excitement, having an opportunity to experience different cultures, and the steady income are the reasons I joined the army.

9. Sylvester Stallone's movies are as violent as Jean-Claude van Damme.

10. Being in the public eye is not only rewarding but also it can help you to win elections.

REVIEW EXERCISES

REVIEW EXERCISE 1

1. Write six simple sentences.

2. Write six compound sentences based on your six simple sentences, using a variety of coordinators. Remember to punctuate.

3. Write six complex sentences, adapting your ideas from the sentences above. Make sure your subordinators are logical.

4. Write six compound-complex sentences. You might use the six simple sentences from number 1 as the starting point.

REVIEW EXERCISE 2

Make up sentences with these subjects, using compound verbs. Do not repeat the subject.
1. a dirt bike
2. George Jetson
3. the province of Saskatchewan
4. lawn mowers
5. Randi and Wayne
6. the neighbours
7. his alibi
8. homicide
9. hang-gliding
10. the magazine subscription

REVIEW EXERCISE 3

Rewrite these compound sentences, using any method of sentence variety you have learned.

1. The house was a large one, and it would require three or four people to pay off the mortgage.

2. The young couple, who were called Leslie and Elliot, went with Penelope, the real estate agent, to look at the house, and then they discussed what down payment they could afford.

3. Elliot liked the study and the patio very much, and Leslie admired the large closets and the whirlpool tub.

4. They disliked the colour scheme in several of the rooms, and they made plans to repaint them.

5. They realized that they would need a large mortgage, but they felt sure their bank manager would agree to it.

6. They planned to build a doghouse in the backyard, and they had already bought a Bouvier to live in it.

7. Penelope then showed them the cost of the mortgage per month, and Leslie and Elliot went pale.

8. They decided they would have to give up dining out, and instead they would be forced to eat peanut butter sandwiches for dinner.

9. A house is certainly an expensive undertaking, but it is a worthwhile investment if you don't mind saving your pennies.

10. Leslie and Elliot decided to buy a trailer instead, and they went camping frequently to get out of their apartment.

REVIEW EXERCISE 4

Convert these simple sentences into complex ones. Choose the most logical method of subordination in each case.

1. Mariano wouldn't pose for the picture. He was too vain to be seen wearing his glasses.

2. The public health nurse made a speech about Elmer the Safety Elephant. The children were not especially interested in it.

3. We will probably never figure out how to connect the modem to the computer. We should not give up.

4. All senior citizens must retake their road test to get their driver's licence. They must take the test once they pass their eightieth birthday.

5. Desmond has a barrow in the marketplace. Molly is a singer in the band.

6. I met your mother last week. She looks just like you.

7. Brock's Monument was built to commemorate the Battle of Queenston Heights fought during the War of 1812. It is a tourist attraction near Niagara Falls.

8. Stephen King published *The Tommyknockers* in 1987. It marked his shift away from horror to other kinds of fiction.

9. The microwave oven is brand new. Ludwig will use it later today to demonstrate how to melt chocolate and fry bacon.

10. Elvis Presley was born in Mississippi. He lived most of his adult life in Tennessee.

REVIEW EXERCISE 5

1. Retell a favorite story in ten to fifteen sentences, using as many of the methods of sentence variety demonstrated in this chapter as possible.

2. When you have written your story, identify the pattern of each sentence (whether simple, compound, complex, or compound-complex) and the method of subordination or coordination used.

REVIEW EXERCISE 6

Correct the faulty parallelism in the following sentences.

1. Computers are useful for writing, doing complicated mathematical procedures, and to pass the time instead of doing something constructive.

2. A hockey player's salary should not be larger than a community college instructor.

3. I was both disgusted by his jokes and his rude behaviour at the party last night.

4. Her backstroke was as smooth if not smoother than that of the competitor from New Zealand.

5. Either you must get off the telephone now or admit your addiction to the long-distance feeling.

6. Not only did primitive man wear a decorative headdress but also a loincloth.

7. Whether I am elected or even if I am rejected as a candidate, I will never give up my political ambitions.

8. Nellie's weight this month is even higher than last month.

9. Alexis refused to believe that her moral standards were lower than her sister.

10. The romance novel was divided into two parts: first, the section where the hero and heroine meet each other and recoil in disgust, and second, they reconcile and fall deeply in love.

REVIEW EXERCISE 7

Correct the faulty parallelism in the following sentences.

1. Everyone knows that students need loans to finance their education, their living expenses, and to afford to go out with their friends.

2. In the opinion of the provincial government, a student's income should never be larger than a departmental chairperson.

3. The form that students must fill out is both repetitive and it is hard to understand.

4. The ministry of education asks that you report your parents' income and you list all your expected earnings from part-time jobs.

5. The questions on the form are as nosy if not nosier than any your neighbours might ever ask.

6. The student loan request is made up of three parts: first, questions that poke into your parents' affairs; second, questions that poke into your personal affairs and, in the last section, you are interrogated about matters completely beyond your knowledge.

7. When students win scholarships, awards, or get bursaries, they are obliged to ask for less money in their student loans.

8. Dishonest students sometimes claim that their prospective income is smaller than a welfare recipient.

9. When you apply for student aid, make sure that your account of your finances is precise, accurate, and above all, that you have not padded your request too noticeably.

10. When your loan comes through, enjoy yourself, but you should also remember that it will be hard to keep up the payments on a Corvette.

CHAPTER
6

REVIEW EXERCISE 8

Applying the principles of parallel construction outlined above, combine each of the following groups of sentences into a single sentence.

The criminal was advised to answer the questions truthfully.
He was advised to get a lawyer.
He was advised to cooperate as fully as possible.

The criminal was advised to answer the questions, to get a lawyer, and to cooperate as fully as possible.

1. A good candidate must look authoritative.
   He must speak persuasively.
   He must not offend any voters.

2. The performers in the telethon entertained off and on for thirty-six hours.
   They answered telephone calls.
   They counted up the pledges.
   They drank coffee to stay awake.
   They tried not to look exhausted.

3. According to a recent study, women in management positions face greater pressures than their male counterparts.
   They run into the problem of "tokenism."
   They have to be more careful about behaviour and appearance.
   They suffer more guilt about neglecting their families.

4. The two houses were built at the same time.
   They both had three bedrooms, a family room, and a two-car garage.
   They both carry substantial mortgages.
   (,Yet) One needs a lot of work.

5. The city planners intend to improve the new approach to the downtown core by widening several streets.
   They intend to turn some blocks into pedestrian-only areas.
   They intend to plant more trees.
   They intend to put up works by local artists.

6. The tobacco pickers' union went on strike because its members wanted higher wages.
   They wanted job security.
   They wanted certain restrictions relaxed.
   They wanted a Christmas party.

7. After the gruelling rounds of competition, the ballroom dancers just couldn't go on.
   They were exhausted.
   They had danced all night.

8. Tom, the Singing Cowboy, made a personal appearance at the shopping mall.
   He was mobbed by a large crowd of adoring fans.
   He performed rope tricks.
   He sang "Buns in My Bedroll."
   Later he was the Grand Marshall in the parade.

9. Although no longer in power, the former king of Albania has been very successful.
   He has invested in real estate.
   He has played the stock market.
   He has become a personal friend of Wayne Newton.

CHAPTER
6

10. The Berlin Wall was taken down in November 1989.
    It has long been a symbol of oppression and East/West conflict.
    It served as a reminder of the Cold War.

Words

SPELLING

Some Suggestions to Improve Your Spelling

1. Buy and use a good dictionary. Your instructor should be able to recommend one.

2. Make a list of the words you usually misspell and consult it as you proof-read.

3. Make friends with a good speller. Ask him or her to look over your work before you submit it.

4. Read to increase your familiarity with language.

5. If you have a computer, you might consider buying a software program that checks spelling.

6. Carefully proofread everything you write; this will eliminate careless errors.

Words That Suffer from Mistaken Identity

accept/except

> I will *accept* your terms *except* your last condition.

accept (verb)—to take what is offered; except—(a preposition) leaving out, other than

adapt/adopt

> If they *adopt* this textbook, it will have to be *adapted* to suit the Canadian market.

adapt (verb)—to change; adopt (verb)—to accept

advice/advise

> Take my *advice*. Those people who would *advise* you to have your stomach stapled are misguided.

advice (noun)—opinion, counsel; advise (verb)—to give advice

affect/effect

> One *effect* of pollution is acid rain. Acid rain *affects* marine and plant life.

effect (usually a noun)—result; affect (usually a verb)—to influence

a lot/allot

One thousand dollars is a *lot* of money.

Each of the canvassers was *allotted* a district of the city.

a lot—a great deal; allot (verb)—to give or put aside

beside/besides

The vampire lurked *beside* her bed.

Besides appearing with Brian Adams, Tina Turner has sung with Robert Cray.

beside (preposition)—next to; besides (adverb)—in addition to

choose/chose

Helen *chose* not to invite her former boyfriend to the wedding. (past tense)

Choose your favorite flower. (present tense)

choose—present tense of the verb "to choose"; chose—past tense of the verb "to choose"

course/coarse

Cedric took a writing *course* in order to improve his style.

Although his manners were *coarse,* his intentions were good.

course (noun)—class; coarse (adjective)—unrefined

compliment/complement

Andrew accepted all the attention as a *compliment.*

He *complimented* her on her biceps.

Since we have hired two more people, we now have a full *complement* of sales people.

Troy bought a sports car to *complement* his leather jacket.

compliment—either a noun meaning "an act of courtesy" as in the first example above, or a verb meaning "to pay a compliment" as in the second example; complement—either a noun meaning "something added to complete a whole" as in the third example, or a verb meaning "to make complete" as in the fourth example

desert/dessert

Robinson Crusoe discovered Friday on a *desert* island.

Why did you *desert* the sinking ship?

For *dessert,* there was a choice of baklava, cherries jubilee, or strawberry Jello.

desert—either a noun meaning "a sandy, barren place" as in the first example, or a verb meaning "to abandon" as in the second example; dessert (noun)—final course of a meal

farther/further

The Smiths' vegetable stand is *farther* down the road.

We will discuss that point *further* along in the course.

farther (adjective, adverb)—literal physical distance; further (adjective, adverb)—usually used to mean to a greater extent or degree

hear/here

Did you ever *hear* anything so revolting?

Here lies the body of the best court jester who ever lived.

hear (verb)—to sense sounds, to listen; here (adverb)—in this place

it's/its

It's raining cats and dogs.

She called the baby Sweetie, but *its* real name was Matilda.

it's—a contraction for "it is"; its—the possessive form of "it," comparable to his or her

lead/led

Use a *lead* pencil to make the diagram.

Champlain *led* the expedition.

lead (noun)—the mineral; led (verb)—the past tense of the verb "to lead"

loose/lose

You must have a screw *loose.*

Aloysius will *lose* his reputation if he keeps hanging around with that crowd.

loose (adjective)—not firmly fastened; lose (verb)—to suffer the loss of

passed/past

> He *passed* the girls' school every morning.
>
> He jogged *past* the girls' school every morning.

passed (past tense of the verb "to pass")—to have gone forward, or from one place to another; past (adverb)—by

peace/piece

> J. Paul Getty's wealth cannot buy him *peace* of mind.
>
> He wanted a *piece* of raspberry pie.

peace (noun)—tranquility; piece (noun)—a part

personal/personnel

> My *personal* choice for *personnel* director is my nephew, Ernie.

personal (adjective)—one's own, private; personnel (noun)—persons employed in an enterprise

principal/principle

> The *principal* of Black Donnelly High, Mr. Berkheimer, was flattened by a steam-roller.
>
> The *principal* colour of her new decorating scheme is red.
>
> The *principle* of freedom of speech is the cause of too many talk shows.

principal—either a noun meaning "a governing officer" as in the first example, or an adjective meaning "first in rank or authority" as in the second example; principle (noun)—a fundamental truth

quiet/quite

> Please be *quiet*.
>
> Henry was *quite* upset when he discovered the soup stain on his new silk necktie.

quiet (adjective)—not noisy; quite (adverb)—very, rather

right/write

> If you think the only way to *write* an essay is with blood, sweat, and tears, you're *right*.

write (verb)—to form words; right (adjective) — correct

sight/cite/site

The teenage boys *sighted* the naked sunbathers.

You're a *sight* for sore eyes.

The judge will *cite* you for contempt if you don't behave in court.

The archaeologists were excavating the *site* of the Indian village.

sight—either a verb meaning "to catch sight of" as in the first of the preceding examples, or a noun meaning "something seen" as in the second example; cite (verb)—summon; site (noun)—location

stationery/stationary

For all her correspondence, Judy preferred pastel *stationery* decorated with pictures of cute animals.

When the sirens sounded, Abdul and Geneva remained *stationary*.

stationery (noun)—paper; stationary (adjective)—not moving

than/then

Anissa said she was better at horseshoe pitching *than* Damian, and *then* she proved it.

than (conjunction, preposition)—in comparison with; then (adjective, adverb)—at that time

there/their/they're

There is no excuse for *their* behaviour: *they're* old enough to know better.

there (adverb)—in that place; their (adjective)—the possessive form of they; they're—a contraction of "they are"

to/too/two

When you go *to* the store, remember to get *two* toothbrushes, some dental floss, and some balloons *too*.

to (preposition)—toward; too (adverb)—also; two (adjective, noun)—a pair

threw/through/thorough

Miguel *threw* the cheap present *through* the window.

Lily made a *thorough* inspection of all her holdings.

threw (past tense of the verb "to throw")—hurled or sent rapidly; through (preposition)—in one side and out the other side of; thorough (in our day, usually used as an adverb)—very exact, complete

weather/whether

If the *weather* is bad on Sunday, Wolfgang and Fanny will be married in the basement.

Do you know *whether* Mr. Posloski has sold his stone birdbath or not?

weather (noun)—atmospheric conditions; whether (conjunction)—if, in case

were/where/we're

The city planners *were* going to put a major thoroughfare through the block *where* Mrs. Paquette had her business.

We're just sick about what happened to your real estate deal.

were (the past tense of the verb "to be"); where (adverb, conjunction, pronoun)—in what place; we're—a contraction of "we are"

whose/who's

Whose pants are these?

Who's that man with Ilona?

whose (possessive pronoun); who's—a contraction of "who is"

you're/your

You're going to have to learn to mind *your* own business.

you're—a contraction of "you are"; your (possessive pronoun)

Words That Are Commonly Misspelled

absence	development	noticeable
accelerate	dilemma	occasion
accidentally	disappoint	occurrence
accommodate	ecstasy	omitted
accustomed	efficiency	parallel
achieve	eighth	pastime
acknowledgment	eligible	perceive
analysis	embarrass	perseverance
appearance	environment	preceding
argument	equipped	privilege
assistance	excel	proceeding
athlete	exercise	psychiatrist
bargain	existence	psychology

basically	explanation	pursue
beginning	extremely	recommend
believe	familiar	relevant
benefited	forcibly	repetition
breath	foreign	referred
breathe	foresee	reminisce
business	forty	resistance
caffeine	friend	rhythm
category	fulfill	sacrifice
ceiling	gauge	safety
cemetery	government	schedule
changeable	grammar	seize
committee	handkerchief	separate
commitment	heroes	sergeant
competent	humorous (or humourous)	severely
conceivable	hypocrisy	sheriff
connoisseur	immediately	similar
conscience	incidentally	species
conscious	independent	superintendent
consistent	indispensable	surprise
continuous	insistent	suspicion
controversial	irrelevant	tendency
convenience	irresistible	truly
corroborate	leisure	unanimous
courageous	loneliness	until
criticize	maintenance	vacuum
curiosity	manageable	vengeance
deficient	mischievous	vicious
definite	ninety	villain
desperate	ninth	weird

CLICHES, JARGON, AND WORDINESS

Clichés

A cliché is an overused expression, a worn-out word or idea that comes into your head as quick as a wink, all at once, like a bolt from the blue. Clichés can be useful; they can provide a colourful way of saying something not meant to be reflected on too deeply. But clichés can detract from your writing because they are so familiar. They suggest that you haven't thought about your subject but are instead falling back on ideas or phrases that are old hat, tried and true, and dull as ditch-water. The following are examples of clichés:

accidents will happen	by the same token	peer group
after all has been said and done	the bottom line	110%
better late than never	at a loss for words	get with it

Jargon

Jargon is technical language or language from a particular discipline that is used inappropriately for the audience. A person who consistently uses jargon chooses long or specialized words when simple ones would serve as well; the muddled thinking of such speakers or writers is also shown in their long, tangled, awkward sentences. Of course some kinds of specialized vocabulary are useful when addressing members of the same profession. Beware, however, of terms from business, advertising, sociology, medicine, and computer technology, among others, when they are used in a misguided attempt to impress or intimidate. The following are examples of jargon:

negative impact	parameters
input	interface
private sector	user-friendly
interpersonal	verbalize
facilitate	prioritize (or most-ize verbs)
liaise	facilitating
mandate	render inoperative
optimal	impact upon
feedback	

Wordiness

If someone describes your writing as wordy, it does not necessarily mean that you use too many words; it may mean that you have used empty words, formulas that take up space on the page without contributing to the meaning. Using wordy expressions will clutter up your writing and make it unclear. Learn to cut them out.

To help you eliminate clichés, jargon, and wordiness from your own writing, you might keep a list of such failures of communication. You will hear and see them everywhere: on radio and television, in the newspapers, and in textbooks.

AVOID	USE
in the near future	soon
end result	result
red in colour	red
totally gone	gone
surrounded on all sides	surrounded
circled around	circled
due to the fact that	because
in the event that	if
until such time as	until
mental attitude	attitude
serious crisis	crisis
complete disaster	disaster
past history	history
personal opinion	opinion
each and every	each
give consideration to	consider
bring to an end	end
be in a position to	can
be dependent on	depend
make assumptions about	assume

EXERCISE 7-1

Complete the expressions below to make them clichés.

1. as high as
2. as hot as
3. as ugly as
4. as poor as
5. to drink like a

6. to work like a
7. to sleep like a
8. as pretty as
9. as strong as
10. as rich as

11 as proud as

12. as meek as

13. as sharp as

14. as clear as

15. as flat as

EXERCISE 7-2

Now complete the expressions in an original way.

EXERCISE 7-3

Find the clichés, jargon, and wordiness in these sentences. Rewrite them using clearer and fresher expressions.

1. Our decision is dependent on a full and complete analysis of the device's marketing potential.

2. Wendell, a big wheel in the automotive parts industry, was facilitating a meeting when he fell head over heels in love with Marlene.

3. Mandy-Beth Thwaite, the keynote speaker at the parenting conference, tried to get feedback about her theory of nonsupportive interpersonal relationships.

4. The admissions office is making a query relative to your status in the nursing program.

5. Send me a memo about the overdue paperwork within the time-frame of two days or the bottom line is you will be terminated.

6. Jergen decided to take a stab at flamenco dancing while he was in the pink and fresh as a daisy.

7. In the foreseeable future it would be inadvisable to interact with Dorcas until your divorce action reaches a satisfactory conclusion.

8. In the final analysis, the self-starting employee must be bright eyed and bushy tailed and raring to go.

9. Benazir made a recommendation that fewer working hours would make the world a better place to live in.

10. During these changing times, in the midst of sweeping changes, our technology definitely must be state-of-the-art in order to be first out of the starting blocks.

CHAPTER

239

REVIEW EXERCISES

REVIEW EXERCISE 1

Find the clichés, jargon, and wordiness in these sentences. Rewrite them using clearer and fresher expressions.

1. Monty and Tad went head-to-head in a combative incident over the affections of Myrtle, who remained as cool as a cucumber.

2. They articulated their feelings of love and tenderness for one another in precise and descriptive verbalization.

3. Alvin was as crazy as a loon, but Simon was busy as a bee, and Theodore was happy as a clam.

4. At some future point in time, Bunty will make an examination of the area of communications in her department.

5. Behaviour of an uncooperative nature serves to create barriers in interpersonal relationships.

6. All these factors serve to illustrate that Tito should take action on the problem as fast as you can say Jack Robinson.

7. To make a long story short, we must keep a low profile in order not to let the cat out of the bag.

8. Lorraine's hands-on experience meant that she had a leg up on the ladder of success.

9. Let's strike while the iron is hot and bring the new plant foreman on stream as soon as possible.

10. Because they were like ships that pass in the night, Althea and Snake shared a meaningful relationship for only three days.

REVIEW EXERCISE 2

Find the clichés, jargon, and wordiness in these sentences. Rewrite them using clearer and fresher expressions.

1. Don't fly off the handle; I can really relate to where you're coming from.

2. This container was made for the purpose of holding water.

3. Mrs. Wadman put her finger on the problem when she outlined the scenario for the sales conference.

4. In this day and age, buying a house is easier said than done, and many young prospective home-buyers find their hopes dashed.

5. As the opening move of his political campaign, Sherman dialogued with his constituents in an effort to make them see the light.

6. Brenda could identify with the aims of the sisterhood, but her attempts to bring the controversy to a head were doomed to failure.

7. Silas, who is a social worker, disagreed with his supervisor with regard to the case in view of the fact that separating the child from his parents would have a negative impact on his development.

8. The downtime on this project was par for the course.

9. Just when all hope had fled, Chino and Anita discovered they were in the proximity of a McDonald's restaurant.

CHAPTER
7

10. It is for this reason that Eppie exhibits a tendency to snore.

REVIEW EXERCISE 3

Choose a technical term from your area of expertise or from a hobby. Define it so that those who are unfamiliar with the specialized language of the subject would be able to understand your definition. Use examples or comparisons to make your definition clear. Make sure you use the proper level of language and avoid jargon.

REVIEW EXERCISE 4

1. Write a paragraph describing the experience of falling in love—without using clichés, if possible.

2. Write a paragraph describing a favourite landscape. Try to avoid clichés.

3. Write a paragraph describing a favourite meal. Try to avoid clichés.

4. Write a paragraph describing your reaction to a recent film or piece of music. Keep the language as original as possible.

5. Write a paragraph or two that retells a familiar story, a joke or a fairy tale, using as many clichés as you can.

Chapter Exercise Answers

CHAPTER 3—SENTENCE CONSTRUCTION

EXERCISE 3-1

1. Sometimes people in trouble turn to a minister for counselling.
2. Counsellors are expected to minister to the needs of their clients confidentially.
3. Remember to consult the computer manual if you can not get the program to function.
4. Manual labour, though it's (it is) hard on the muscles, is good for the soul.
5. The arrows will guide you to the nearest washroom.
6. The tour guide at the Festival Theatre showed the audience the gong.
7. Don't (Do not) ruffle your feathers; I'm (I am) coming.
8. The ruffle on his dress shirt needs to be starched.
9. Poindexter felt that life was short, transient, and basically dull.
10. The transients huddled in the bus station for warmth.

EXERCISE 3-2

1. Bertram would like to preface his remarks with a warning to the audience to keep silent during the remainder of his speech.
2. The preface of his first book was long winded, tiresome, and full of typographical errors.
3. Dara wore a tangerine dress to her prom.
4. The camel ate the tangerine greedily.
5. Huck noticed that the table was covered with a beautiful piece of linoleum.
6. A linoleum floor is not as stylish as hardwood.
7. The collector discovered to his chagrin that the painting he had been duped into buying was a counterfeit.

8. Counterfeit money is sometimes very difficult to spot if the serial numbers are done correctly.

9. The would-be actor wants to audition for a part on the new soap opera, *The Old and the Ruthless.*

10. His audition went well, but he didn't get the role of the veteran hockey player because he still has all his teeth.

EXERCISE 3-3

1. The Montgolfier brothers invented the balloon in France in 1783.

2. The first balloon flight covered a distance of a mile and a half before it landed safely.

3. Other early balloonists were not so lucky.

4. Superstitious peasants attacked one "monster" with scythes and pitchforks as it descended from the sky.

5. Balloons were used to carry mail and passengers and for military surveillance.

6. Both the North and the South used observation balloons during the American Civil War.

7. The world's first practical powered airplane was invented by Orville and Wilbur Wright.

8. Orville made the first manned mechanical flight in history at Kitty Hawk, North Carolina.

9. Charles Lindbergh, in his plane "The Spirit of St. Louis," made the first nonstop flight from New York to Paris in thirty-three hours and thirty-three minutes.

10. Whatever happened to Amelia Earhart?

EXERCISE 3-4

1. (S) couple; (V) acted
2. (S) they; (V) bought
3. (S) godmother; (V) purchased
4. (S) godfather; (V) wore
5. (S) baby; (V) was not impressed and screamed
6. (S) minister; (V) baptized
7. (S) godparents; (V) swore
8. (S) baby; (V) was carried
9. (S) godparents; (V) should have brought
10. (S) Flora, Fauna, and Merriweather; (V) were

EXERCISE 3-5

1. (S) Boredom; (V) can be
2. (S) Falling asleep; (V) is
3. (S) What; (V) can be done
4. (S) you (understood); (V) try
5. (S) you (understood); (V) prop
6. (S) you (understood); (V) scribble
7. (S) Passing; (V) can be
8. (S) students; (V) make
9. (S) You; (V) should be
10. (S) Skipping; (V) might be

EXERCISE 3-6

1. (S) Emmeline; (V) loved
2. (S) She; (V) made
3. (S) She; (V) designed
4. (S) She; (V) enjoyed
5. (S) noodles; (V) must be added
6. (S) experience; (V) was
7. (S) He; (V) did dislike
8. (S) Stories; (V) worried
9. (S) He; (V) managed
10. (S) He; (V) became

EXERCISE 3-7

1. (S) terrier; (V) was
2. (S) she; (V) was
3. (S) she; (V) ate
4. (S) he; (V) was

5. (S) She; (V) ate

6. (S) master; (V) took

7. (S) she; (V) had

8. (S) health; (V) was

9. (S) terrier; (V) was

10. (S) you; (V) do think; (S) she; (V) was

EXERCISE 3-8

1. (S) Max; (V) has

2. (S) He; (V) drinks, eats, does

3. (S) sleep; (V) does not come

4. (S) Counting; (V) has

5. (S) Max; (V) is

6. (S) he; (V) should hang

7. (S) story; (V) would soothe

8. (S) Reading; (V) might prove

9. (S) you (understood); (V) think

10. (S) staying; (V) might be

EXERCISE 3-9

1. (S) Griselda; (V) needed

2. (S) She; (V) took off and stretched out

3. (S) telephone; (V) rang

4. (S) she; (V) ran

5. (S) caller; (V) was doing

6. (S) Griselda; (V) had not owned

7. (S) mother; (V) had flushed

8. (S) she; (V) vowed

9. (S) Griselda; (V) returned

10. (S) law; (V) ought to be

EXERCISE 3-10

1. (S) Making; (V) can be

2. (S) you; (V) should cook

3. (S) solution; (V) is

4. (S) you (understood); (V) go

5. (S) packages; (V) are stacked

6. (S) Eating; (V) can be

7. (S) we; (V) don't buy

8. (S) we; (V) won't need

9. (S) Nothing; (V) is

10. (S) you; (V) wouldn't have

EXERCISE 3-11

Because many correct answers are possible in these exercises, we will simply identify F (fragments) and C (correct sentences).

1. F	5. C	8. F
2. C	6. F	9. C
3. F	7. C	10. F
4. C		

EXERCISE 3-12

1. F	5. F	8. C
2. F	6. C	9. F
3. C	7. F	10. F
4. F		

EXERCISE 3-13

1. C	5. F	8. F
2. C	6. F	9. F
3. F	7. F	10. C
4. F		

EXERCISE 3-14

1. F	5. C	8. F
2. F	6. C	9. F
3. F	7. C	10. F
4. F		

EXERCISE 3-15

1. F	5. F	8. F
2. F	6. F	9. C
3. C	7. C	10. C
4. C		

EXERCISE 3-16

1. F	5. F	8. F
2. F	6. F	9. C
3. F	7. F	10. C
4. F		

EXERCISE 3-17

1. C	5. F	8. F
2. C	6. F	9. C
3. F	7. F	10. F
4. F		

EXERCISE 3-18

The following are intended as suggested solutions only; other combinations might also be correct.

1. Here is the plunger. I will unclog your toilet.

2. Jessye and Frank went to the First National Bank: they wanted to make a withdrawal.

3. Going to Jamaica sounds wonderful, but, on the other hand, I don't have the money for air fare.

4. He loved video games; she preferred checkers.

5. His dentist reminded him of the dangers of gum disease; now he flosses daily.

249

6. Please be quiet. I'm very upset.

7. She objected to the price of the Porsche; nevertheless, the salesperson insisted it was fair.

8. Some people who live in cold countries believe that fur coats are not a luxury; they're a necessity.

9. He hated having to mow the lawn; therefore, he bought a flock of sheep.

10. Lotteries are extremely popular in Canada. Those who like to gamble spend thousands of dollars a year on them.

EXERCISE 3-19

The following are intended as suggested solutions only; other combinations might also be correct.

1. The Beatles were originally called the Quarrymen, but later they changed their name to the Silver Beetles.

2. Most people remember John, Paul, George, and Ringo, yet only a few people know that Pete Best was the group's first drummer.

3. Correct.

4. At first, they were popular only in England and in Germany where they had performed when starting out; they became a hit in America in 1964.

5. The Beatles arrived in the U.S.A. in February 1964. They made their television debut on "The Ed Sullivan Show."

6. They had five best-selling singles in the top ten in March 1964; this record has never been equalled.

7. Two movies followed, the first in 1964 and the second in 1965: *A Hard Day's Night* and *Help*. These films were well received; consequently, the group met with increasing financial success.

8. About 100,000 people watched them perform at Shea Stadium in New York during their last tour in 1966; however, they decided to give up live performances.

9. Many of the songs the group wrote and performed in the late sixties were considered controversial; for example, "Lucy in the Sky with Diamonds" was thought to be a song celebrating the use of LSD.

250

10. Despite their success, and to their fans' dismay, the Beatles disbanded in 1970. Paul McCartney sued the others in order to break their contract.

EXERCISE 3-20

The following are intended as suggested solutions only; other combinations might also be correct.

1. Elvis is alive and living in a trailer park in Red Deer, Alberta. He now weighs 350 pounds.

2. If you hear it thunder, don't run under a tree; there will be pennies from heaven for you and me.

3. Correct.

4. Harriet baked cookies in order to impress Mr. Elton, the new minister; unfortunately, he got indigestion.

5. Correct.

6. The painting caused a scandal when it was unveiled. The artist was charged with creating a public nuisance.

7. The professor continued to lecture, unaware that his class was falling asleep; however, the fire alarm woke them up.

8. Correct.

9. When she consulted the psychic, Belva discovered the ring was cursed; nevertheless, she decided to wear it.

10. Damian and Jojo were introduced to one another by a publisher; subsequently, they had successful writing careers and an unsuccessful marriage.

EXERCISE 3-21

The following are intended as suggested solutions only; other combinations might also be correct.

1. Run to the store. Buy some bandages.

2. Although this part of the jungle was supposedly undisturbed, Come-by-Chance Smith, the intrepid explorer, was surprised to find evidence of civilization near the waterfall. He found Mars bar wrappers and an old *Chatelaine* magazine.

3. Correct.

4. Chess is an absorbing intellectual challenge. It is nonetheless more interesting to play than to watch.

251

5. The sun will come up tomorrow; bet your bottom dollar that tomorrow there will be sun.

6. The return of spring had a noticeable effect on Sterling's mental outlook; as a result, he gave up smoking and drinking and became a priest.

7. After she fired her entire administrative staff, the director of the art gallery held a press conference to explain her managerial style. "A new broom sweeps clean," she said.

8. Correct.

9. Don't cry for me Argentina; the truth is I never left you.

10. By day Mrs. Luciani appeared to be the image of the traditional grandmother; by night she was "Grey Panther Woman," a tireless champion of senior citizens.

EXERCISE 3-22

The following are intended as suggested solutions only; other combinations might also be correct.

A. For decades we have sent terminally ill patients to the hospital to die. In hospitals, visiting was restricted, patients were isolated, and a strict schedule was maintained. These measures were often employed to prolong life even though everyone knew the patient would die anyway. Discussions about the patient's coming death were discouraged. Family members were cut off from their loved ones; they had no one to help them cope with their grief. There is now a much-needed alternative to our traditional methods of caring for the terminally ill, which is called Palliative Care.

B. In a Palliative Care Unit, overall care is provided by a multi-disciplinary team. This team includes nursing staff, social workers, pharmacist, dietician, chaplain, occupational therapist, physiotherapist, speech pathologist, and trained volunteers, as well as physicians. When the patient arrives, he is welcomed by members of the staff who encourage him to call them by their first names. To make him feel at home, they encourage him to bring and use his personal belongings. Visiting is not restricted; family may help with day-to-day care; relatives often stay overnight especially when death is near; and even pets are allowed to visit occasionally.

C. Most patients know they are going to die. They become angry and upset when people attempt to hide this reality from them. Staff members in a

Palliative Care Unit help patients to cope with the facts. Patients are encouraged, but not forced, to talk about their feelings. PCU staff are trained to recognize signs that patients are ready and willing to talk to others; members of the family are also encouraged to lend support. Because patients are made aware of any changes in their condition, the family may help them work through their feelings as death comes closer.

D. Palliative Care offers us a far more satisfactory method of caring for the terminally ill than standard hospital treatment. Patients and their families receive encouragement and support from the Palliative Care team. Patients are treated like contributing members of society; this treatment reduces or eliminates their feelings of alienation. Patients remain alert; they are free of pain; and they die with their families close by. The Palliative Care concept allows patients to die peacefully and with dignity. It therefore provides us with a humane method of caring for the terminally ill.

CHAPTER 4—COMMON ERRORS

EXERCISE 4-1

1. dove/dived
2. forgotten
3. chose
4. bitten
5. risen

6. shrank
7. hung
8. ridden
9. given
10. rung

EXERCISE 4-2

1. paid
2. proven/proved
3. tore
4. written
5. shaken

6. seen
7. dug
8. frozen
9. lit
10. sprung

EXERCISE 4-3

1. taken
2. spoke, spoken
3. showed
4. lose, lost
5. rise, risen

6. slunk
7. dragged
8. eaten, drank
9. blown
10. threw, slid

EXERCISE 4-4

1. left, knew, burned/burnt
2. believed, was, ate
3. became, tried
4. searched, realized, was
5. started, didn't know

6. asked, would tell
7. had, was
8. kept, owed, didn't
9. was striking, pulled
10. was sleeping, went, bought, woke, heard, shut

EXERCISE 4-5

1. has been waiting, has made
2. received, could
3. gasped, bought
4. put, had
5. turned, made

6. was, has been telling
7. got, told, was paid, was lacking
8. yelled, made up, decided
9. was considered, could play
10. could, didn't stay

EXERCISE 4-6

1. said, didn't
2. asked, agreed
3. revealed, knew, was
4. believed, paid, paid
5. claimed

6. asserted, was
7. would have finished, had kept
8. asked, was
9. assured, would arrive
10. wondered, would rain, had

EXERCISE 4-7

1. hoped, would behave/ behaved
2. expected, went
3. reported, was, was
4. was completed, returned
5. leaked, wrung
6. was, didn't know
7. enjoyed, found
8. were, had decided
9. was, couldn't
10. reacted, got, looked

EXERCISE 4-8

1. passive
2. passive
3. passive
4. active
5. active
6. passive
7. passive
8. active
9. active
10. passive

EXERCISE 4-9

1. passive
2. passive
3. active
4. passive
5. active
6. passive
7. active
8. active
9. passive
10. active

EXERCISE 4-10

1. Cathy broke her arm when she fell from her bicycle.

2. The godmother gave Marietta's baby a bath after the ball game was over.

3. Mara injured her knee in a fall, and a team of orthopedic surgeons operated on it.

4. The respiratory infection clogged Dave's sinuses.

5. The conference's sponsor was paying the hotel bills of the noisy, eager tourists who crowded the beach.

6. Throughout the house the owners had displayed photographs that a friend of the family had taken.

7. The government paid the wages of the work-study student who had done the photocopying.

8. A trained psychologist, whose autographed collected works were available in the bookstore for $150 plus tax, conducted the workshop.

9. Fiona, whose father had encouraged her to buy jewellery, purchased an amber necklace.

10. Luckily, a registered nurse, invited to the reception, performed the Heimlich manoeuvre on the choking dinner guest.

EXERCISE 4-11

1. Patsy's brother Charles owned and managed the nursing home.

2. The freedom that Rebecca allowed her dog Fluffy pleased him when they spent a week at the cottage.

3. The women of the community prepared the sandwiches for the meeting that the council planned on Monday.

4. The government axed the department when the press relayed the news that several officials had been lining their pockets.

5. The folk singers cancelled the bus trip when they put off their performance for two months.

6. The skunk sprayed the husky, and its owner gave the dog a bath.

7. The owner mounted the moosehead, a trophy from Vern's garage sale, ostentatiously above the bar.

8. Garcia stuffed the chicken with breadcrumbs and fruit.

9. When they were tidying up the room, the children laid the doll on the bed.

10. As a finishing touch, the electrician screwed in the lightbulbs.

EXERCISE 4-12

1. attends
2. wants
3. is
4. hopes

5. plan
6. Is
7. form

8. have
9. like
10. smokes

EXERCISE 4-13

1. has
2. provide
3. Has
4. are, become

5. remain
6. are, helps, creates
7. is, sees

8. needs
9. hates
10. smells

EXERCISE 4-14

1. does
2. are
3. was
4. lie

5. were
6. is, goes
7. has

8. attends
9. is
10. were

EXERCISE 4-15

1. is
2. makes
3. has
4. functions

5. sings
6. is
7. am

8. was
9. were
10. makes

EXERCISE 4-16

1. is
2. was
3. was
4. does

5. cause
6. are
7. wants

8. is
9. are, characterize
10. has (not have)

EXERCISE 4-17

1. is
2. meets
3. Correct
4. was

5. is
6. feels
7. concerns

8. does
9. mean
10. are

EXERCISE 4-18

1. sleeps, rises
2. want
3. sponsors
4. is

5. bring
6. leaves
7. interests

8. is
9. takes
10. offer

EXERCISE 4-19

1. is
2. talks
3. is
4. consists

5. has
6. is
7. accepts

8. was, were, is
9. has
10. stands

EXERCISE 4-20

1. is
2. tastes
3. seems
4. has

5. is
6. overwhelms, offers
7. is

8. screams
9. wants
10. is, are

EXERCISE 4-21

Answers will vary.

EXERCISE 4-22

1. Everyone who rides in a car should use his or her air bag, or his or her seat belt to ensure safety.

2. Each of the sisters knows how to operate the jackhammer herself.

3. No one with any sense wants to see herself or himself gain forty pounds.

4. Unless you stop cracking your knuckles, no one will get his or her necessary hours of sleep.

5. None of the awards shows on television is ever entertaining in itself; though such programs celebrate excellence, they bore me to tears.

6. All TV evangelists swear that their programs are dedicated to saving souls rather than to making money.

7. Everyone must ask himself/herself if he/she really wants to buy an ant farm or if he/she is just succumbing to peer pressure.

8. The child who reads *Winnie the Pooh* will learn the importance of playing by itself.

9. Business and economics were valuable even though they demanded a great deal of work from students deficient in mathematics.

10. Everyone who goes scuba diving should make sure his or her oxygen tank is securely fastened and his or her life insurance is paid up.

EXERCISE 4-23

1. The master chef showed the apprentice cooks the oyster shells and explained how he shucks them.

2. The front runner knew every member of the community and was counting on his or her vote to win the election.

3. Do you think any one of these respected citizens will admit that he or she saw a UFO after the New Year's party?

4. All men, women, and children who prefer this brand of popcorn are cordially invited to attend the film festival in their honour.

5. Everybody living in Canada secretly wishes he or she could move to California during the winter months.

6. The survey reported that each of the animals in the taste test preferred its usual brand of cat food to Brand X.

7. No one watching that soap opera really believes that his or her favorite character will not recover from amnesia.

8. One or other of the brothers always insists on showing everyone his tattoo.

9. Anybody who eats lunch regularly in the school cafeteria will find that his or her health suffers from a lack of the four basic food groups.

10. One of the boys had a mosquito bite on his elbow.

EXERCISE 4-24

1. One irate woman told Yvette, "Stay away from my husband."

2. Eating too much salt leads to hypertension, kidney problems, and heart disease, and we should control these.

3. Millicent asked the woman if she thought Millicent should divorce her husband because of his chronic fits of temper.

4. Delbert's report card said that he never paid attention in class.

5. The supervisor in the exam room said that if any cheating was discovered, the school would demand the suspension of those caught, no matter what their excuse might be.

6. The second chapter of this book discusses the formation of a thesis statement.

7. The crowded department store plays soothing Muzak to prevent riots from breaking out during special sales.

8. Herbert sucked his thumb while sitting beside his four-year-old brother.

9. We fed the jujubes, on which we had been snacking throughout the field trip, to the monkeys.

10. Even though Mark never did get the hang of the parallel bars, he thought that his gym teacher was a good coach.

EXERCISE 4-25

1. Christie told Jaclyn, "You have dandruff."

2. Whenever her mother makes lunch for her, Queenie eats too much.

3. When Alain patted the horse's mane, the horse kicked him.

4. Elwy loves to go to movies and does so a lot.

5. I have always liked nursing sick animals, and after a year at veterinary school, I'm going to be a veterinarian.

6. The first chapter of the book on basic car maintenance tells how to do a lube job.

7. When it hit its head, the baby screamed.

8. Whenever Yuri and Sergei play monopoly, the latter cheats shamelessly.

9. When they finally step into the ring, Farley will hit Gore below the belt until the referee has to step in.

10. The night-shift workers rallied for wage parity because they all believed their salaries should be higher.

EXERCISE 4-26

1. The dinner guests whom she served flatly refused to eat hearts of palm because, in their opinion, the vegetables looked like popsicle sticks.

2. The agency asked specifically for the model whom she recommended, not the one who had thick ankles.

3. My brother purchased Frieda, a red-haired doll, for my mother and me.

4. I know whom you are speaking of.

5. Frederick gave the canned goods and the money for the food bank to her and me.

6. The Petersons have a dog that is as big as I.

7. We always believe that other people are happier, richer, and thinner than we.

8. They presented the award to him and me.

9. Jim and I usually eat too many doughnuts when we get together.

10. Correct.

EXERCISE 4-27

1. Tina gets more out of the aerobics class than they.

2. The boss will give the raise to whoever is most competent.

3. At whom did Francine throw the bouquet?

4. Miss Fishbane didn't like my working on the assignment in class.

5. The bears asked who had been sleeping in their beds.

6. Between you and me, his life is a mess.

7. After work, Norton and he left for the fishing trip.

8. Mr. Weller disapproved of their playing loud music late at night.

9. Correct.

10. The change in the hiring policy will affect you more than her.

EXERCISE 4-28

1. The nurse who attended the elderly gentlemen was working during the night shift only.

2. In September, my astrologer predicted that I would become rich and famous. OR My astrologer predicted that I would become rich and famous in September.

3. From the last row of the orchestra, using their opera glasses, they watched Mr. Roffey's Amazing Canine Friends on stage.

4. There on the doorstep, screaming at the top of its lungs, was a tiny newborn baby wrapped in newspaper.

5. Dolly had worked as a short-order cook for years before becoming the owner and manager of Vancouver's best restaurant.

6. She has a fur coat with a hood in her closet.

7. The hostess immediately warned us not to smoke.

8. What did you say with such a nasty sneer to that woman?

9. On their way to the orthodontist, they almost got run over by an ice cream truck.

10. They have no intention of buying those blue jeans unless they're on sale.

EXERCISE 4-29

1. Rocko was lying lazily on the couch all the time his mother was visiting.

2. The customers wait just a minute before they are served with their hamburgers and french fries.

3. The teller gave the robber one hundred dollars in a plain brown bag.

4. Some people, such as union leaders, are paid to make demands.

5. That actress has a terrible case of stage fright; she loses her nerve before nearly every single performance.

6. The troubled patient told her counsellor secretly that she wanted to talk to someone.

7. He couldn't believe that he drank almost the whole case of beer himself.

8. The parlour maid spotted the cobweb hanging from the ceiling.

9. Taking odd jobs, the bankrupt couple did their best to pay their overdue bills.

10. Barking at passing cars, the German shepherd woke up the neighbourhood.

EXERCISE 4-30

1. After having moved several times over the past eight years, I have extensive knowledge of the process.

2. During my last relocation, taking inventory of what I had to move, I discovered lots of heavy books and cumbersome possessions.

3. When I prepared for the move, my new home seemed threatened by the loads of debris I had accumulated over the years.

4. Resolving never again to keep cards and letters for sentimental reasons, I destroyed the contents of my desk drawers before leaving my old apartment.

5. Once you decide what is no longer needed, it is time either to throw things out or to find people who can use them.

6. Correct.

7. When packing fragile items, you may find it convenient to use boxes with lids to prevent breakage, soiling, and invasion of your privacy.

263

8. To avoid excessive moving costs, you can bribe your friends into helping you in return for a case of beer or a meal.

9. If moving gradually into your new place, you should pack everything but the bare necessities.

10. Having accomplished the task painlessly, you will probably see a larger, cheaper, and nicer apartment than your new one advertised in the paper the following week.

EXERCISE 4-31

1. When attending classes, you can see that there are two kinds of people enrolled in any educational institution: students and pupils.

2. To distinguish between the two groups, you should know that a student is someone who studies various subjects, whereas a pupil is merely registered in courses.

3. Differing from the pupil, not only in academic pursuits but also in social disposition, the student finds that hard work and dedication are important.

4. When walking through the library, you can see the student sitting quietly in a corner reading a lab manual.

5. Finding pupils is not so difficult. Listening to the sounds of chatter, you can hear Biff and Bob talking to Betty and Buffy, rather than studying biology.

6. After going for a coffee, a pupil mainly occupies himself gossiping.

7. Taking a cigarette break, the pupil exhibits signs of restlessness.

8. Writing essays in a single night, he often thinks that getting a diploma is easy.

9. Cramming for exams, the pupil rewards his academic efforts with massive amounts of alcohol.

10. Correct.

EXERCISE 4-32

1. Eating a chocolate bar, he broke his tooth.

2. Before giving a party, you should clean the house.

3. Ralph knows that, being a forgiving woman, Trixie can be counted on for sympathy even when he doesn't deserve it.

4. Watching television, I noticed that the picture suddenly became cloudy.

5. Learning to write, we were instructed to stay inside the lines by our teacher.

6. Realizing that she couldn't help it, I wasn't distracted during my talk by her hacking cough.

7. Hoping to win, she let the ski pole slip out of her hand in her nervousness and cost herself a medal.

8. After calling me names, he asked me to leave.

9. The panda seemed to pose for the tourist who was aiming his camera.

10. As a track and field runner, I need special care for my feet.

EXERCISE 4-33

1. Admiring the football star, the cheerleader didn't care about his weak academic record.

2. Her mother complained that she was lazy after she refused to help with the dishes three nights in a row.

3. Slaving over the stove all day, she was disappointed that her lasagne was devoured in five minutes.

4. Withdrawing so much money, I was refused my request for a loan by the bank manager.

5. When you compare these animal acts, you will find that both the trained penguins and the gorilla are excellent, but the pit bull terrier is more exciting.

6. Believed to be dangerous, an escaped convict accosted an old lady on the street and stole her purse.

7. Correct.

8. Battling the elements for days, the crew reached the North Pole as it snowed.

9. Writing a letter home, she begged her parents for extra money to finance her trip to Barbados.

10. When eating, you should clean your hands.

EXERCISE 4-34

1. When he was eating a chocolate bar, his tooth broke.

2. The house should be cleaned before you give a party.

3. Ralph knows that he can count on Trixie's sympathy even when he doesn't deserve it because she is a forgiving woman.

4. While I was watching television, the picture suddenly became cloudy.

5. When we learned to write, our teacher instructed us to stay inside the lines.

6. Because I realized that she couldn't help it, her hacking cough didn't distract me during my talk.

7. Although she hoped to win, the ski pole slipped out of her hand in her nervousness and cost her a medal.

8. After he called me names, I was asked to leave.

9. As the tourist aimed his camera, the panda seemed to pose for the picture.

10. As I am a track and field runner, my feet need special care.

EXERCISE 4-35

1. Since she admired the football star, his weak academic record didn't matter to the cheerleader.

2. Her mother complained about her laziness after she refused to help with the dishes three nights in a row.

3. After she had slaved over the stove all day, her lasagne was devoured in five minutes.

4. Because I withdrew so much money, the bank manager refused to grant my request for a loan.

5. When you compare these animal acts, both the trained penguins and the gorilla are excellent, but the pit bull terrier is more exciting.

6. An escaped convict who was believed to be dangerous accosted an old lady on the street and stole her purse.

7. Because they didn't want to offend anyone, they kept their opinions to themselves.

8. After they battled the elements for days, it snowed as the crew reached the North Pole.

9. When she wrote home, her letter begged her parents for extra money to finance her trip to Barbados.

10. When you eat, your hands should be clean.

EXERCISE 4-36

1. As a health-conscious Senior citizen, Mr. Littlejohn thinks bran and prune juice are important.

2. After allowing it originally, the students' council banned smoking.

3. As he blushed furiously, the audience laughed at the game-show host who lost his pants.

4. It is important to make a will while you are of sound mind and body.

5. Trapped in the basement, the political prisoner could not see the sun.

6. The Canadian tourists saw a duck-billed platypus, nursing its young.

7. When Michael was three months old, his father changed his diaper for the first time.

8. I see in *The Globe and Mail* that a national election is going to be held.

9. After accusing me of cheating, the proctor tore my exam paper up.

10. When using my credit card, I consider price to be of minor importance.

EXERCISE 4-37

1. The acting dean of the library school was accused, in the press, of incompetency before she could defend her actions.

2. The feminist group asserted that civil servants at the Unemployment Insurance Commission were biassed against them because they were women.

3. Licking David's face affectionately, the cocker spaniel showed that he was grateful for his new toy.

4. Because he is suffering from a highly contagious social disease, his friends have stopped visiting him in the hospital.

5. Lobster, broiled in butter and covered with béchamel sauce, was served at the gynecologists' convention.

6. As a home owner, I believe the high rates for property taxes in this area are unjustified.

7. To succeed in life, one must accept responsibility.

8. Wanting to see her old flame one more time, she invited the other guests merely as camouflage.

9. In order to win the game, you must plan a strategy.

10. As a meat eater, I find vegetarians pale, thin, and undernourished.

CHAPTER 5—PUNCTUATION

EXERCISE 5-1

1. Heather wondered if she could sue for defamation of character.

2. "What do you mean by 'tragic business loss'?" the tax auditor inquired.

3. Wipe your feet before walking on my white carpet!

4. The mechanics rioted when they saw the final examination.

5. Would you bring two coffees and a danish when you come back.

6. When will I be eligible to collect unemployment insurance?

7. The manager was insulted by his employees' lack of attention to him at his retirement party.

8. Look at that!

9. What colour do you want your office painted?

10. For his project on black history, John asked what conditions on slave ships were like.

EXERCISE 5-2

1. During the interview, the celebrated author was asked why none of her friends spoke to her anymore.

2. Which do you prefer: brains or money?

3. Where would you like your temperature taken?

4. Thank you for not smoking.

5. "I can't believe I've been charged with careless driving!" shouted Renato angrily.

6. Did the murder take place in the conservatory or in the billiard room?

7. The policewoman wondered if the suspect knew where his family was.

8. Ms. Banerjee, a radiologist from the U.S., is now living in Edmonton, Alta., and working for IBM.

9. When keyboarding, leave two spaces after a period.

10. Are you hoping to win "Cash for Life"?

EXERCISE 5-3

1. For his vacation, Alex was trying to decide among skiing, big game hunting, body-surfing, and watching television.

2. The tall, dark, handsome stranger was disappointed; Jane was looking for a famous, short, blond millionaire.

3. At the concert, the choir performed difficult, unmelodic modern music; unfortunately, the audience was more in the mood for the familiar old standards.

4. The restaurant has paid the hospital bills and offered cash settlement, so there will be no need for a lawsuit.

5. Betting on the horses, buying lottery tickets, and playing bingo are effective ways to spend extra cash.

6. Those expensive shoes look wonderful, yet they are very uncomfortable.

7. Today you are successful if you have a job, are able to meet your mortgage payments, go to aerobics at least once a week, and keep your sanity.

8. This calls for a tall, cold glass of chocolate milk.

9. Correct.

10. The first meeting of the joint committee proceeded smoothly, but there are hidden agendas to be considered and personality conflicts to be resolved before the merger can be declared a success.

EXERCISE 5-4

1. He refused to drink at the party, for he was the designated driver.

2. A really good vacation would mean no emergencies, no phone calls, no calories in the food, and no bills waiting at home.

3. That ugly, old vase was the only one of its kind.

4. Merv and Bernice are coming for a visit; they will want to see Ethel and Bill, Paul and Nancy, and Lucy and Desi.

5. The very last piece of that delicious, low-calorie strawberry cheesecake was sold ten minutes ago.

6. He took a swing at the ball, and he missed.

7. Loreena McKennitt, a singer, has released a number of albums, including *Elemental, Parallel Dreams, To Drive the Cold Winter Away*, and *The Visit*.

8. When writing an ad for the newspaper, remember to be as precise as possible, for the fewer words you use the lower the cost.

9. Mary-Lou will gain extra points for every new customer, and she will soon have enough to qualify for the car.

10. Tuponia, Cabotia, Hochelaga, Borealia, and Transatlantica were names that were not chosen when in 1867 the four colonies joined in Confederation.

EXERCISE 5-5

1. That is why, my fellow Canadians, I am asking for your vote in the up-coming election.

2. The real Laura Secord, a heroine of the War of 1812, bears little or no resemblance to the woman on the boxes of chocolate.

3. Obviously, you can't give them that for a wedding present!

4. Whatever do you mean, Mr. Johnson?

5. For example, it is still possible in some parts of the country to be fined for leaving your horse unattended for too long a time.

6. My white angora cat, Mrs. Bates, has just devoured an entire box of After Eights, a present I intended to give to Marion.

7. Weather permitting, the balloon launch should take place at the usual time.

8. In order to buy the outfit that she wore to the christening, she had to sell the silver tea service.

9. Bellowing and waving the newspaper, the enraged businessman strode into the editor's office.

10. Mrs. White, who used to be a cook, now runs the Clue Detective Agency in partnership with Professor Plum.

EXERCISE 5-6

1. On the contrary, I'm sure Susan doesn't mind paying her own way when she goes out on a date with you.

2. Correct.

3. Zabaglione, a dessert made of eggs and sugar stirred over high heat, is difficult to make; if you make one wrong move, you have something for breakfast: scrambled eggs.

4. Yes, I think you should apologize to the neighbours for what you did to their plants during their absence.

5. Correct.

6. To be perfectly honest, I don't think that complete candour is advisable or healthy.

7. As a matter of fact, I don't think that black leather, spiked hair, and heavy mascara are appropriate for a primary school teacher.

8. In spite of the terrific view and the up-to-date recreational facilities, the rent for this apartment is still too high.

9. Sally, I would like you to meet the most notorious and most often photographed member of my family, my cousin Scarface.

10. Sydney Biddle Barrows, who was the Mayflower Madam, now appears on TV talk shows discussing business management.

EXERCISE 5-7

1. Mackenzie King was, without a doubt, the only Canadian prime minister to govern by crystal ball.

2. Following the revolution, the dictator and his wife opened a Burger King franchise.

3. That is the correct answer, and you win a million dollars.

4. In order to compete with the novelty of television in the late 1950s and early 1960s, Hollywood filmmakers had to resort to some gimmicks of their own, including an increased screen size called Cinerama, a technique which released smells into the theatre called Odorama, and a process called 3-D that created the illusion that certain objects emerged from the screen.

5. When the students arrived for the class, they found the classroom door locked and the instructor pacing in the hall.

6. The vice-principal, naturally, made all the necessary arrangements to ensure the school picnic would be a success; he has purchased large quantities of hot dogs, ice cream, lemonade, and shark repellent.

7. If the chips are down, it's best to pass the dice to the next player.

8. Jennifer will eat anything except lima beans, squash, bread pudding, and Big Macs.

9. A Mercedes, a Rolls-Royce, and a BMW are among his most valued possessions.

10. Correct.

EXERCISE 5-8

1. Mountain biking, wall climbing, and roller blading are strenuous ways to keep fit.

2. When filming a scene, a director can use a long shot, a medium shot, a close-up, or an overhead shot.

3. To play baseball well, you need to be able to hit the ball out of the park, to catch it on the fly, to run like hell, and to slide on your stomach in the dirt.

4. Although some people think that hard work, perseverance, and talent will get them to the top, others believe that connections and a complete lack of morals will get them there sooner.

5. Money can't buy health and happiness, but there are compensations.

6. Schoolwork used to be confined to reading, writing, and arithmetic; now

advanced calculus, pottery, and restaurant management can be found on the curriculum.

7. Before we can close up the cottage, we will have to put on the storm windows and repair the screens.

8. Unfortunately, John was the only one who remembered to bring the insect repellent.

9. Working out with weights is an effective way to relax after school, build up your body, and meet new friends.

10. Although he searched through all the documents, at least those he could find, he was never able to discover with any certainty who his father was.

EXERCISE 5-9

1. Many popular movie stars these days get their acting experience on daytime TV soaps, sitcoms, and commercials.

2. Despite their apparent happiness, their marriage, to my knowledge anyway, is based on mutual infidelity and greed.

3. James, despite his success with women, has never met one who is willing to marry him.

4. If were you Fred, I would look for a less dangerous, not to say exposed, profession than hang-gliding.

5. At her shower, Lisa was, according to rumour, given three coffee makers, four pairs of towels, one toaster, and eight electric kettles.

6. He is an expert, so he claims, at solving computer crimes.

7. About seventy-five percent of the foods we eat contain chemical additives, yet many people remain unaware of this fact.

8. Lying on the couch, Judith recounted her dream to the analyst, including her sense of liberation as she flew around St. Paul's Cathedral with a doughnut in her mouth.

9. Although Emily says she is a careful driver, she has been involved in five minor accidents in the past six months, and her insurance premiums have risen dramatically.

10. You can have the strawberry mousse, or you can have the pumpkin cheesecake.

EXERCISE 5-10

1. His only living relative, who used to be a movie star, is coming to visit him.
   "who used to be a movie star"—non-restrictive clause

2. Lulu's cat, which just got its shots last week, is safe from the threat of rabies.
   "which just got its shots last week"—non-restrictive clause

3. Her dinner, which consisted of three leaves of lettuce, a tomato, and a few carrots, was intended to help her lose weight.
   "which consisted of three leaves of lettuce, a tomato, and a few carrots"—non-restrictive clause

4. People like my neighbours ought to be taught to respect the privacy of others.
   "like my neighbours"—restrictive phrase

5. His previous wife Myrtle had written a book about the time they spent together.
   "Myrtle"—restrictive phrase
   "they spent together"—restrictive clause

6. Students who have never taken a language course will find the advanced section of the course too difficult.
   "who have never taken a language course"—restrictive clause

7. Those who expect too much will be disappointed.
   "who expect too much"—restrictive clause

8. Aristotle gave the corsage to that woman over there wearing the green evening dress.
   "wearing the green evening dress"—restrictive phrase

9. The tenants in this apartment building, who are, for the most part students, are protesting the latest increase in rent.
   "who are, for the most part students"—non-restrictive clause

10. Two of her sisters, Emily and Charlotte, preferred sports to reading.
    "Emily and Charlotte"—non-restrictive phrase

EXERCISE 5-11

1. The Corvette was travelling along the highway at great speed; it failed to negotiate a turn.

2. Knowledge comes; wisdom lingers.

3. At the staff party, all the men gathered in the den to watch the hockey game; the women sat in the living room.

4. The baker mixed the ingredients of the cake; then he turned the batter into the pans.

5. When the teacher came down the hall, the students hid in the stairway; they didn't want to be caught.

6. Nancy and Harold just bought a new car; consequently, they sent their daughters out to work.

7. Writing letters is a chore; still, it is the only way to prevent losing your friends or paying large phone bills.

8. To make the most of her new swimming pool, Betty has recently acquired new lawn furniture, purchased at Canadian Tire; a cordless phone, on sale at Radio Shack; and a string bikini, found in the lingerie department at Kmart.

9. He got his tax rebate today; therefore, he's having a party tomorrow.

10. The celebration was cancelled, however, when he discovered the cheque had been sent to the wrong address.

EXERCISE 5-12

1. The newcomers entered the auditorium noisily; they were unaware that they were late for the recital.

2. A good artist must paint the subject and, at the same time, show his or her reaction to it; while the first is easy, the second is unusually difficult.

3. Going to the hairstylist is hard on my nerves; I'm afraid I'll wind up looking like something the cat dragged in.

4. Often the stylist will show you pictures of the latest cuts; however, these are always worn by handsome men and glamorous women who would look good bald.

5. Correct.

6. Usually the next day my hair stands straight up; worse, it may develop a cowlick.

7. You know that your haircut is not a success when your friends make no comment; instead they greet you with looks of startled surprise.

8. Maintaining a style is frequently a challenge; however, if you use enough mousse, gel, and spray your hair should stay put for about a week though it will be as hard as a football helmet.

9. Correct.

10. The ideal stylist has to have the patience of Job, in order to deal with the public; the invention of Leonardo da Vinci, to adapt unsuitable cuts for demanding clients; and the acting talent of Greta Garbo, to be able to say "You look great!" whatever happens.

EXERCISE 5-13

1. Cookbooks have become an important mainstay of the publishing industry; each year many different books appear presenting a variety of new ways to prepare food.

2. One of the earliest ones to survive to the present is called *The Learned Banquet*; it was written by a Greek gourmet in the second century B.C.

3. We may think that cheesecake is a recent discovery; however, *The Learned Banquet* contains several recipes for it.

4. Apicius, a Roman merchant who lived during the first century A.D., held enormous parties whose cost eventually led him to bankruptcy and suicide; although his cookbook has been preserved, it is not recommended to people on budgets.

5. Correct.

6. Cooking was revolutionized by the printing press; as a result of this invention, cookbooks were widely available for the first time.

7. The first printed cookbook was written in Italian and appeared in 1485; it says a lot about the human appetite that the majority of the recipes in this book were for candy and sweets.

8. One of the most successful and popular books, *The Boston Cooking-School Cook Book*, was originally published in 1896; it has, however, been reprinted many times since.

9. Its editor was Fannie Farmer; she was the first to standardize her recipes, guaranteeing reliable results to her readers.

10. Today you can find a cookbook on any subject; there are vegetarian ones with instructions on how to prepare tofu; there are Cajun ones that show

how to cook squirrel and possum; and there are even "natural" ones with hints on how to harvest edible mushrooms and flowers.

EXERCISE 5-14

1. At her divorce settlement, Brenda thought of the words of the old philosopher: "God is love—but get it in writing."

2. For their new apartment, Chip, Robbie, and Ernie made up a list of necessities: candles, TV dinners, toilet paper, and a roach motel.

3. Pat lived for one thing: salmon fishing.

4. Larry and Liz are getting a divorce: he's decided he can't stand her perfume anymore.

5. Although foreign travel is not new, the modern travel industry was really invented in the nineteenth century by one man: Thomas Cook.

6. In 1841 he persuaded the Midland Counties Railway Company to run a special train to take passengers to a temperance meeting: it was the first excursion train in England.

7. Later in his career he expanded the business to include conducting tours to France and Europe, selling tickets for local and overseas travel, and organizing military transport for the British army.

8. Today Thomas Cook offices throughout the world provide assistance: at any one of these offices harried tourists can cash their travellers cheques.

9. It has been said that travel is broadening which is especially true if you go on a cruise which offers nine meals a day.

10. Correct.

EXERCISE 5-15

1. Before his job interview, Rico was so nervous that he forgot what he ordered for lunch: a donut and a coffee.

2. Edward knew his insurance rates would go up after the accident: he was a single male driver under thirty-five and the owner of a brand new sports car.

3. Delores guessed correctly and won the game: the murder was committed by Colonel Mustard in the conservatory with the wrench.

4. Correct.

5. If you plan to sit on the committee for student government, you will need patience, determination, and Tylenol.

6. The two things Lucy wants in life are real estate and Schroeder.

7. Gamblers suffer from a hopeless addiction whether they win or lose.

8. I'll never forget you mother: you gave away my dog.

9. Mark Twain was cynical about journalists; he once made this comment on the practice of reporting: "Get your facts first, and then you can distort 'em as much as you please."

10. Snapper's favorite parts of the newspaper are the TV guide, the comics, and the want ads.

EXERCISE 5-16

1. *The Origin of Intelligence in Children* and *The Early Growth of Logic* are books written by Jean Piaget.

2. According to Piaget, there are four stages in the development of the child.

3. First the child learns from experience: this stage lasts approximately two years.

4. Next, at the pre-operational stage, the child experiments with words, in the same way as he or she at first learned about concrete objects; this stage occurs from ages two to seven.

5. In stage three, children's logic continues to develop; they learn to classify and compare objects.

6. In the final stage, children learn formal logical operations, a stage which continues into adulthood.

7. All of Piaget's major research was conducted at the Sorbonne; while he was there he initiated a study of the failure of children's reasoning powers.

8. Piaget himself was a child prodigy; did you know, for example, that he wrote his first article at the age of ten?

9. Like Jean Piaget, Maria Montessori believed in "periods of sensitivity," ages at which children are best suited to acquire certain kinds of knowledge.

10. In her schools, Montessori stressed a curriculum based on her research: physical freedom for students, early reading and writing skills, and individual self-instruction.

EXERCISE 5-17

1. The qualities of a good prizefight are action, an enthusiastic crowd, and lots of blood.

2. The guests ate the meal quickly; then they left the hostess without offering to wash the dishes.

3. The Blue Jays are my favorite team; therefore, I always watch their games on television.

4. He won a year's free subscription to *Big Pecs*, a magazine devoted to body building.

5. The only thing that this candidate lacks is brains.

6. Unless you commit perjury, your brother will be sent to the slammer.

7. Snakes deserve a much better reputation than they have; for example, they help keep the frog and rat populations down.

8. Despite the hardships of winter, many Canadians take consolation in one thing: a trip to Florida is cheap.

9. Writer and publisher Robert Fulford once expressed this sentiment: "My own observation is that there is no Canadian community which is as dull as the newspaper it reads."

10. The party was successful: there are two gaping holes in the plaster; there's nothing left to eat in the house; the host is still sleeping in the bathtub.

EXERCISE 5-18

1. Country and western music, the Roller Derby, and burritos—these are Lance's least favorite things.

2. AIDS (Acquired Immune Deficiency Syndrome) is of international concern to the health-care profession.

3. A week ago—or was it two—my bird, Mr. Biddle, died.

4. Abraham Lincoln once said of an incompetent general, "Sending men to that army is shoveling fleas across a barnyard—not half of them get there."

5. My favorite nineteenth-century authors of children's literature are Louisa May Alcott (1832–88) and Lewis Carroll (1832–98).

6. To many historians, the sinking of the Titanic (April 15, 1912) signals the start of the twentieth century.

7. Vern, how nice to see you after your trip to Paris—or was it Rome?

8. Rosalita Feldman (née Gonzalez) is the new office manager at my bank.

9. Our get-rich-quick system is foolproof—you pay us money and we get rich quick.

10. The Association of Canadian Television and Radio Artists (ACTRA) is hosting its annual awards next week.

EXERCISE 5-19

1. Stupidity—that's what's wrong with the world today.

2. Several pieces of the new bedroom suite—bed, chest of drawers, and mirrors—arrived in damaged condition.

3. Many environmental factors—for example, holes in the ozone layer—are thought to be causes of the "greenhouse effect."

4. The rising costs of production and advertising (see Exhibits A and B) are responsible for the decline in profits (Table 1).

5. Mary Anne Evans (a.k.a. George Eliot) shocked Victorian society by living for many years with a married man.

6. His theory—doubtless many will disagree—is that a woman's place is in the home.

7. The epitaph of Dorothy Parker (1893–1967) reads, "Pardon my dust."

8. Some of the players' parents disapprove of the violence in junior hockey—or for that matter in all sports.

9. Utilitarianism (the theory that happiness lies in the greatest good for the greatest number) was first developed by Jeremy Bentham.

10. Mrs. Larsen—I think she's the oldest woman in the city—celebrated her 105th birthday on Tuesday.

EXERCISE 5-20

1. Nutritional food isn't necessarily boring: just because it's good for you doesn't mean you'll hate it.

2. Although people generally believe that only brussel sprouts and lima beans constitute healthy food, they're wrong: there's as much nutritional value in a dish of ice cream, for example, as in a glass of skim milk.

3. There's one difference, of course; if you're one of those people who must watch their weight, the skim milk may well be your choice.

4. Nevertheless, it isn't a bad idea for people to learn something about the nutritional value of their foods, so that they'll be free to enjoy many of the things they like.

5. It's never advisable to go on a diet that obliges you to eat cottage cheese and melba toast if these foods are unappetizing to you; you'd do better eating smaller portions of your usual foods.

6. If your weight or a sluggish energy level indicates that a change of diet is called for, you'll be most successful if you don't attempt to diet too drastically.

7. A diet won't necessarily be rigorous; it'll just demand an adjustment in your daily habits.

8. Admittedly, some people are spared the necessity of dieting: they're able to eat anything without gaining a pound; if you aren't so lucky, don't despair.

9. There's some hope if you keep these rules in mind: don't expect miracles and don't cheat even if the diet doesn't show results immediately.

10. Here's one more bit of advice: if you can't stop eating too much, ask your dentist if he's willing to wire your jaws shut.

EXERCISE 5-21

1. It's often frightening for people to discover that they're in need of dental work.

2. Whenever I've had to go to the dentist, I've always tried to trick myself into thinking that it won't hurt.

3. Once she's got the drill in her hand, however, it's almost impossible to feel that you're safe.

4. What's most annoying is the way that dentists often ask questions of you just as you're incapable of answering them.

5. Dentists aren't really sadistic, though; they're just trying to do their job.

6. Nevertheless, if you've had any bad experiences with them, you'll find yourself shivering whenever you hear the words, "Spit and rinse."

7. I'm not really sure why my fear of pain never seems to inspire me to use the dental floss that she's recommended.

8. Wouldn't it make sense, after all, for me to take care of my teeth as I've been instructed to do?

9. What's your excuse for not brushing your teeth regularly?

10. Who's going to suffer for your negligence? It's not a problem for dentists: they'll go on charging you for cleaning and fillings regardless.

EXERCISE 5-22

1. Thursday's
2. Kathleen's
3. turtle's
4. everyone's

5. briefcase's
6. saleswomen's
7. hero's

8. dress's
9. cutlass's
10. elephants'

EXERCISE 5-23

1. weekend's
2. tomorrow's
3. Emily's
4. Camrose's

5. seamstresses'
6. somebody's
7. Dickens's or Dickens'

8. theirs
9. whose
10. Honduras'

EXERCISE 5-24

1. "What was that?" they cried in amazement.

2. "How many of you are coming on the trip?" the instructor asked.

3. Alva inquired if I had seen her new article, "Adventures in a Canoe," in *Equinox.*

4. "Politics," Lester Pearson said, "is the skilled use of blunt objects."

5. Bob Hope made the following comment about Toronto: "You're going to have a great town here if you ever get it finished."

6. "If you are moving at the speed of light you're already there," Marshall McLuhan has noted.

7. Correct.

8. On reaching sixty, Coco Chanel said, "Cut off my head and I'm thirteen."

9. In *Casablanca* Dooley Wilson plays "As Time Goes By" for Ingrid Bergman, not for Humphrey Bogart as everybody thinks.

10. After reading *Carrie,* Heidi told Conrad, "I don't want to go to the prom."

EXERCISE 5-25

1. Correct.

2. The Red Queen yelled, "Off with her head!"

3. Correct.

4. Jack Kerouac dubbed his peers "the beat generation."

5. "In spite of everything," Anne Frank writes at the end of *The Diary of a Young Girl,*" I still believe that people are really good at heart."

6. "Oh brother," sighed Jodie, "here comes Gino in his sportscar."

7. Joey Smallwood has called Newfoundland "this poor bald rock."

8. Explaining why he had not hired her for the job, he said that "many are called but few are chosen"; she was not amused and called the Human Rights Commission.

9. "Don't call us: we'll call you" is what most job applicants hear at the end of an interview.

10. Correct.

EXERCISE 5-26

1. The doctor worked for the Ministry of Health after graduating from medical school at The University of Western Ontario in London.

2. This year Christmas falls on the third Sunday in December.

3. Mr. and Mrs. Sheepshanks are going camping in Algonquin Park either in the spring or in July.

4. Professor Erickson will present a lecture entitled "Taking Your Money Seriously" on Monday, November 13, in Room 253 of the Social Sciences Building.

5. "To die will be an awfully big adventure," said Peter Pan.

6. The counsellor wanted me to take Business 200 and English, but I'm taking chemistry instead.

7. Her Uncle Floyd and Aunt Eppie are taking Joanne to Kalamazoo to visit her cousins.

8. On her summer vacation, Karen read *Something I've Been Meaning to Tell You* by Alice Munro, *The Closing of the American Mind*, and *Remembrance of Things Past* in the original French.

9. "I would never put my money in that bank," said the Reverend Peabody, "because it still has investments in South Africa."

10. This week the ambassador from the Netherlands will be conferring with the prime minister in Ottawa and touring the Maritimes.

EXERCISE 5-27

1. Captain Preston of the Royal Canadian Mounted Police came to R.B. Bennett High School to recruit for the force.

2. When I was younger, a variety show hosted by Juliette would follow "Hockey Night in Canada" on television.

3. The Blessed Virgin Mary appeared to Bernadette Soubirous at Lourdes in France in the mid-nineteenth century.

4. This semester I'm taking Comparative Religion 310; we have read parts of the Koran, the Talmud, and the teachings of Buddha.

5. The Progressive Conservative Party will be holding its annual convention at the Banff Springs Hotel in April.

6. Doctors Haycock and Toth are chairing the fundraising campaign for The Hospital for Sick Children in Toronto.

7. Most of the songs on the Beatles' *Sergeant Pepper's Lonely Hearts Club Band* album are pop classics, especially "With a Little Help from My Friends," "She's Leaving Home," and "When I'm Sixty-four."

8. When you are out in British Columbia, make sure you visit Stanley Park.

9. The opening sentence of Daphne du Maurier's novel *Rebecca* is "Last night I dreamed I went to Manderley again."

10. For his uncle's fiftieth birthday party, Dick is renting *A Day at the Races* with the Marx Brothers, Woody Allen's *Everything You Always Wanted to Know About Sex But Were Afraid to Ask*, and *Casablanca* with Bogart and Bergman.

CHAPTER 6—SENTENCE PATTERNS

EXERCISE 6-1

1. compound	5. simple	8. complex
2. compound-complex	6. simple	9. complex
3. complex	7. compound	10. complex
4. simple		

EXERCISE 6-2

1. complex	8. simple	15. simple
2. simple	9. complex	16. compound-complex
3. simple	10. simple	17. simple
4. complex	11. compound-complex	18. complex
5. complex	12. compound	19. complex
6. simple	13. simple	20. compound-complex
7. compound	14. simple	

EXERCISE 6-3

(While these sentences are correct, there are other ways to join the sentence pairs that would also be correct.)

1. Kent does not smoke, nor does he drink.

2. The students listened to the teacher with complete indifference, but, undaunted, he continued to speak.

3. Myrna was hardworking and gifted, and she practised the piano every day, never complaining about the difficulty of the exercises.

4. The dog slept on the landing of the stairs; the cat prowled through the house all night.

5. Jean-Paul worked at McDonald's during the day and at Arby's at night, for he needed the money.

6. The progress report must be on my desk tomorrow at nine, or heads will roll.

7. Most of the people at the party ate scallops, but the guest of honour was allergic to shellfish and ate perogies instead.

8. Mr. and Mrs. Osbourne didn't holiday in the Caribbean, nor did they cruise the Mediterranean.

9. Leigh-Anne looked directly at me, but I pretended not to notice.

10. Elvira claimed not to be offended by his silly remarks, but she never came to another of his parties.

EXERCISE 6-4

(While these sentences are correct, there are other ways to join the sentence pairs that would also be correct.)

1. We were led into the theatre by an usher who was showing people to their seats in the balcony.

2. The sports fans entered the stadium from which came a lot of noise.

3. Melody went directly to the toy department where she stopped to look over the dump trucks.

4. The firemen, who had been called away by a false alarm, returned to the station house.

5. None of Malcolm's friends were warned that his pet aardvark had a wicked disposition.

6. There was a YMCA in the town where the unemployed often stayed.

7. The boss walked over to the podium on which the text of her speech was resting.

8. Cornelia, the debutante, toyed with her beads jadedly while she was waiting for her chauffeur.

9. The bartender introduced a husky man, who had just been hired as the bouncer, to the bar patrons.

10. The Continis put the personal notice, which they had removed two weeks before, back in the paper.

EXERCISE 6-5

(While these sentences are correct, there are other ways to join the sentence pairs that would also be correct.)

1. There is a rose bush, which has huge thorns growing on it, climbing up our trellis.

2. Joan and Sandy wandered along the beach where they saw driftwood, some broken shells, and the remains of an old pirate ship.

3. Luther idly picked up the lint which was lying on the carpet.

4. Charlie Brown thought of another scheme by which he hoped to capture the attention of the little red-haired girl once and for all.

5. When Angelica discovered what was in the bouquet sent by her unknown admirer, she let go of it quickly.

6. The police officer gave a ticket to the driver of the green Corvette, who had been speeding.

7. Because it seeks vengeance, the phantom of the murdered duke appears regularly in the upper hall of the castle.

8. We tried to talk to the hotel clerk whose language we did not speak.

9. When Rupert accidentally broke his aunt's favorite china figure, he hid the fragments under the cushions of the sofa.

10. After the travellers lost their map and their bearings, they wandered in the forest aimlessly for several hours.

EXERCISE 6-6

(While these sentences are correct, there are other ways to join the sentence pairs that would also be correct.)

1. Geoffrey, a teacher for many years, did not think it was appropriate to wear shorts to class.

2. Lizzie Borden's house, an ordinary-looking building located in Fall River, has become a tourist attraction for those with a macabre curiosity.

3. This grammar book, the product of many months of hard work, will be largely unappreciated by the students who use it.

4. Janet Gaynor, one of the first to win the Oscar for Best Actress, played the lead in the film *A Star is Born*.

5. Tanya's father, a minister, disapproved of her tattoos.

6. The squirrels, new patients at the veterinary clinic, ran from one corner of the cage to another.

7. Frederica hated her new glasses, pink-tinted granny glasses.

8. Mel, a pilot with the Canadian Armed Forces, wants to open his own flying school after retiring.

9. Lima beans and squash, two vegetables I hate, are actually her favorites.

10. *Kiss of the Spider Woman*, a musical about the friendship between two prison inmates, won the Tony Award for Best Musical in 1993.

EXERCISE 6-7

1. The elephant roared and sprayed the spectators with water.

2. The twins ran away from home but were found next door.

3. You may wish to order off the menu or choose à la carte.

4. The band played a free concert in the park and was later interviewed on a local television show.

5. The columnist printed the letter but chose to delete the writer's name.

6. The coven enlisted new members because it needed thirteen for spell-casting and also had a spare broom.

7. Every morning Brandon jogs five kilometres before work and rides his bicycle every evening after work.

8. Cotton is a cool, comfortable natural fabric but needs to be ironed if it is to look attractive.

9. The hiring committee offered the job to an American but passed over five local applicants.

10. The nurse came in to take my temperature and also intended to take my blood pressure.

EXERCISE 6-8

1. The criminal mastermind scooped up the defense plans and hid them in his trench coat.

2. The stranger swung open the doors of the saloon and entered with guns blazing.

3. Answer the phone, or the caller will think you're not home.

4. The toddler burst into tears, for his mother had forgotten to change him.

5. At the end of the performance, the skater picked the flowers off the ice and proceeded to skate into the boards.

6. Leaping to her feet, Barbarella grabbed the electro-synergetic laser, so she could draw the enemy's fire and cover the princess's escape.

7. With only minutes to spare, Dr. Who ran to the Tardis, but the Daleks were there before.

8. Hal the computer cut off the life-support system to the rest of the space-craft and jettisoned the escape vehicles.

9. The incident occurred at 2:45 p.m., but the nurse forgot to mark it on the patient's chart.

10. Searching for dinner, the shark cruised through the shallow waters close to the beach, but the bathers did not see it.

EXERCISE 6-9

1. Searching for monsters, the boys approached the old house cautiously.

2. Nervously glancing over their shoulders all the time, Jason and Norm opened the front door.

3. Pausing on the threshold, they peered into the entrance hall which was large and filled with ominous shadows.

4. Looking to the left and to the right, they could see many rooms crowded with furniture covered in sheets.

5. Suddenly hearing a noise like a low moan, they froze in their tracks.

EXERCISE 6-10

1. Forgetting to set the VCR timer, Minh went out to dinner with her friends.

2. Found at the scene of the crash, the survivor was delirious.

3. Thinking he was in the clear, the suspect tried to leave town but was apprehended at the airport.

4. Encouraged by the response to her new album, Debbie signed a contract for a thirty-six week tour of North America and Europe.

5. Borne by the wind, the dandelion seeds blew all over the field.

6. Fed up with Kurt's wisecracks, Jennifer threw a mug of beer in his face.

7. Having spoken in favour of the motion, the member of Parliament began the filibuster.

8. Tripping over the fallen log, the hiker sprained his ankle.

9. Tearing down the stairs, the child and the dog ran to answer the doorbell.

10. Hoping to find the remains of the ancient settlement, the archaeological team excavated the site.

EXERCISE 6-11

1. Waiting in his car outside the apartment building, the detective drank coffee and ate doughnuts to stay awake during the stakeout.

2. A shadowy figure, hidden by the fog, crept close to the car.

3. Carefully taking aim, the figure fired a revolver at the unsuspecting victim.

4. Thrown into the bay, the murder weapon sank without a trace.

5. The detective, murdered by an unknown assailant, was found the next day slumped over the steering wheel of his car.

6. Angered by the lack of police cooperation, the widow swore to track down her husband's killer herself.

7. Following a lead provided by an anonymous phone call, she discovered that someone had been embezzling from the firm and cooking the books.

8. Having gathered the incriminating evidence, she confronted her husband's partner and tricked him into a confession.

9. The killer, realizing that he had spilled the beans into a tape recorder, tried to escape, but the police were waiting for him.

10. Pleased at her success, the widow decided to keep the detective agency open and run it herself.

EXERCISE 6-12

1. This van may seat eight people comfortably or twenty people uncomfortably.

2. Angrily, bitterly, and tearfully, the child filed a lawsuit against his parents.

3. This summer he visited New York, the Rockies, and his mother's house in Toronto.

4. If Dolly was given the choice of doing the laundry or going to a movie, she would choose the laundry.

5. Babs not only enjoys eating snails but also enjoys eating squid.

6. Cricket is more popular in England than in Canada.

7. The instructor advised the members of the class to work diligently and not to ask for extensions.

8. Elton works either at a library or at a car wash after school each day.

9. Matilda believes in and is an advocate of women's rights.

10. Bill and Hillary not only have high-paying professions but also are the proud parents of some perfectly awful children.

EXERCISE 6-13

1. Phil is neither working nor attending college.

2. Ferdinand the Bull is shy, peaceful, and fond of smelling the daisies.

3. Al and Peg are basically compatible, considering their constant fighting, their problems with children, and their different attitudes towards money.

4. Make sure all prospective employees are polite, hard working, and without a criminal record.

5. Rousseau's theory of perception is as valid as Dewey's.

6. He will either have to give up a promising career as a movie director or will fail his freshman courses.

7. You can pass the time in the bus station reading a magazine, striking up a conversation with other people who are waiting, or loitering in the coffee shop.

8. I would be willing to contribute to the construction fund in order to get a tax deduction or to have a building named in my honour.

9. The marriage ceremony has changed its wording: wives swear to love and honour their husbands, and they disregard obedience.

10. The rising birth rate among unwed teenage mothers can be attributed to a lack of knowledge of contraceptive devices, and more parental tolerance of promiscuous behaviour.

EXERCISE 6-14

1. Not only did he lose the match but lost his chances of winning a medal.

2. A job search involves finding an appropriate opening, writing an effective letter of application, and creating the right impression at an interview.

3. Correct.

4. Her jokes are often much funnier than Waldo's.

5. I wanted to find a man with Paul's looks, Tim's charm, and Keith's intelligence.

6. The travel agent will want to know whether you want to go to Tahiti or to Finland.

7. Correct.

8. Excitement, an opportunity to experience different cultures, and the steady income are the reasons I joined the army.

9. Sylvester Stallone's movies are as violent as those of Jean Claude van Damme.

10. Being in the public eye is not only rewarding but also helpful in winning elections.

CHAPTER 7—WORDS

EXERCISE 7-1

1. as high as a kite
2. as hot as hell
3. as ugly as sin
4. as poor as a church mouse
5. to drink like a fish
6. to work like a dog
7. to sleep like a log
8. as pretty as a picture
9. as strong as an ox
10. as rich as Croesus
11. as proud as a peacock
12. as meek as a lamb
13. as sharp as a tack
14. as clear as a bell
15. as flat as a pancake

Index

295